PLAYS

Frederick Lonsdale

PLAYS ONE

AREN'T WE ALL?
THE LAST OF MRS CHEYNEY
ON APPROVAL
CANARIES SOMETIMES SING

edited with
introductory notes by

Clifford Williams

OBERON BOOKS
LONDON

Aren't We All? first published in the USA by Brentano's, inc. in 1924.
First published in the UK by Samuel French Ltd in 1925
The Last of Mrs Cheyney first published by Davis-Poynter Ltd in 1925
On Approval first published by Samuel French Ltd in 1928
Canaries Sometimes Sing first published by Samuel French Ltd in 1931

First published in this collection in 2000 by Oberon Books Ltd.
(incorporating Absolute Classics)
521 Caledonian Road, London N7 9RH
Tel: 020 7607 3637 / Fax: 020 7607 3629
e-mail: oberon.books@btinternet.com

Contents

INTRODUCTION

Clifford Williams

Frederick Lonsdale was born in St. Helier, Jersey in the Channel Islands, in 1881. His father was an assistant in a tobacconist's shop, and he and his wife brought up their family on very modest means. Freddy's sister, Frances, said that her brother was a 'heart-breakingly wilful child. It was accepted from his earliest years that he was a very bad boy.'

He was not a thief or a trouble-maker. He was not malicious or stupid. He was simply without interest in the small rules which help to make family life agreeable, and he entirely rejected the idea of being educated. He roved around St. Helier with his cronies by day and night. Now and then, he was dragged back to school where he was caned. The next day he was on the streets again.

His father eventually opened a shop of his own, and the family lived in the rooms above. Freddy occasionally served in the shop, but when he was seventeen, he signed up for seven years in the army, joining the South Lancashire Regiment. He was immediately miserable. His only way out of the army was to be bought out, but his family had not the money, and probably not the inclination. But he managed to obtain a discharge on the grounds of a dangerous heart condition. This was the only time he experienced this particular medical problem.

There may be another explanation for his early release. In Aldershot, he had written a sketch for the annual regimental entertainment in which he made fun of the General and other officers. He was reprimanded. A little later, he fell mildly ill and was put in the camp hospital. The General's wife visited him. She thought his sketch had been brilliant. Really amusing. Why didn't he write plays? Lonsdale replied that such a vocation was not compatible with his army duties. The General's wife replied that the vocation made the discharge essential. The head doctor was a friend of hers. Lonsdale was discharged.

He returned to St. Helier and became a clerk in the enquiry office of the London and South Western Railway. The work was not congenial and, in any case, Lonsdale was distracted by a Canadian girl, who was in Jersey to learn the French patois of the island. They spent a scandalous weekend in Southampton, whereupon the girl's irate father arrived to escort her back to Canada. Lonsdale found a job as steward on a liner, and followed. Father became more irate and drew a pistol. The romance terminated, and Lonsdale returned to England to do odd jobs in the Southampton docks.

He pitched up again in Jersey in 1903. He had written a play, *Who's Hamilton*, which had toured the mainland, been praised by the famous critic, Clement Scott, and was now to play St. Helier. The island was agog. Some people remembered Lonsdale only as the black sheep son of the local tobacconist. Others were intrigued, including Leslie Hoggan, daughter of Colonel Hoggan, retired, Royal Artillery, (India). Leslie was engaged to Bertie Grey, a wealthy Scottish friend of her family, but she told Lonsdale that she did not love Bertie. Lonsdale promptly abducted her. She was staying in Scotland with the Grey family at Auchterarder, Gleneagles. Lonsdale arrived secretly by train. Leslie broke off her engagement with Bertie. The love-birds departed Auchterarder, but had to wait all day in Glasgow for Leslie's luggage. The elders of the Grey family arrived to plead with Leslie to return. Leslie could not be persuaded. She and Lonsdale departed by the night train south. He sat upright, and she did not rest her head on his shoulder.

They were married in Weymouth in 1904. Neither of them had any money, and Lonsdale had to persuade the vicar to pay for the special licence. After the wedding, Leslie went back to stay with her parents in Jersey, and Lonsdale remained in England. He was penniless, and had creditors in Jersey where the law allowed a man to be imprisoned for debt. For four years, Leslie visited Lonsdale when funds permitted, and when they ran out she returned home.

Lonsdale sold a play, *The Follies of the Foolish*, to Willie Edouin, a famous comedian, for £500. This was a large sum of money at that time and Leslie was able to rejoin her husband. But there were many bills and loans to be paid, and the couple were soon living on a diet of porridge in Herne Hill. Edouin died, and the play was never performed although Lonsdale rewrote it years later as *On Approval*.

Frank Curzon, an actor turned manager, saw some of Lonsdale's writing. He put him on a weekly retainer of £3 which more or less kept the Lonsdales going until 1908 when Curzon produced *The King of Cadonia* at the Prince of Wales Theatre. It was billed as a musical play with lyrics by Adrian Ross, music by Sidney Jones and libretto by Frederick Lonsdale, and it was reckoned to have a stronger plot than many of its popular predecessors such as *In Town*, *Belle of New York* and *Floradora* which relied on vaudeville, burlesque, hummable tunes and *les girls*.

The critic of the *Daily Graphic* noted that the story was the familiar one of a young couple who have been betrothed before they have met, and who then fall in love without being aware of each other's identity. He praised the manner in which the plot was never allowed to get out of hand, but made steady progress from the rise to the fall of the curtain. Most of the critics were of the same opinion, although one of them, when asked whether he liked *The King of Cadonia* replied: 'I like it very much. But then I always have. I liked it when it was *The Prisoner of Zenda*.'

The King of Cadonia was an instant success, and ran for 330 performances. Only four days after its première, Lonsdale had a second winner when his play *The Early Worm* opened at Wyndham's Theatre, again presented by Curzon and welcomed by the *Daily Graphic*:

> It is exceedingly amusingly written, with light and pointed dialogue, it is admirably cast, and it is beautifully played. It is a mere trifle, light as air, but for an after-dinner nine o'clock entertainment it is exactly the thing...

It really did start at 9 o'clock, being preceded at 8.30 p.m. by *Filby The Faker*, a melodrama by Leon M Lion. An orchestra played selections from Mendelssohn, Edward German and

Alexandre Luigini, and all this from one shilling in the gallery to ten shillings and sixpence in the stalls ('Dainty Teas' an extra sixpence).

A E Matthews played George, Duke of Tadcaster, in *The Early Worm*. 'Matty' was already established as a fine and popular actor. The ease with which he slipped into his roles, his spontaneity and effortless timing, concealed wonderful technical skills. He was the ideal actor for Lonsdale.

Lonsdale's second play *Best People* appeared the next year (1909) with Frederick Kerr, who became another Lonsdale favourite. He played Lord Emsworth, an easy-going, cynical, cool and shrewd man of the world, whose instincts for good a selfish and self-centred life had failed wholly to dull.

In 1910, *The Balkan Princess*, a musical comedy with book by Lonsdale and music by Paul Rubens, was produced by Frank Curzon at the Prince of Wales Theatre. It put the seal on Lonsdale's reputation, and he was now able to live comfortably at Westgate-on-Sea with Leslie, the children, a cook and a parlourmaid.

Lonsdale's father travelled to London to see his son's plays, but he could not believe that the ill-educated St. Helier urchin was their author. He thought they had probably been written by Jim, his eldest son, who had died before he was thirty.

Life at Westgate was delightful and expensive. Lonsdale did not work for five years, and then the money ran out. He quickly wrote the book for a musical, *Teresa*, and sent it to Curzon, who turned it down. Fortunately, Lonsdale then fell in with George Edwardes, who ran Daly's Theatre, the great home of musical comedy. Edwardes had pioneered the genre in England at the Gaiety Theatre with its beautiful chorus of 'Gaiety Girls', and afterwards with *The Country Girl*, *The Shop Girl*, *The Runaway Girl* and *The Quaker Girl*. Edwardes clearly understood what the young men in the audience appreciated. Girls!

In collaboration with Gladys Unger, and with music by Paul Rubens, Lonsdale wrote *Betty*, which opened at Daly's Theatre in 1915, and ran for 391 performances. Although Edwardes died soon afterwards (not, one trusts, out of shock at the lack of a *Girl* in the title), the management of Daly's was carried on by his associate, Robert Evett. Lonsdale showed Evett the rejected script for *Teresa*. Evett accepted it, Harold Fraser-Simpson was engaged to compose the music, Harry Graham (of *Ruthless Rhymes* fame) supplied the lyrics, and Oscar Ashe, who had created *Chu Chin Chow* took charge of design and direction. Ashe suggested a change of title from *Teresa* to *The Maid of the Mountains*. The show opened under that title at Daly's Theatre in 1917, with José Collins, a fiery soprano, as Teresa, the mountain maid.

It won great praise, although Allardyce Nichol, the respected theatre historian, later judged Lonsdale's libretto to be mediocre, a criticism which librettists have often endured.

Teresa loves Baldasarre, a brigand chief, who is held in prison by General Malona, who loves Teresa:

TERESA: May I speak to you?
GENERAL: Yes – what is it?
TERESA: I want you to give me something.
GENERAL: Well, what is it?
  (*They both laugh.*)
TERESA: Have you ever been in love?
GENERAL: Have I ever been in love? Don't you
  read your News of The World? Just sit down and
  I'll tell you all about it –
  (*TERESA sits on barrel near wall.*)
  Well, many years ago, when I was a comparatively
  young man – not quite as young as that perhaps –
  I was appointed President of a Girls' Friendly
  Society. It didn't last very long.
TERESA: Why?
GENERAL: I got a bit too friendly. Well, time
  passed on, and I did not have many love affairs –
  I must say it willy nilly – until I met you, and
  then my heart began to suzzle and sizzle and
  sizzle and suzzle. And I know it's love, because
  I've got all the symptoms…
TERESA: Then you know what love is?
GENERAL: Yes.
TERESA: Well enough to understand it?

GENERAL: Yes.

TERESA: Isn't love wonderful?

GENERAL: Yes.

TERESA: Could you love me?

GENERAL: Yes.

TERESA: Well enough to give me anything?

GENERAL: Yes.

TERESA: Then give me Baldasarre.

GENERAL: Yes – (*Turning quickly.*) Yesterday was a very nice day. I can understand Baldasarre liking you, but not you liking him.

TERESA: You don't know Baldasarre, or you'd understand.

TERESA/GENERAL: (*Sing.*) When You're in Love…

The Maid of the Mountains ran for 1352 performance, which did not put it in the same league as *Chu Chin Chow* (2238), but alongside *Charley's Aunt* and *Me and My Girl* in London, or *Hellzapoppin* and *Oklahoma* in New York.

Just prior to *The Maid*, Lonsdale had another musical at the Adelphi Theatre, *High Jinks* (Music: Rudolph Friml). Its success enabled him and his family to move along the Kent coast to a larger house at Birchington. *The Maid of the Mountains* brought dividends of a different order. Not only the means to pay off all his debts (including those in Jersey), but acceptance by Daly's which confirmed his professional standing.

He was elected to the Garrick Club, where he met fellow wits, thespian and judicial, and made friends with Arnold Bennett and H G Wells. Lonsdale was teased by Wells – 'I will not discuss this question with you, Freddy. You are too uneducated.'

Birchington became a fashionable resort, and Lonsdale took pleasure in the company of Gerald du Maurier, Gladys Cooper, Ivor Novello, and Lord Edward Carson. He was bitten by the dancing bug in the early nineteen-twenties, helped by his daughters and a pile of gramophone records. One day, practising alone in the drawing-room, he noticed that a man was watching him through the doorway.

'Ain't ye *ashamed* of yeself?' Lord Carson said, in his thickest brogue.

He wrote a romantic opera *Monsieur Beaucaire* (Music: Andre Messager), adapted from Booth Tarkington's famous story, with the incomparable Maggie Teyte, and presented by Gibert Miller, the American impresario, at the Prince's Theatre. Then he went back to Daly's with a new musical play *The Lady of the Rose*. In 1923 he sold Birchington and went to London.

The nineteen-twenties were a golden period for the Jersey boy. He continued to write musicals – *Madame Pompadour* (1923), which made Evelyn Laye a star, *The Street Singer* (1924), and *Katja the Dancer* (1925). But he also began to write plays again. *Aren't We All?* (1923) was the first of a quartet of comedies which established him as a dramatist in his own right.

> *The Times*: Musical comedy doubtless has many attractions, but we have always understood that witty dialogue is not one of them. Indeed, amid cues for song and dance, wit might lie superfluous. Judge of the general surprise – and gratification – when the distinguished author of many musical comedy libretti writes a straight play (if the stage jargon may be pardoned) which is witty from end to end.

> *Daily Telegraph*: When, on the fall of the curtain at the Globe last night, Miss Marie Lohr declared that it was a pleasure to welcome Mr Lonsdale from musical comedy to legitimate theatre, she obviously and indubitably voiced the feelings of everyone present. For nothing could be more clear than that in the case of a man capable of writing so witty, so human and so delightful a piece as *Aren't We All?* the one right and proper place for him to occupy is the stage of the latter.

Lonsdale's 1924 offering *The Fake* could be described as a serious melodrama. A young girl is obliged by her father to marry an alcoholic, from which misery she is finally delivered by the deliberate murder of her husband by an old family friend. It was well received in London, with Franklyn Bellamy as the husband, and Godfrey Tearle as the murderer, but it failed in New York where audiences preferred the lighter side of Lonsdale.

Spring Cleaning was produced in London in 1925, following an earlier New York staging in which A E Matthews played the role of Ernest Steele, a professional Don Juan. He had a line to speak: 'With a charm of manner, there's a hell of a lot of fun to be had in cathedral towns.'

At rehearsal Matty came on and said:

'There's a lot of fun to be had in cathedral town.'

Lonsdale spoke from the stalls:

'With a charm of manner, Matty.'

Matty tried the line again:

'There's a lot of fun to be had in cathedral towns.'

Lonsdale said again:

'With a charm of manner, Matty.'

Matty stormed off the stage and Lonsdale went to look for him. He found him hunched and glowering. Lonsdale said: 'Matty, the line in the play is: With a charm of manner, there's a hell of a lot of fun to be had in cathedral towns.' 'Oh!' said Matty, jumping up, 'I thought you were criticising my acting.'

The Sketch, in London, deemed it a brilliant, cynical comedy of modern 'manners' in which the depravity and folly of the 'wrong' circle were daringly portrayed. The play did extremely well in both countries, although Lonsdale was such a 'classic' by now that critics hardly affected the box-office queues. Ronald Squire played Ernest in London, and made a triumvirate with Matty and Fred Kerr – the dramatist's favourite players.

The Last of Mrs Cheyney is probably the most performed of all his plays. It opened at the St. James's Theatre in September 1925, with a cast including Gerald du Maurier, Ronald Squire and Gladys Cooper. At the end of the performance, the audience called for Lonsdale to join the actors lined up on stage. He entered to tremendous applause. 'Ladies and Gentlemen', he said, 'this morning I composed a most brilliant little speech to make to you this evening, but this afternoon I read it to Sir Gerald du Maurier in his dressing-room. He liked it so much that he insists on making it himself'. Lonsdale then left the stage, Du Maurier, taken by surprise, stepped forward and sang:

> I want to be happy
> But I can't be happy
> Till I've made you happy too.

The notices were mixed.

Illustrated Sporting / Dramatic News: If a good play, despite the intelligentsia, is any one which amuses you all the time the curtain is up, *The Last of Mrs Cheyney* is a good play to most people. Of course, some people's definition of a good play is one in which Miss Gladys Cooper is appearing, while the hallmark for others is one in which the name of Sir Gerald du Maurier is printed in the programme. Some people swear by Chekhov, and others insist on a chorus, but not a Greek one. When the curtain goes up at the present time at the St. James's the auditorium is as neatly and tightly packed with people as the hold of an outgoing ship is with goods, while during matinées you may also see, outside on the pavement, firm souls on camp stools, ardently waiting for the evening performance. So camp stool makers probably swear that Frederick Lonsdale is the master dramatist of the age. It is all a matter of taste.

Sunday Times: West End audiences take no interest in low life except on condition that it is above stairs. Mr Lonsdale owes his success to his perfect realisation of this fact. There is no secret about successful playwriting. Avoidance of any kind of truth, wit which does not rise out of character but is an important distribution from the author's private storehouse, and, as to players, stars of whoppingest magnitude with no nonsense about team-work – this cannot be wrong. The success of *The Last of Mrs Cheyney* will, I imagine, be found to correspond exactly with the faithful carrying out of this formula. It is not a good sort of play, but it is a very good play of its sort.

In 1927, *On Approval* opened at the Fortune where it ran for 469 performances (*Cheyney* ran 514). *Theatre World* did not enjoy a matinée:

> On the whole, it was a depressing afternoon. I am old-fashioned enough to be rather careful of the company I keep. I do not enjoy the contemplation of a Duke who grossly insults a lady who happens to be his hostess; and I resent having to spend an afternoon in the presence of a 'nice' girl who tells people to 'go to hell'. Neither is my scant 'enjoyment' of such society much mitigated by the fact that I have had to pay for the privilege!

James Agate in *The Sunday Times* suggested that the French who knew froth for what it was 'would not have made the mistake of insisting at quite so much length upon an agreeable folly, preferring to imitate the spider who spins his web from twig to twig, and not from tree to tree'. Agate felt that the play should have been cut by an hour, but he conceded that it was all very amusing, and 'one needed not to believe a word of it'. *Sporting and Dramatic* was interesting:

> Since Mr Frederick Lonsdale left off writing the words for musical comedies and trod the severer paths of the 'legitimate', he has been extremely successful, and yet his plays have left you with the impression that the musical comedy libretto is his true métier. For the situations to be the weakest part of your work and the jokes the strongest, for your characters to be chosen from fast-living Society people and to be types and not individuals, these things are the stock-in-trade of both musical comedies and of Mr Lonsdale's plays. His attributes will, perhaps, prevent his ever writing a great play, so meantime we must laugh at his dialogue and love him, like England, with all his faults.

There was always some critical huffing if Lonsdale slipped a serious moment or situation into a play. The received opinion was that he should stick to providing witty, diverting and plot-less (or, at least, improbable) entertainments. 'Forget that sometimes Mr Lonsdale will be solemn; remember only his graceful nonsense' was the conclusion of *The Times* review of his new play *The High Road* in the autumn of 1927.

The solemnity consisted of having a poignant, sad ending. Edward, Duke of Warrington, and Elsie Hilary, actress, fall in love with each other. They are both sincere and sensitive people, and when something unforeseen occurs they realise they must part. There is an echo here of Eliza leaving Higgins in Shaw's *Pygmalion*, and one recalls that Shaw was obliged to defend the unromantic ending to his play.

Lonsdale reached the end of the Twenties with his final musical *Lady Mary* which made little stir, and a brand new comedy *Canaries Sometimes Sing*. Geoffrey is an easy-going playwright, bored with his silly, socially ambitious wife, Anne. Ernest, a school friend from the past, who is not such a fool as he looks, and Elma, his chorus-girl wife, come to visit. Geoffrey takes a shine to Elma, and they both hope that their spouses will hit it off together. But, at the last moment, Geoffrey chickens out. He lacks the courage to leave Anne. But Elma cannot face returning to life with Edward.

> EDWARD: Where – where – are you going?
> ELMA: I – I'm going to find another co-respondent.
> (*ELMA exits.*)
>
> *The End.*

Ronald Squire, who played Geoffrey, hailed Lonsdale in the first night curtain call as the 'Sheridan of our time'. Some critics were troubled that a brilliant comedy, a 'near master-piece' was spoilt by its 'jarring finish'. Others were taken by the skill with which Lonsdale emptied quivers-full of poisoned shafts into that Aunt Sally which is British hypocrisy. The *Sunday Times* reviewer thought Lonsdale's world of four people too restricted. He found himself 'hankering for a housemaid, or yearning for the postman. Even a jobbing gardener, or a district visitor'.

The *Last of Mrs Cheyney* with Norma Shearer and Basil Rathbone was filmed in 1929, and *On Approval* in 1930.

Lonsdale's reputation in the USA was very high, the talkies industry was beginning, and Lonsdale was bewitched by Hollywood. His first original film *The Devil to Pay* (1930), strong in story and few of words, featured Ronald Colman and Loretta Young, with Myrna Loy beginning her career. *Lovers Courageous* (1932) starred Robert Montgomery in a story based on Lonsdale's own life, Herne Hill included!

In the same year, he was back in London with a new play *Never Come Back*. Raymond Massey and Adrienne Allen were excellent, but the play failed. Ernest Lubitsch wanted him to write a screen play of Melchior Lengyel's *Angel* for Marlene Dietrich. He started work on this but inexplicably withdrew.

Lubitsch pressed on with the film, and later directed Greta Garbo in *Ninotchka*, so Lonsdale missed out on a pair of Hollywood legends. Instead, he collaborated with Lajos Biró on *The Private Life of Don Juan* (1934) which involved two other legends, Douglas Fairbanks and Merle Oberon, directed by Alexander Korda.

He had a new play *Once is Enough* produced in New York in 1938. Richard Watts reviewed it in the *Herald Tribune*:

> It is consoling to know that in a changing chaotic world, England and Frederick Lonsdale stand undismayed and unaltered. House parties given by the Duke and Duchess of Hampshire are still attended by Reggie, Archie, Hugo and Johnny and their wives, who talk amusingly about adultery, and practice it a bit...

It ran a modest 107 performances (it was not put on in London until 1959 as *Let Them Eat Cake*).

He had been thinking about another play for many years to be called *The League of Nations*, a satire on human folly and the futility of war. There were firm plans for Tallulah Bankhead to appear in it under a new title – *Foreigners* – but Lonsdale failed to complete the script in time, and the production was abandoned. Eventually, the play opened in New York in 1939. The critics did not respond well. Nor, for once, did the public. It was withdrawn after 7 performances. It was the first flop he had ever experienced.

Lonsdale was winded by the blow, or at the least he took a deep and very long breath. His next play *Another Love Story* did not open in New York (where he spent the war years) until 1943. The *Daily Mirror* wrote:

> *Another Love Story* is as thin as the roast beef in a drug-store sandwich, and about as filling.

In England in 1944, it toured the provinces with Roland Culver, Zena Dare, A E Matthews and Anton Walbrook, before London. It was perceptively welcomed by the *Manchester Guardian*:

> ...and all with the deftest sense of the theatre and to our constant merriment and sustained interest. And all, it may be added without grossness or offence, and that in spite of a bedroom scene of quite unusual implications and comic subtlety. Peace to the ancients, but our new Restoration comedy has prettier manners than the old – even, perhaps, a hint that, if the social deluge should follow, it would not be undeserved.

Lonsdale, at sixty-three, remained the very picture of a successful playwright, but he was unhappy in his personal life. He had parted from his wife many years before. He cared deeply for her and his family and supported them financially, but he had become a restless spirit, easily bored, aggressive, changeable, stubborn, full of temper, and increasingly of savage independence. He had loved company, but he became a lonely man – disappointed, it seemed, with life.

There is a hint of this in *But for the Grace of God* (1946) which treats of theft, adultery, blackmail and murder. Ernest Betts:

> What happens then? Mr Lonsdale gives you suspense, cynicism and dissection of the human soul caught in a ghastly crime – with a whisky and soda, good manners and devastating epigrams.

The Way Things Go (1950) another title with undertones, was Lonsdale's last play. George, Duke of Bristol, is bankrupt and hopes that he may be able to reside in the future with his old butler. George's extensive family of the idle-now-not-so-rich and other hangers-on are in a state of terminal shock. The New World drops by in the person of a shrewd but soft-hearted American big business man and his delightful (rich) daughter. The family is temporarily rescued, but it is clear that their society, their way of living, is on the way out. The play did marvellously at the Phoenix Theatre, a great deal being due to Glynis Johns, who captivated London as the rich daughter, and Kenneth More, in his first comedy role, as the Duke's young dipsomaniac brother.

In 1925, in a profile of Lonsdale for *The Sketch*, Beverley Nichols wrote:

> His plays, brilliant as they are today, are for today only. In a hundred years' time St. James's Street may well be buzzing with aeroplanes carrying our great-grandchildren to see a revival of Somerset Maugham's *The Circle*. But I doubt if they will be going to see a similar revival of *The Last Days of Mrs Cheyney*.

Nichols, happily, was wrong. Lonsdale's snobs and egoists and dullards and bores and boors and hedonists and brutes and idiots were not culled from the pages of Debrett's Peerage (although some may well be found there). They were the creatures of the author's jaunty conceit, and they stood in, as it were, for the arrogant modesty and the clever vacuity and the grimacing charm to be found anywhere and anytime in society. *Once is Enough* (1938):

> EMILY: (*Lady Bletchley.*) The more I see of our set,
>   the more dreadful I realise they are!
> NANCY: (*Duchess of Hampshire.*) Our set is the same
>   as any other set – but with more opportunity!

Clifford Williams
London, 2000

AREN'T WE ALL?

"AREN'T WE ALL . . . ?"

There are two missing words, one of which is the epithet to which Mr. Bernard Shaw first introduced play-goers. The other word is "fools!" Left to right in this collection of striking portraits are: Miss Marie Löhr as Margot Tatham, the heroine, who eventually discovers that those who will love in glass houses must see that the blinds are drawn; Mr. Julian Royce as Lord Grenham, the wily old raisonneur, who makes Margot "forgive" her husband, who has been so stupid as to be discovered kissing a lady named Kitty; Miss Ellis Jeffreys as Lady Frinton, who thinks she would like to change her name to Grenham; and Mr. Eric Lewis as the Rev. Ernest Lyndon, whom Lord Grenham calls a "something" old fool. The play has had a big success at the Globe, and is most amusing

Characters

MORTON

HON. WILLIE TATHAM

LADY FRINTON

ARTHUR WELLS

MARTIN STEELE

KITTY LAKE

LORD GRENHAM

HON. MRS W TATHAM (MARGOT)

ROBERTS

ANGELA LYNTON

REVEREND ERNEST LYNTON

JOHN WILLOCKS

Act I: Willie Tatham's House in Mayfair. Evening.

Act II: Grenham Court. Afternoon. Two weeks later.

Act III: The same. The next morning.

Aren't We All? was first performed at the Globe Theatre, London, on 10 April 1923, with the following cast:

MORTON, E. Vivian Reynolds

WILLIE, Herbert Marshall

LADY FRINTON, Ellis Jeffreys

ARTHUR, Charles Hickman

MARTIN, Patrick Gover

KITTY, Cyllene Moxon

LORD GRENHAM, Julian Royce

MARGOT, Marie Löhr

ROBERTS, E. A. Walker

ANGELA, Elizabeth Chesney

VICAR, Eric Lewis

WILLOCKS Martin Lewis

The play was revived at the Fortune Theatre (1929) and the Royal Court (1935) where Marie Löhr, who had played Margot Tatham in the original production, now took on the Ellis Jeffreys role of Lady Frinton.

Reviewers of a 1953 revival at the Haymarket felt that the play was beginning to creak. Was it really witty, or was it adroitly facetious? Was it a comedy of manners, or merely a sentimental comedy? Kenneth Tynan in the *Evening Standard*:

> *Aren't We All?* snappily enquire the posters outside the Haymarket Theatre. Well, we were: but are we still?

> Frederick Lonsdale's comedy, first produced almost eighty years ago, is what some would call gentle and others toothless...where Somerset Maugham chews and digests his characters, Lonsdale merely mumbles them... Tennent Productions, who presented the play,

have had one sensible impulse: they did not trust it. Hence they and their designer, Cecil Beaton, decked it out in the costumes of 1914, nearly a decade before it was written. But of all unfortunate decades! Lonsdale's style was ever a sentimental hangover from Oscar Wilde's – and you do not help a man with a hangover by reminding him of the night before.

May I take leave to dissuade the management from doing moderately well plays that are not worth doing at all?

Aren't We All? was up and running again at the Savoy Theatre in 1967, but Felix Barker in the *Evening Standard* concluded that the author was 'making a mountain of adultery out of an amorous molehill'. I directed the play in 1984, its last major twentieth-century production, again at the Haymarket, with Rex Harrison and Claudette Colbert. The audiences were extremely enthusiastic. The following year we went to New York. The critic of the *New York Times*, Frank Rich (known as 'The Butcher of Broadway'), found the play 'no other than an antique trifle, not without passing pleasure'.

But he went wild about Colbert's legs, enjoyed Lonsdale's *bon mots* such as 'How angry the monkeys must be when they hear that men are descended from them', and in the Rich way of things was moderately complimentary about my contribution: 'Williams cannot camouflage the dated vintage of Lonsdale's caprice, but his airy staging does keep rigor mortis at bay.'

Walter Kerr, doyen of the New York critics, wrote that Lonsdale made the seemingly entirely plausible. He added:

Is there really a theatrical activity more deserving of our giddy gratitude than the business of improvising artifice. Artifice that will induce a whole bunch of charismatic actors to come together to employ the charms they have spent a lifetime acquiring? Not for me, lads, not for me. I am a fervent admirer of *Oedipus Rex*, mind you, and I don't honestly think Mr Lonsdale could have written it. But if *Oedipus Rex* stands for theatre on its best and most virtuous behaviour, there's room left over for cakes and ale. Somebody important said so. And, for your information, Claudette Colbert, Rex Harrison, Lynn Redgrave, Brenda Forbes, Jeremy Brett are cakes and ale and after-dinner mints besides, separately and jointly delicious.

After New York, Harrison and Colbert led the production on a long tour of the USA *and* Australia. Troupers! Incidentally, among the many reviewers I think only Sheridan Morley in *Punch* appreciated that *Aren't We All?* was Lonsdale's reworking of *The Best People*, which he had written in 1909 at the beginning of his career.

ACT ONE

The room has a central door and an archway leading to other parts of the house. The sound of dance music comes through the archway as MORTON enters by the door with letters on a salver. He puts the letters on a desk, goes to the archway and looks off. He watches the dancers, beating time to the music with the salver. WILLIE comes through the door.

WILLIE: (*Going quickly to the table, on which the letters are lying, and looking through them.*) Is this all?

MORTON: (*Turning.*) Yes, sir!

WILLIE: (*Opening some of the letters.*) You're sure there's no message or cable from my wife?

MORTON: Certain, sir! (*He goes up to the door.*)

WILLIE: Extraordinary! Extraordinary! Give me a whisky and soda, please!

MORTON: Certainly, sir. (*He goes to a table and pours whisky into a glass. He then puts some soda water in. WILLIE turns to him. The music stops.*)

WILLIE: Not too much soda.

(*MORTON puts the glass on the salver and brings it over to WILLIE.*)

I'm frightfully worried, Morton!

MORTON: I'm sorry, sir.

WILLIE: (*Taking the glass from him.*) Not a word of any sort from my wife for the last eight days! (*He drinks.*)

MORTON: The mails from Egypt are all wrong nowadays, sir.

WILLIE: But I have cabled her three times and no reply! I'm terrified she's ill again!

MORTON: Then you would have heard, sir!

WILLIE: That's true! But if I don't hear tomorrow, I'll cable the manager of the hotel.

MORTON: Yes, sir. Anything else you want, sir?

WILLIE: Nothing, thank you.

MORTON: Oh! I forgot, sir, Miss Lake rang you up!

WILLIE: Did she leave any message?

MORTON: I told her you were out, sir, and that you were expected back later in the evening.

WILLIE: Ho! Alright.

(*MORTON exits.*

LADY FRINTON enters through the archway.)

WILLIE: Hullo, my dear! You look wonderful; 'pon my soul, you become younger every day.

LADY FRINTON: I'm glad of that because it takes most of the day to become it!

WILLIE: (*Laughing.*) Splendid!

LADY FRINTON: Willie, dear, it's sweet of you to lend me your house to give this dance to-night.

WILLIE: You're not a bit grateful.

LADY FRINTON: Why do you say that?

WILLIE: Because you have asked me to it, and you know how I loathe dancing!

LADY FRINTON: Nonsense!

WILLIE: Who's here?

LADY FRINTON: Well, the usual lot. At the last moment some of them insisted on coming in fancy dress; not serious – just anything, you know. Arthur Wells, I'm told, is coming as George Robey, and Martin Steele as Charlie Chaplin, and –

WILLIE: How frightfully original!

LADY FRINTON: My dear, you are not suggesting that two men, each born with twenty thousand a year, should be expected to have heard of Mr Clynes or Mr. Baldwin, are you?

WILLIE: I'm sorry.

LADY FRINTON: You must be more tolerant; and lots of other people – amongst them, your father!

WILLIE: You don't mean to tell me that dear old gentleman still goes out at night?

LADY FRINTON: I'm very worried about your father.

WILLIE: You are?

LADY FRINTON: Remembering the affection I had for your dear mother, and you; unless your father really gets old, and soon, I fear I shall be called upon to make the supreme sacrifice.

WILLIE: What do you mean?

LADY FRINTON: I shall have to marry him!

WILLIE: Do you know anything?

LADY FRINTON: Do I? By accident, this afternoon, I met him with a young and extremely over-dressed young person –

WILLIE: (*Anxiously.*) Who was she?

LADY FRINTON: I don't know. But it was quite evident it was early-closing day!

WILLIE: Did he see you?

LADY FRINTON: Oh, no; I saw to that. He called a taxi, put her into it, and to my amazement said, 'British Museum!'

WILLIE: Why the British Museum?

LADY FRINTON: Don't you realise, he knows perfectly well only an air raid would drive his own class into it!

WILLIE: This is very worrying, you know.

LADY FRINTON: That's not all! His photograph, the other day, was in one of the illustrated morning papers playing with two little children; underneath it was written: 'The distinguished old sportsman, Lord Grenham, whose great affection for little children regularly takes him to the park.'

WILLIE: Well?

LADY FRINTON: Unfortunately for him they included the nurse in the photograph.

WILLIE: But this is perfectly dreadful.

LADY FRINTON: The worst is yet to come.

WILLIE: He's going to marry her?

LADY FRINTON: The reverse; he's having dancing lessons.

WILLIE: Good God! He's fifty-nine.

LADY FRINTON: He told Mademoiselle de Salis, the dancing mistress, he was forty-six.

WILLIE: Have you danced with him?

LADY FRINTON: He becomes acutely sciatic the moment he's asked to dance with a woman over twenty-four.

WILLIE: This must be stopped!

LADY FRINTON: It must! Unless he gives me his word of honour to become, within three months, the most popular member of the Athenaeum, I marry him. Tell me, any news of Margot?

WILLIE: Not a word. I'm worried out of my life.

LADY FRINTON: Poor dear, I'm sorry; but it's alright, the posts are all wrong!

WILLIE: But I got no answer to my cable. I can't understand it. I tell you I'm worried out of my life.

LADY FRINTON: I know you are, and I'm awfully sorry for you, but you must remember, if she were ill they would have cabled you. When did you hear from her last?

WILLIE: A fortnight ago. Exactly what I expected happened; the moment she arrived, everybody begging her to sing for their cursed charities. The very thing she went away to avoid.

LADY FRINTON: What a divine voice it is, though, Willie!

WILLIE: Nevertheless, I sometimes wish she had never possessed it; singing night after night for various charities was the cause of her breakdown.

LADY FRINTON: I agree. How long has she been away? (*The music starts.*)

WILLIE: Four months; and, thank heaven, only another two months and she will be home again; and I may tell you, this house, during the last four months without her, has been perfectly damnable. I've hated it!

LADY FRINTON: I'm sure you have. (*Looking at picture of MARGOT over the mantelpiece.*) What a dear she is!

WILLIE: Is there such a thing as a superlative angel?

LADY FRINTON: I like you for that, Willie. Do you know it's wonderful the way you have settled down? You were a gay lad yourself once upon a time! Tell me, how much did your past cost you?

WILLIE: My father always told me it cost less to be generous!

LADY FRINTON: Well, he knows!

(*ARTHUR and MARTIN enter by the door. ARTHUR is dressed as George Robey and MARTIN as Charlie Chaplin.*)

LADY FRINTON: (*Seeing ARTHUR.*) Isn't he sweet!

WILLIE: Congratulations. By the way, if you are asked to a dance at nine o'clock, what do you mean by coming at ten thirty?

ARTHUR: These things take a little time to put on, old
    friend. How are you, Lady Frinton? (*They shake hands.*)
    Here, Willie, I say, why are you in those clothes?

WILLIE: I'll tell you if you'll tell me why you are in those.

ARTHUR: I don't know! Some one asked me to!

LADY FRINTON: What are you supposed to be, Arthur?

ARTHUR: Isn't it obvious? Chu Chin Chow!

LADY FRINTON: Then keep humming the music, dear, or
    we'll never know.

MARTIN. How are you, Lady Frinton? (*They shake hands.*)

LADY FRINTON: Now please don't tell me who this is!
    (*Looking at him.*) I give it up!

WILLIE: Martin Steele.

LADY FRINTON: But how perfectly wonderful. And who
    are you supposed to be, Martin?

MARTIN: Really, Lady Frinton, really! Charlie Chaplin, of
    course. (*He imitates Charlie Chaplin's walk.*)

LADY FRINTON: But isn't that interesting, and so many
    people have told me he was funny.
    (*The music stops. MORTON enters by the door.*)

MORTON: Miss Lake!
    (*KITTY LAKE enters. MORTON exits.*)

LADY FRINTON: Kitty dear, how delightful! You told me
    you were going to the country today.

KITTY: I altered my mind at the last moment. You wanted
    me to come tonight.

LADY FRINTON: Of course I did.
    (*KITTY looks over at ARTHUR and MARTIN. They bow.*)

KITTY: I think you are right.

ARTHUR: I say, I didn't want to come in these beastly
    things. I only put them on to oblige.

LADY FRINTON: Quite right, Arthur, you must
    occasionally do something to justify your existence!
    (*The music starts.*)

MARTIN: I say, Kitty, I was told today that you are going
    back to the stage!

KITTY: Never, my dear. There isn't enough money in the
    world to even tempt me.

WILLIE: I'm sorry to hear it.

KITTY: When you have made a reputation, keep it, don't come back and lose it.

LADY FRINTON: Wise child!

MARTIN: But you wouldn't.

KITTY: Thank you, Martin, but I haven't the courage to risk it.

LADY FRINTON: Come along, all of you; you must come and dance.

(*She goes through the archway, followed by ARTHUR and MARTIN.*)

KITTY: Yes, do let us! (*To WILLIE.*) You're going to ask me?

WILLIE: I'm hopeless!

KITTY: What nonsense! We danced splendidly together the other evening.

WILLIE: Yes, because you are so good!

KITTY: Then I must be as good tonight!

WILLIE: Then I'd love to.

(*They go through the archway.*
MORTON enters by the door. He tidies the room. After a moment LORD GRENHAM enters by the door.)

LORD GRENHAM: Evening, Morton!

MORTON: Good evening, my lord!

LORD GRENHAM: The band alright?

MORTON: Very good, I think, my lord!

LORD GRENHAM: That's alright! To us young people, the band is all important, Morton!

MORTON: (*Smiling.*) Yes, my lord!

LORD GRENHAM: You dance, Morton?

MORTON: My wife doesn't care for it, my lord!

LORD GRENHAM: Quite! Quite! How is my son?

MORTON: He's very well, my lord. He's dancing at the moment!

LORD GRENHAM: Splendid! (*Walking to the archway and looking off.*) Tell me the name of the lady dancing with my son!

MORTON: Miss Lake, my lord!

LORD GRENHAM: Miss Lake! You're well, I hope, Morton?

MORTON: Thank you, my lord! And I'm glad to see your lordship looking so well!

LORD GRENHAM: I'm alright, thanks! I was too generous that day, Morton, I lent you to my son!

MORTON: It's very kind of you to say so, my lord!

LORD GRENHAM: I miss you, Morton! However, I've no doubt you are very happy, so that's everything, isn't it?

MORTON: Mrs Lynton well, my lord?

LORD GRENHAM: Very, thanks! My sister and her husband, the Vicar, by the way, arrive next week to spend their annual holiday with me!

(*MORTON smiles and turns to suppress a laugh, then turns again.*)

MORTON: Is there anything I can get you, my lord?

LORD GRENHAM: No, thanks. (*He crosses to pick up a paper from the settee and sits.*)

(*MORTON exits. The music stops. WILLIE enters through the archway.*)

WILLIE: Hullo, Father, how long have you been here?

LORD GRENHAM: Just arrived, my boy, just arrived!

WILLIE: What brings you up to town?

LORD GRENHAM: Just filling my lungs with a little of the oxygen of life in preparation for my sister and her husband the Vicar's annual visit to me!

WILLIE: Oh! Awful! I don't know how you can bear to have them with you!

LORD GRENHAM: I have to, because nobody else will.

WILLIE: I wouldn't, personally! Well, how are you?

LORD GRENHAM: I'm alright, my boy, still gettin' about a bit!

WILLIE: You're a marvel, really you are. I was trying to remember your exact age today.

LORD GRENHAM: Thirty-one or thirty-two! Never more than thirty-five! So you're giving a little dance, are you?

WILLIE: I'm not. I've merely lent my house to Mary Frinton, who is.

LORD GRENHAM: There's great excitement coming to that woman one of these days; she'll pay for something, herself! (*WILLIE laughs.*) Who's here? That pretty creature, Miss Lake, coming by any chance?

WILLIE: Yes! She's already here.

LORD GRENHAM: Already here, is she? That's good! Damned attractive woman, that, Willie.

WILLIE: And a nice one.

LORD GRENHAM: Experience has taught me that's the last thing we find out. We know she's attractive. You get about with her a bit, don't you?

WILLIE: I meet her occasionally, if that's what you mean?

LORD GRENHAM: That's what I mean! I saw you lunching with her in her box at the races –

WILLIE: So were heaps of other people!

LORD GRENHAM: You dined together the other night at the Ritz.

WILLIE: If I remember rightly there were five of us dining together.

LORD GRENHAM: Numbers mean nothing to me, Willie! Many a woman has carried on a long conversation with me without opening her mouth when there have been twenty of us dining together! Tell me, is she fond of the telephone?

WILLIE: I don't know. How should I?

LORD GRENHAM: I mean, has she started to ring you up?

WILLIE: (*Pause.*) No!

LORD GRENHAM: Good! If she should ring you up one day and ask if you – if you could help her to find a good architect and you're prepared to find him, Willie, take my advice, have the telephone disconnected and take a long trip to Australia!

WILLIE: I should very much like to know what you are suggesting?

LORD GRENHAM: I'm suggesting, Willie, she's a damned attractive woman, and you're a foolish fellow to see so much of her!

WILLIE: You mean, I'm in love with her?

LORD GRENHAM: I have had enough experience of life to know if you were in love with her, that it would be waste of time to talk to you.

WILLIE: Then what do you mean?

LORD GRENHAM: Just simply this! Since the world began, and up to the day that the world ends, it has been arranged for us that when an attractive man and an attractive woman have the desire to meet each other, then they meet; then, when they have agreed that the weather for this time of the year is most unreasonable and the last novel is most indifferent, he is left with only one thing to say to her, and that is goodbye – or tell her she is the most beautiful thing he has ever seen!

WILLIE: (*With a little laugh.*) Nonsense! Nonsense!

LORD GRENHAM: A Wesleyan minister once said that to me; they tell me he travels in jam now! (*Another laugh from WILLIE.*) And, in addition, I'm not saying a word against the dear creature; a woman of her attraction is bound to be, shall we say, sought; so, understanding as I do, I say frankly, this is not the place to ask her.

WILLIE: Indeed! Where do you suggest I should ask her? The British Museum?

LORD GRENHAM: (*Innocently.*) There are many more unhealthy places than the British Museum, Willie.

WILLIE: That's why you were there this afternoon, I suppose?

LORD GRENHAM: How did you know I was there?

WILLIE: One of the mummies was so depressed at seeing a man in your position with an overdressed young shop girl, she wrote and told me.

LORD GRENHAM: Mary Frinton told you.

WILLIE: How do you know?

LORD GRENHAM: The moment you said 'Mummy'! Let me tell you something about Mary Frinton. She's started at her age the ringing up business; she's got her eye on me, Willie.

WILLIE: At all events, I think we can leave Miss Lake alone, don't you?

LORD GRENHAM: Just as you like, my boy.

WILLIE: Don't you sometimes regret what a bad man you have been, Father?

LORD GRENHAM: (*Sadly.*) Often! Often! There's only one
thing I regret more.

WILLIE: What's that?

LORD GRENHAM: The opportunities I have missed that
would have made me a worse one.

WILLIE: I don't mean it unkindly, but I wish I could think
you had done one good thing in this world.

LORD GRENHAM: Have you ever heard of the Boy
Scouts?

WILLIE: Yes.

LORD GRENHAM: I was the origin of them.

WILLIE: (*Amused.*) In what way?

LORD GRENHAM: Before I ever accepted any amusement
any one day in my life, I made it a point of honour to
walk down Bond Street and hand the glad eye to three of
the ugliest women I could find, thereby filling their sad
hearts with pleasure, encouragement, and even that thing
which I today live on – hope!

(*The music starts.*)

WILLIE: That's pretty good.

LORD GRENHAM: Oh! I've done a lot of unadvertised
good in the world, Willie! Tell me, any news of our
darling Margot?

WILLIE: Not a line! Not a syllable. I'm distracted.

LORD GRENHAM: Worrying? I'm sorry for you! She was
alright in her last letter?

WILLIE: Perfectly. (*He takes the letter out of his pocket.*) Here
it is.

(*LORD GRENHAM reads the letter.*)

LORD GRENHAM: She seems to be enjoying herself.
Who's this young man she refers to several times?

WILLIE: I don't know; some fellow she's with!

LORD GRENHAM: (*Reading.*) 'I'm ever so much better,
and enjoying myself in a way. The whole thing is spoilt
for me by the number of people begging me to sing. If it
goes on I shall adopt some way of avoiding them. Oh,
Willie, how I ache to put my arms round you and
smother your dear sweet face with kisses.' That's the

stuff. I have always complained there are not nearly enough of those fine creatures in the world! (*He hands back the letter to WILLIE.*)

WILLIE: She refers to you at the end. (*He shows him the place and gives him the letter again.*)

LORD GRENHAM: (*Reading.*) 'As I sit here thinking of your father, I could scream with fear that there may be something in heredity!' Bless her heart, I don't blame her. (*He gives him the letter and pats him affectionately on the arm.*) You're a damn lucky fellow; your mother and your wife are the two nicest women I have ever known.

WILLIE: I often see why women liked you so much.

LORD GRENHAM: Thank you, Willie. Well, I'm goin' to have a look at the little pretties. Coming?

WILLIE: Not I. Besides, I'm going to send another cable to Margot.

LORD GRENHAM: Right you are. I like these jazz dances, Willie; it doesn't matter a damn whether you can or whether you can't! (*He exits through the archway.*)
(*WILLIE goes to a desk, tears off a foreign telegraph form and sits down at the desk and begins to write out a message. KITTY appears in the archway.*)

KITTY: Oh! I'm sorry; you're busy.

WILLIE: Not at all! (*He rises.*) Come in! Why aren't you dancing?

KITTY: My dear, I suppose I'm getting old, but I'm so bored with the men you meet at dances nowadays.

WILLIE: (*Smiling.*) I danced with you.

KITTY: But so badly.

WILLIE: (*Laughing.*) That's unfortunate.

KITTY: Nonsense! You don't need to dance. Oh, I forgot to tell you, I rang you up this evening, but you weren't in.

WILLIE: So my man told me. I'm sorry.

KITTY: I was dining alone, and I thought if you were, you might like to dine with me.

WILLIE: I wish I had known. I dined at the club alone.

KITTY: What a dreadful thing to think of, two people dining alone! May I have a cigarette?

WILLIE: I beg your pardon. (*He takes up cigarette-box from desk and offers her one, then lights it for her; also takes one himself and puts the box back on the desk.*)

KITTY: (*Sitting on the settee.*) Thank you. (*She leans back.*) My dear, I feel so dreadfully tired! Truly, do I look terribly haggard?

WILLIE: The reverse; you look charming.

KITTY: One would expect that remark from a good dancer. Look at me and tell me the truth.

WILLIE: You look very, very pretty.

KITTY: (*Laughing.*) That helps me through tomorrow, doesn't it? (*They look at each other. Pause, KITTY looks around the room.*) I adore your house.

WILLIE: It is nice, isn't it?

KITTY: Charming! (*Seeing the picture of MARGOT over the mantelpiece.*) Is that your wife's picture?

WILLIE: Yes. I had her painted in fancy dress.

KITTY: But how perfectly divine!

WILLIE: You think her pretty?

KITTY: Pretty! I think her too charming.

WILLIE: So do I. Frankly, I often wonder why she married me.

KITTY: (*Looking at him.*) Pity you said that.

WILLIE: Why?

KITTY: I don't know; it makes you so ordinary.

WILLIE: I meant it.

KITTY: (*Still looking at him.*) Ridiculous. You know you are most attractive.

WILLIE: I don't, I assure you, and very few other people do, really.

KITTY: Well, that makes you even more attractive to the few who do, doesn't it?

WILLIE: Well, I –

KITTY: And, being a man, you don't know how frightfully nice it is to be able to say the pleasant thing, when you are compelled so often to think the other.

WILLIE: I understand that perfectly.

KITTY: You do? (*She sighs.*) Oh dear! But I should hate not to be a woman. You were writing. I disturbed you. (*Rising.*) I'm so sorry.

(*The music stops.*)

WILLIE: No, no, don't go.

KITTY: I'm not in the way?

WILLIE: Not in the least.

KITTY: And I don't bore you?

WILLIE: Pity you said that.

KITTY: Why?

WILLIE: It makes you so ordinary.

KITTY: (*Laughing.*) And I am.

WILLIE: (*Getting near to her.*) You know you're most attractive.

KITTY: But how thrilling, particularly as I had no idea you thought I was.

WILLIE: You must be told it every day.

KITTY: But I so seldom want to hear it. But you said it rather charmingly.

WILLIE: Because it's true.

KITTY: Nevertheless, I adore to hear you say you think I am. (*She takes his hand, in which he is holding his cigarette.*) May I take a light off your cigarette?

(*He holds it up for her. She removes the cigarette from her mouth; looks at him appealingly. He hesitates, bends over and kisses her. The door opens and MARGOT enters. She appears very excited and happy, but her manner at once changes as she catches sight of them embracing. She has her furs and bag in her hands.*)

WILLIE: Margot!

MARGOT: Won't you introduce me?

(*She puts the furs on the back of a chair.*)

WILLIE: Er – er–

MARGOT: I should like to know who it is I have to thank for so admirably filling my place during my absence.

WILLIE: Margot! This is Miss Lake!

MARGOT: Willie, in his delight at seeing me again, has entirely forgotten to tell you who I am. I am his wife.

KITTY: I know.

MARGOT: You know! You knew he had a wife! But how interesting!

WILLIE: Margot, you must let me explain to you.

MARGOT: But you did, most lucidly, as I entered the room.

WILLIE: I admit appearances are against me, but that kiss you saw meant nothing at all.

MARGOT: I suppose it was merely your way of explaining to Miss Lake how very much you had missed me, and how glad you would be when I came home again?

WILLIE: No, no, but –

MARGOT: I am entirely to blame.

WILLIE: You? Why?

MARGOT: It was careless of me. I ought to have knocked at my own door before I came into my own room. I ask Miss Lake's forgiveness. (*She puts her bag on the desk and begins to take off her gloves.*)

KITTY: I'm sorry this has happened. I should have liked you.

MARGOT: How very flattering.

KITTY: You're entitled to say what you like, of course. As a matter of fact, I envy you. I would give anything to be in a similar position myself. But, as a woman, you know it had nothing to do with him. I'm going to be quite frank with you. I intended it, I like him, and I didn't know you, and quite honestly you never entered my mind.

MARGOT: How very interesting. And, having listened to your curious explanation, you mustn't let me detain you any longer.

KITTY: (*Looking at her angrily.*) You must a moment longer; it isn't quite finished! To your husband, I only appeared as attractive women do to most men – nothing else.

MARGOT: Is that so, Willie?

KITTY: That's not fair; you might have waited until I had gone to ask him that question.

MARGOT: I prefer to ask him while you are here!
(*To WILLIE.*) Won't you answer my question? Well?

WILLIE: I – I – will tell you everything later.

MARGOT: This is your only opportunity. I mean it! Do you understand, Willie?

WILLIE: Yes.

MARGOT: Well?

(*The music starts.*)

WILLIE: I'm sorry, I can't now.

MARGOT: Very well. (*She starts to move to the door.*)

WILLIE: Margot!

MARGOT: (*Looking through the archway.*) What's that?

WILLIE: A lot of infernal idiots dancing.

KITTY: They are not coming in here.

WILLIE: I'll stop them if they do. (*Crossing to the archway.*)

MARGOT: What are you doing?

WILLIE: We don't want every one to know!

MARGOT: Do you mean you think it's likely I will tell them? It might occur to you, Miss Lake has much more to gain by telling them than I have.

WILLIE: But they will notice by your manner.

MARGOT: (*Smiling.*) I don't think so.

(*LADY FRINTON enters through the archway, followed by ARTHUR.*)

LADY FRINTON: Margot, my darling! (*Kisses her.*) But, my dear, this is the most beautiful surprise I have ever known.

MARGOT: And I'm so glad to see you. How are you, Arthur? It is Arthur, isn't it?

ARTHUR: Yes; in the pink, and delighted to see you again.

MARGOT: Thank you.

LADY FRINTON: Let me look at you; quite alright again?

MARGOT: Perfectly.

LADY FRINTON: But I didn't expect to see you for another two months.

MARGOT: Neither did Willie, did you, dear?

WILLIE: No.

LADY FRINTON: (*To KITTY.*) Don't you think she looks splendid?

KITTY: I, unfortunately, never met Mrs Tatham until tonight, but she certainly looks very, very splendid!

LADY FRINTON: Wonderful!

KITTY: (*Going to ARTHUR.*) I have a great desire to dance. Come along.

ARTHUR: I'd love to.

(*KITTY and ARTHUR exit.*)

41

LADY FRINTON: Tell me, what brought you home so soon?

MARGOT: (*Taking WILLIE's arm.*) Does it need any telling? But I will if you like. I left Egypt because I was terribly in love.

LADY FRINTON: Of course, how stupid of me! But you must forgive me, my dear, because nowadays most people go there because they are not! Do come and see them all! They'd love to see you.

MARGOT: Please! I'm so tired. I've been travelling all day.

LADY FRINTON: Of course. And I'm quite sure you don't want me here. I'll come and say goodbye before I go! (*LADY FRINTON exits.*)

MARGOT: (*Removing her arm from WILLIE.*) Another scene in high life avoided, Willie. You might thank me.

WILLIE: I do, but –

MARGOT: But how are we going to avoid it in the future? However, that's for another day! (*She picks up her furs and her bag, then starts to walk to the door.*) Good night!

WILLIE: Margot!

MARGOT: Yes.

WILLIE: I can't let you go like this; you must listen.

MARGOT: Well?

WILLIE: I tell you that kiss meant nothing to me.

MARGOT: Then I deplore your intelligence when you wish it to mean nothing to me. It's meant everything to me. Do you understand you've crushed every single hope of happiness out of me. I stand here cold with misery.

WILLIE: Margot, please.

MARGOT: That you could have dared ask this woman to this house, and then dared to protect her against me.

WILLIE: I couldn't do otherwise, but I give you my word of honour, she means nothing to me. I would give everything I possess in the world for this not to have happened. Won't you believe me?

MARGOT: Believe you? I came back because I love you so much. I couldn't stay away another minute from you! All the way over on the steamer I cried out again and again: – quicker, quicker. Each day seemed like a hundred years, and when I reached the house I flew up the stairs to rush into your arms with happiness, only to find another woman in them! And, as I stand here at this minute, I am ashamed that I can hate anyone as much as I do you!

WILLIE: Please, please.

MARGOT: That's all I have to say. (*She goes to the door.*) (*The music stops. LORD GRENHAM enters through the archway.*)

LORD GRENHAM: In the name of all that's wonderful, it's Margot! Why, what's the matter?

MARGOT: Nothing, nothing! Forgive me, Willie will explain. (*MARGOT exits.*)

LORD GRENHAM: What the devil has happened?

WILLIE: I must go to her. Don't you go, do you understand, don't you go! I'll tell you everything later. (*WILLIE exits.*
LORD GRENHAM watches WILLIE go out. LADY FRINTON comes through the archway.)

LADY FRINTON: Where's Margot?

LORD GRENHAM: Have you seen her?

LADY FRINTON: Yes, of course. What's the matter?

LORD GRENHAM: Mary, there's been a row.

LADY FRINTON: A row? Who with?

LORD GRENHAM: Margot and Willie.

LADY FRINTON: You don't mean it! What about?

LORD GRENHAM: What did you usually row with your husband about?

LADY FRINTON: A woman.

LORD GRENHAM: Well, there's no exception to the rule, even in Margot's case.

LADY FRINTON: Are you suggesting that Willie's being his father's son?

LORD GRENHAM: The opposite! He's been found out.

LADY FRINTON: Poor dear Margot!

LORD GRENHAM: Poor dear Willie!

LADY FRINTON: Do you think I can do anything?

LORD GRENHAM: You can. Go home and pray for forgiveness for asking Kitty Lake to your beastly party.

LADY FRINTON: So that's what it is?

LORD GRENHAM: I imagine so. I know it would be so in my case.

LADY FRINTON: What brutes you men really are!

LORD GRENHAM: Not at all. It's our tender moments that tell against us! Mary, you'd better hop it. I've got myself out of these damn difficulties many times, but I'm not so certain I can lie my son out of them. However, I am going to have a dash. I may appear to be a very indifferent parent but, believe me, I have a great affection for Willie, and more than that, I admire his wife.

LADY FRINTON: So you should. You'll give me lunch tomorrow, and tell me all about it, you understand?

LORD GRENHAM: Right you are!

LADY FRINTON: Oh dear, what a place this world would be if there were no men in it.

LORD GRENHAM: If that were the case, believe me, your name would head the petition.

LADY FRINTON: Well, I must go back to my guests.

LORD GRENHAM: And, by the way, don't let any of your comic friends come in here – they are not wanted at the moment, believe me.

LADY FRINTON: Good night, you old fool. (*She exits through the archway.*)

(*LORD GRENHAM sits on the settee. WILLIE enters.*)

LORD GRENHAM: Come on, tell me all about it.

WILLIE: It's awful, it's terrible!

LORD GRENHAM: I know! I know! She copped you, so to speak.

WILLIE: Yes.

LORD GRENHAM: Well, come on!

WILLIE: Meaning nothing, on my honour, nothing at all, I kissed her.

LORD GRENHAM: Margot didn't see you?

WILLIE: Yes.

LORD GRENHAM: I knew you would kiss her, but I never believed you could be such a fool as to let anybody see you.

WILLIE: It was done in a second. I never meant it. Oh, I can't explain. I assure you, I don't care a damn for her.

LORD GRENHAM: You needn't explain to me, I should have done exactly the same thing. I'll stand by you, Willie, but for heaven's sake, when I've got you out of this, stand by experience. Believe me, the British Museum is much more interesting than it appears from the outside.

WILLIE: I don't know that she will come down! She won't for me, so I sent a message to say you wanted to see her. She swears she's going to leave me!

LORD GRENHAM: Never take any notice of that, first words they always say.

WILLIE: But she means it.

LORD GRENHAM: Nonsense! You leave it to me. I'll tell her the tale.

WILLIE: You'll do nothing of the sort. I only want you to tell her the truth.

LORD GRENHAM: My boy, there are more men separated from their wives whom they love, for that crime, than you and I could ever count. The most fatal thing in the world, believe me. Put out some of the lights, let the atmosphere be sympathetic.

(*WILLIE switches off some of the lights.*)

Good! Now, quiet a moment, I must try and get myself in the frame of mind that you have done something I could never think of doing.

(*The door opens. MARGOT enters.*)

Thank you, Margot. Come over here.

(*He moves to the right end of settee to make room for her beside him. She ignores this and remains standing.*)

MARGOT: Well?

LORD GRENHAM: This is really a most regrettable and unfortunate business, my dear.

MARGOT: Have you sent for me to tell me that?

LORD GRENHAM: Certainly not. I want to help you to put it right.

MARGOT: And you think you'll be able to?

LORD GRENHAM: I'm confident.

MARGOT: Well, you're wrong. I've made up my mind.

LORD GRENHAM: Come, come, that's usually the act of a person who hasn't any, and that doesn't apply to you! Willie never meant anything by that kiss.

MARGOT: So he tells me.

LORD GRENHAM: And you don't believe him?

MARGOT: Do you?

LORD GRENHAM: Absolutely!

MARGOT: How interesting! I should have thought you the one man in the world who would have known better.

LORD GRENHAM: My dear, an innocent kiss, bah! What is that in a man's life?

MARGOT: Everything! Should you happen to be the woman who doesn't receive it.

LORD GRENHAM: Willie! Now, on your honour, have you ever kissed that girl before, or any other during Margot's absence?

WILLIE: Never, never, on my honour!

LORD GRENHAM: There you are! And I'll come out in the open. I don't know how you have done it. (*To MARGOT.*) The whole thing may be described as an accident.

MARGOT: I'm very tired. Is there anything else?

WILLIE: Margot, my darling, please try and understand.

MARGOT: What is there to understand?

WILLIE: Don't you realise that –

MARGOT: I realise a number of ridiculous people in ridiculous clothing being entertained in my house, as an excuse for a notorious young person to be included amongst them, with the knowledge of who she is and what she is, without even the association of a delicate atmosphere. I enter the room, and it might have been some one else, and find you kissing her! That I can neither understand nor forgive. (*She goes to door.*)

LORD GRENHAM: Well, I don't agree with you, and if you will allow me to say so, it's particularly small and un-understanding of you.

(*The music starts.*)

MARGOT: (*Turning.*) You dare say that to me?

LORD GRENHAM: I dare!

MARGOT: Then you ought to be ashamed of yourself.

LORD GRENHAM: I'm not! And I repeat it's very unworthy of you and I am deeply disappointed in you.

WILLIE: Father, please!

LORD GRENHAM: (*Rising.*) My dear boy, Margot is a girl who evidently is unable to understand anything.

MARGOT: Indeed!

LORD GRENHAM: Do you deny it?

MARGOT: Absolutely!

LORD GRENHAM: Then what could you understand?

MARGOT: Many things! If it had been a garden of warmth and beauty, a wonderful moon, for instance, shining on the water and in the distance a violin playing the most divine music, and she had been an attractive woman, then I might have understood! (*She exits.*)
(*LORD GRENHAM turns to WILLIE.*)

LORD GRENHAM: It sounds attractive, but I still stand by museums.

End of Act One.

ACT TWO

Grenham Court. Afternoon. Two weeks later. The room has French windows leading to the garden and doors to the other parts of the house. LORD GRENHAM comes through the windows and places his hat and stick in a corner. ROBERTS enters with 'Pall Mall' and the 'Evening Standard'. As he puts them down he sees LORD GRENHAM.

ROBERTS: Sorry, my lord, I didn't know you had returned.

LORD GRENHAM: I came through the garden. I noticed during my absence in London during the last three days the position of the furniture in this room has been changed. Why?

ROBERTS: Mrs Lynton, my lord, ordered it to be done.

LORD GRENHAM: (*Nodding his head with meaning.*) Ah! A considerable improvement. Tell me, has the geographical position of any other of our rooms been altered?

ROBERTS: You will find your study also considerably improved, my lord.

LORD GRENHAM: Ah!

ROBERTS: (*In a manner which suggests he has something serious to say.*) My lord!

LORD GRENHAM: Yes, Roberts?

ROBERTS: Polly, the parlour maid, has given us notice to leave at the end of the month.

LORD GRENHAM: (*Sighing.*) I was afraid it was going to be the cook!

ROBERTS: If I may say so, my lord, you will find it very difficult to replace Polly. An excellent servant, my lord.

LORD GRENHAM: In that case, you might, in a subtle manner, let her know that when my sister leaves here on Monday, the furniture will be replaced to the position that she and I prefer.

ROBERTS: I will, my lord.

(WILLIE enters. ROBERTS stands aside for him to pass, then goes off.)

48

WILLIE: Hullo, Father!

LORD GRENHAM: Hullo, Willie!

WILLIE: Had a good time in town? (*He gives the impression of being very depressed and miserable.*)

LORD GRENHAM: Very! (*Looking at him.*) To the most casual observer it is evident that during my absence our domestic relations have undergone no change?

WILLIE: None! And if there had been any chance of Margot forgiving me, your sister and that Vicar she married would have entirely disposed of it!

LORD GRENHAM: It was a pity their yearly visit to me should have happened at this time.

WILLIE: I wish they were in hell or anywhere except here!

LORD GRENHAM: Leave me something to look forward to, Willie; I may be there myself in a year or two!

WILLIE: They have never stopped praying for my misdeeds ever since you left. How glad they are my mother has been spared this unhappiness! You realise, of course, they assume the worst.

LORD GRENHAM: Half the joy of life would be gone for them if they didn't.

WILLIE: Some of these Christians are odd people.

LORD GRENHAM: I am bound to say, my boy, in moments of despair, I prefer the hearty understanding of a money-lender! But Margot doesn't take them seriously.

WILLIE: Every time either of them opens their mouth, Margot looks at me and says 'There', and, as I told you on the telephone this morning, Margot leaves me on Monday and goes to her mother for a month! (*In anguish.*) What am I to do?

LORD GRENHAM: (*Smiling.*) Go to the Lakes for a month.

WILLIE: What a beastly thing to suggest!

LORD GRENHAM: Possibly! But if your wife had the slightest idea you would, her mother wouldn't see her again for years!

WILLIE: You know very little about women like Margot.

LORD GRENHAM: Very, Willie, except they are identically the same as all other women.

49

WILLIE: You make me laugh! Why do you suppose I married her?

LORD GRENHAM: For the same reason that every other man marries his wife, because she is different from any other woman he has ever known.

WILLIE: Oh, it's waste of time to talk to you.

LORD GRENHAM: Not at all! Your wife leaves you for four months, returns and finds you in the arms of another woman! I am full of sympathy! But, since her return a fortnight ago, despite every demonstration of regret and affection, she refuses even to allow you to hold her hand, let alone let you kiss her. Surely that's very like all other women, isn't it?

WILLIE: (*Shaking his head.*) Don't you understand, with her nature she can't. I have horrified her.

LORD GRENHAM: You have done more than that.

WILLIE: What do you mean?

LORD GRENHAM: You've frightened her. She's terrified you might do it again, so she's learning you, Willie. She is slowly but surely putting you in the position of never kissing any woman but her again!

WILLIE: And I never want to.

LORD GRENHAM: A noble sentiment, but a terribly cramped position to be in, believe me.

WILLIE: Unless you are prepared to discuss my wife in a very different manner from this, I'll ask you to be good enough not to discuss her at all!

LORD GRENHAM: Just as you like, Willie.

WILLIE: Margot is incapable of forgiving, because she's incapable of understanding.

LORD GRENHAM: What you wish me to believe is, that Margot, given similar circumstances, provoked by admiration, her vanity sincerely appealed to, would not do what you did?

WILLIE: Certainly not! How dare you make such a suggestion?

LORD GRENHAM: I'm sorry, and I congratulate you very sincerely. Supposing some one were to suggest, under similar circumstances, your wife would be as human as you were, what would you do?

WILLIE: If it were a man, knock him down!

LORD GRENHAM: An effective way of encouraging reticence! (*Picking up a case of pearls on the mantelpiece.*) Charming! For Margot?

WILLIE: Yes.

LORD GRENHAM: You must have paid quite a lot of money for these.

WILLIE: Well?

LORD GRENHAM: I'm not criticising! I was only wondering, speaking metaphorically, of course, if a shilling cane wouldn't have been more appreciated? (*ROBERTS enters, leaving the door open; he is carrying tea on a tray; he places it on the small tea-table, then goes off. ANGELA enters. ROBERTS re-enters with the cake-stand then leaves again.*)

ANGELA: (*To LORD GRENHAM, offering him her cheek.*) So you're back again, Grenham?

LORD GRENHAM: (*Kissing ANGELA.*) And delighted to see you, my dear Angela.

ANGELA: (*Sitting at the tea-table.*) And what have you been doing in London?

LORD GRENHAM: (*Smiling.*) When a man reaches a certain age, there is nothing left him but to watch what other people do.

ANGELA: (*She begins to pour out LORD GRENHAM's tea, then pours out WILLIE's.*) Do I understand you have at last reached that age?

LORD GRENHAM: Not yet! Two lumps, please.

ANGELA: When do you propose to?

LORD GRENHAM: The day I do you will find it announced on the same page as my biography in *The Times.* (*He gets his tea.*)

ANGELA: (*To WILLIE.*) Like your father in other things, you take two lumps in your tea?

WILLIE: (*Angrily.*) Three! (*He gets his tea and a cake from the stand, then sits drinking his tea and looking at a magazine.*)

ANGELA: Really! (*To LORD GRENHAM.*) Does your friend, Lady Frinton, know that tea is ready? (*She pours out her own tea.*)

LORD GRENHAM: My experience of my friend Lady Frinton is that she knows most things.

ANGELA: She'll be some time yet, I expect. She's painting her face to make herself look beautiful for you.

LORD GRENHAM: I hope so. The fear I have is, she one day may forget to paint it.

ANGELA: Horrid woman! I don't know how you can bear to have her here!

LORD GRENHAM: It's only fair, my dear sister, you should know Lady Frinton's intentions towards me are perfectly honourable. During the last ten days she has been here she has done me the honour of asking me to be her husband three times.

ANGELA: You are not thinking of doing such a terrible thing, are you?

LORD GRENHAM: All my life I have found it very difficult to refuse a woman anything; except marriage! (*WILLIE laughs.*)

ANGELA: (*Looking at WILLIE.*) And you, young man, would be much better employed repenting of your own sins, than laughing at your father's.

WILLIE: (*Angrily.*) I shall laugh exactly when I like.

ANGELA: And please don't be rude to me.

LORD GRENHAM: Inability to sacrifice one's character for good manners is hardly rudeness, my dear Angela.

ANGELA: I say he was extremely rude to me!

LORD GRENHAM: (*Quietly.*) No, no, only an indifferently phrased, but deserved, rebuke, my dear.

ANGELA: (*Staring at WILLIE.*) Really!
(*LADY FRINTON enters.*)

LADY FRINTON: Hullo, Grenham dear! I saw you pass my window, but I had so little on I resisted the temptation of greeting you!
(*A look of horror from ANGELA.*)
Tea ready, dear?

ANGELA: Tea has been ready for a quarter of an hour!

LADY FRINTON: Then it's undrinkable. Ring the bell, Grenham dear, and we'll have some fresh made.

(*LORD GRENHAM rings the bell above the fireplace.*)

ANGELA: I wonder how you people keep your servants.

LADY FRINTON: By not drinking undrinkable tea, darling, thereby not apologising to them for being a little late.

LORD GRENHAM: I agree!

(*ROBERTS enters.*)

LADY FRINTON: Some fresh tea, please, Roberts.

ROBERTS: Yes, my lady! (*He takes the teapot and exits.*)

LADY FRINTON: There you are! Even the ordering of a little fresh tea impresses him that we are the right people!

LORD GRENHAM: Quite right! Democracy will go no distance so long as there are democrats!

LADY FRINTON: (*Smiling at LORD GRENHAM, she turns to ANGELA.*) Now tell me, dear, all the exciting things you have done this afternoon.

ANGELA: I rested on my bed for two hours.

LADY FRINTON: But how thrilling! And I from my bedroom window was fascinated by your dear husband, the Vicar, feeding the chickens and carrying on with all the beautiful simplicity of life. And he in return, unknown to the chickens, gazed up at my window, and was equally fascinated watching me put a little black on my eyelids.

ANGELA: Lady Frinton, my husband disapproves of that habit as strongly as I do!

LADY FRINTON: Not at all! The chickens were a mere subterfuge, the accomplices of a shy man!

(*ROBERTS enters, places the tea on the tray.*)

Thank you, Roberts.

(*ANGELA has the greatest difficulty controlling herself and begins to pour out LADY FRINTON's tea. ROBERTS exits.*)

ANGELA: Kindly understand I strongly resent my husband being talked of in this manner.

LADY FRINTON: Sorry, darling, we won't do it anymore.

(*ANGELA is about to put sugar in LADY FRINTON's cup.*)

No sugar, it ruins the figure.

(*ANGELA gives LADY FRINTON her tea, and LORD GRENHAM offers her the cake-stand. She takes a biscuit and he puts down the stand again.*)

Where's Margot? Does she know tea is ready?

WILLIE: She's having it in her room.

LADY FRINTON: Are you sure? She told me she was coming down.

WILLIE: She did? I'll go and tell her! (*Rising, he moves to the door.*)

(*The VICAR enters.*)

VICAR: (*As WILLIE passes him.*) Ah, Willie.

(*WILLIE exits. The VICAR takes a seat. ANGELA pours out his tea, hands it to him and then begins to knit.*)

LADY FRINTON: You look worried, Vicar dear!

VICAR: I am! I am! It distresses me to see those two young people separated in this manner.

LORD GRENHAM: It's entirely Margot's fault that they are. Willie has done all he can to make it up.

VICAR: The light way you treat this matter, Grenham, sometimes suggests to me you do not remember what your son did.

LORD GRENHAM: Of course I do, my dear friend. He kissed another woman that wasn't his wife, and his wife had the good luck to catch him at it.

VICAR: The good luck?

LORD GRENHAM: Of course! How many women of your acquaintance have had the privilege of actually catching their husbands in the arms of another woman?

VICAR: (*Indignantly.*) The men of my acquaintance are not in the habit of doing such things, Grenham.

LORD GRENHAM: Then they have a lot to learn (*He pauses.*) or is it you who have?

ANGELA: He is my brother, but he is a very, very bad man!

LORD GRENHAM: What you don't seem to grasp, Vicar, is that Margot is not angry with Willie because he kissed another woman! She's angry with herself because he should want to.

VICAR: I must be forgiven, but I do not understand.

LORD GRENHAM: Well, if some one were to tell you that the sermon you preached last Sunday was one of the dullest he had ever heard, (*LADY FRINTON laughs.*) you'd find yourself leaving him out of your prayers that night! Vanity, the most vulnerable spot in any of us.

VICAR: Indeed! Nevertheless, I still wonder, with her noble high-minded character, if she will ever be able to forgive him.

LADY FRINTON: She'll never forget, but in time she will forgive! (*She finishes her tea and puts it down on the tray.*)

VICAR: Ah, my dear lady, apply it to yourself. Supposing you had gone into your room and found your husband wrapped in the arms of another woman, how would it have occurred to you?

LADY FRINTON: My husband's ideas of women were rather curious. If I had caught him in that position, I should have known at once he had at last found someone who could teach him golf.

LORD GRENHAM: (*Laughing.*) Mary, there are moments when I adore you.

LADY FRINTON: (*Blowing him a kiss.*) Darling! You fill me with hope.

ANGELA: You're wasting your time, Ernest. My brother looks upon his son as a hero for having broken his dear wife's heart! Even the criminal in the dock would receive my brother's sympathy.

LORD GRENHAM: Not at all, my sympathy would entirely be with the other twelve criminals in the jury box.

VICAR: (*Shaking his head.*) Deplorable cynicism, Grenham, deplorable!

LORD GRENHAM: Come, come, Vicar, you take this matter too seriously. What are the facts? Willie, provoked by admiration for a beautiful woman, stands today in the position, but for the grace of God, you, Margot, I, and heaps of other people would be in.

VICAR: Grenham, I protest!

LORD GRENHAM: I knew you would, my dear fellow!

VICAR: I have never even looked at any other woman but my wife in my life!

LORD GRENHAM: No more would Willie if he hadn't been caught in the act.

ANGELA: Oh you bad, bad man!

LORD GRENHAM: An understanding man, my dear, who accepts the elementary facts of life! Men and women crave for appreciation more than for anything else; it's the great driving force of the world! And in our different ways we all succumb to it. Some, instead of buying a pair of socks at the hosier's for the curate, sit at home and knit them.

ANGELA: (*Stopping knitting.*) If you are referring to me, Grenham, I have knitted socks for many curates.

LORD GRENHAM: That's all I said, darling.

ANGELA: But understand I was not in love with them.

LORD GRENHAM: No more was Willie! But, unfortunately, he doesn't knit.

(*LADY FRINTON laughs. ANGELA puts down her knitting, annoyed.*)

ANGELA: You should be ashamed of yourself laughing at him!

LADY FRINTON: Can't help it, my dear. Grenham in this mood tickles me to death!

LORD GRENHAM: So if we could remove for a moment conventionality, which is only a more musical word than hypocrisy, and in a spirit of tolerance realise we are all capable of falling to some form of temptation, we might begin to understand, as I say, that even Margot given equal provocation might have done what Willie did!

VICAR: Margot is incapable of even thinking such a thought, and to speak of a girl with her beautiful character in that way, is a mean defence of your son, for whom I can find no excuse.

LORD GRENHAM: Miss Lake was a beautiful woman.

VICAR: Then are we all to fall at the feet of a woman merely because she is beautiful!

LORD GRENHAM: Some man does!

(*MARGOT enters with her hat in her hand and an unstamped letter.*)

MARGOT. Some man does what? (*She goes to LADY FRINTON, kisses her, goes to ANGELA, squeezes the hand she offers her and puts her hat on a table.*)

LORD GRENHAM: I have been endeavouring to persuade our Vicar, Margot dear, that to a man, a beautiful woman, and to a woman an attractive man, makes heaven temporarily a much nearer place than he would have us believe it is.

MARGOT: I hope he doesn't believe you.

VICAR: I don't, my dear.

MARGOT: I'm glad! (*To LORD GRENHAM.*) I am right in saying that it was I who inspired the platitude?

LORD GRENHAM: You are.

MARGOT: (*Sighing.*) I would be so grateful if I might be once left out of your conversation.

VICAR: It distresses me so much, my dear, to see you and Willie estranged in this manner.

MARGOT: If I am unable to fill Miss Lake's place in my husband's arms with the alacrity that Miss Lake filled mine, I must be forgiven! Has anyone a stamp?

LORD GRENHAM: (*Smiling.*) Happily I have. (*He takes out a book of stamps and hands it to her.*)

MARGOT: Thank you so much! (*As she is tearing off a stamp she notices ANGELA is not knitting.*) Why, Aunt Angela, this is the first time I have seen you without your knitting.
(*She puts the stamped letter on the table and returns the book to LORD GRENHAM.*)

ANGELA: I shall never knit again in this house.

MARGOT: Why not?

ANGELA: It's misunderstood!

MARGOT: (*Laughing.*) But how funny! By whom?

ANGELA: By your father-in-law.

MARGOT: But you surely don't take any notice of what my father-in-law says, do you? (*Turning to him.*) Well, what did you do in London?

LORD GRENHAM: Several things!

MARGOT: Oh!

LADY FRINTON: What I want to know is, what took you up to town so suddenly the other morning?

LORD GRENHAM: The honour of a lady to whom I am very devoted!

LADY FRINTON: I knew there was a woman in it!

LORD GRENHAM: Quite, but I was not the man. The man I'm referring to in this case, wrote to me about the lady, but instead of answering his letter by post I called on him personally.

LADY FRINTON: What was the lady's name?

LORD GRENHAM: (*He pauses, then speaks with great meaning.*) If I told, not one of you would believe me.

ANGELA: Personally, I don't wish to know. (*She rises and picks up her knitting.*) I am going to fill my mind and body with purer air! Ernest, I am going to walk! (*She goes off to the garden.*)

LORD GRENHAM: (*Smiling at the VICAR.*) Which means, Ernest, you are going to walk.

VICAR: But I like it, Grenham – I like it!

(*He goes off, humming a hymn: 'Come, ye thankful people, come'. MARGOT helps herself to tea.*)

MARGOT: It amazes me how those two people care to take their holidays with you.

LORD GRENHAM: The house is comfortable, the food is excellent, and in their hearts they like me well enough to come and put my house in disorder for me once a year!

MARGOT: That could be avoided by your settling down and marrying again.

LORD GRENHAM: I agree. But who would have me?

LADY FRINTON: I would.

LORD GRENHAM: Mary darling, I didn't intend you to pick me up quite so quickly.

LADY FRINTON: You may not know it, Grenham, but we are being talked about.

LORD GRENHAM: Impossible, why should we be?

LADY FRINTON: Because I have seen to it that we are! For months at a time I come down here and stay here, to all intents and purposes as your lady housekeeper; did you know any woman who took on that job without being full of hope?

LORD GRENHAM: Never!

LADY FRINTON: Exactly! I only told the Vicar this afternoon how dreadfully you snored!

LORD GRENHAM: What did he say?

LADY FRINTON: He became quite animated, and asked me how I knew, and I told him because my room is next to yours.

LORD GRENHAM: But it isn't.

LADY FRINTON: The Vicar would prefer that it was, so I leave the rest to him.

LORD GRENHAM: You're a very determined party, Mary dear.

LADY FRINTON: I am; I'm very fond of you, and I have made up my mind to marry you!

LORD GRENHAM: My dear! You mustn't make up your young mind in too great a hurry, think it over and come to me in five years' time, and if you still think the same way, we'll think about it.

LADY FRINTON: It's no use, Grenham, you're for it.

LORD GRENHAM: Mary dear, I am a man of very determined character.

MARGOT: Nonsense. You've already got one foot in the registrar's office.

LADY FRINTON: (*With a sigh.*) Yes, but alas the other's still firmly planted in the British Museum. (*She rises.*) Nevertheless, amongst other qualities that I possess, which I commend to you, Grenham, one is, I too am a determined character. (*She exits.*)

MARGOT: And when a woman's making up her mind – well – but she's a darling, why don't you marry her?

LORD GRENHAM: It would be wrong for a young man of my elastic propensities to marry anyone yet. Besides, I couldn't bear to part with my freedom.

MARGOT: Selfish rather, isn't it?

LORD GRENHAM: I don't think so! Didn't you enjoy yours in Egypt?

MARGOT: Do you know it never occurred to me that
    I had it?

LORD GRENHAM: Pity.

MARGOT: Why?

LORD GRENHAM: I would have helped you to
    understand and forgive Willie so much quicker.

MARGOT: I hope you haven't forgotten you promised
    never to return to this subject?

LORD GRENHAM: I remember! So I assume you are not
    yet able to forgive your erring husband?

MARGOT: For the last time, I shall forgive Willie exactly
    when I choose.

LORD GRENHAM: Don't leave it too late.

MARGOT: What do you mean?

LORD GRENHAM: I mean, even the novelty of making
    love to a charming but unreciprocative wife wears off!

MARGOT: Really! Well, I don't wish to discuss it.
    (*WILLIE enters.*)

LORD GRENHAM: Ah, Willie, my boy. Margot, my dear,
    I have just remembered, I wonder if you would do
    something for me?

MARGOT: That's all I live for.

LORD GRENHAM: Angel! I have a young friend of mine
    coming by the four fifty-five, and as I promised to run in
    and see old Garnet who is ill, it's just possible I may not
    be back in time to greet him, so would you give him
    some tea and look after him for me until I return?

WILLIE: Who is he?

LORD GRENHAM: A young man you have never met,
    Willie, but you'll like him.

WILLIE: (*Annoyed.*) Thoughtful of you to ask a stranger
    down here in these times.

LORD GRENHAM: (*Rising.*) Very, my dear boy. It
    occurred to me in London our diagnosis of Margot's case
    is entirely wrong; we are all of us treating her for a
    broken heart. Whereas – I was suddenly inspired and
    with joy – it's nothing of the sort! It's just a very
    ordinary complaint, but to effect a cure we have only to

restore to her her sense of humour. And I rather think our young friend might considerably help. (*He takes MARGOT's hand and kisses it.*) Bless you!
(*LORD GRENHAM goes into the garden, taking his hat and stick with him. MARGOT picks up a paper and begins to read.*)

WILLIE: It's no use sulking with me; it's not my fault my father's a damned fool.

MARGOT: Or yours that he ever had a son!

WILLIE: That's a charming thing to say to me.

MARGOT: Wouldn't apt be more correct?

WILLIE: Does it ever occur to you that you are my wife?

MARGOT: Oh, yes! Like yourself, on occasions.

WILLIE: Margot, I have stood all that I can stand of this attitude of yours to me, and this has got to be settled now once and for all! (*She doesn't answer.*) Put that paper down!

MARGOT: (*Still reading.*) I'm engrossed in a case, Willie, of a woman who forgave her husband four times, and she is now doing what she should have done the first time.
(*WILLIE tears the paper out of her hand and throws it away. She picks up the other paper and reads.*)
Well?

WILLIE: How much longer do you propose to treat me in this way?

MARGOT: I have told you that is something that I have no control over.

WILLIE: (*Laughing normally.*) And all because I kissed a woman once!

MARGOT: Even if it was only once, you forget I saw it, and when you can remove from my mind the picture of Miss Lake in your arms being passionately kissed by you that once, I'll take her place.

WILLIE: It's hopeless! Can't you – can't you see that I am truly repentant?

MARGOT: Is any man truly repentant at having kissed a beautiful woman?

WILLIE: Of course!

MARGOT: All men are truly repentant at having been caught kissing one, which means they will never let it happen again.

WILLIE: It will never happen again in my case.

MARGOT: You were always a pessimist, Willie dear.

WILLIE: It's no use. I can't bear it any longer. If you can't forgive me, why not have done with it, and send me away?

MARGOT: How can I? I can't trust you.

WILLIE: There you are! There you are!

MARGOT: Willie, supposing you had come into a room, and found me being kissed in the same way as I saw you kissing Miss Lake, what would your attitude be to me?

WILLIE: Such a thing is impossible!

MARGOT: I'm not as human as you are? (*He doesn't answer.*) But supposing I had, would you have spoken to me again?

WILLIE: No, I shouldn't.

MARGOT: Then why should I?

WILLIE: Because it would be quite different.

MARGOT: In what way?

WILLIE: Because you couldn't have, unless you were in love with him, and I wasn't.

MARGOT: Oh dear, I wish men knew more about women than they do! Tell me this, what would have happened if I hadn't come back that night?

WILLIE: Nothing!

MARGOT: If you mean that, you evidently know very little about yourself or Miss Lake.

WILLIE: Don't you understand? I was lonely, bored; she was an amusing companion. I never meant anything. I swear it.

MARGOT: I admit that's the silver lining; it's always the woman's fault.

WILLIE: I wouldn't go as far as that,

MARGOT: You're not expected to! But, nevertheless, it's always the woman's fault! Shall I tell you how she got you?
(*WILLIE looks at her.*)

You were so unlike any other man she had ever met, it was so refreshing to be appreciated by a man merely because she was a nice woman! And when she looked at my picture she was amazed at my beauty, and told you I was one of the prettiest women she had ever seen! Did she?

WILLIE: (*Hesitating.*) Yes.

MARGOT: Of course! I wonder why, but that never fails with any man. (*She sighs.*) How angry the monkeys must be when they hear that men were descended from them!

WILLIE: (*Taking her hand.*) Margot, I beg of you! Please! Please! (*He kisses the palm of her hand.*)

MARGOT: That's new, Willie! (*She snatches her hand away.*) Did Miss Lake teach you that?

WILLIE: (*Rising.*) Oh! Oh! Damn Miss Lake! Damn everything! (*He exits.*)

(*MARGOT watches him go out. She smiles. LORD GRENHAM returns with his hat and stick in hand.*)

LORD GRENHAM: Where's Willie?

MARGOT: I don't know. I only know he left me in a horrid temper.

LORD GRENHAM: Ah! I'm sorry! You won't forget to look after my young friend for me?

MARGOT: I'll give him some tea and hand him over to Willie.

LORD GRENHAM: As a matter of fact, Margot, I don't think Willie will like my young friend who's coming for the weekend.

MARGOT: Why not?

LORD GRENHAM: Well, I don't know! He's a charming fellow, you know, an Australian.

(*MARGOT starts a little.*)

By the way, now I come to think of it, I remember he told me he was out in Egypt; and when I come to think further, it must have been about the same time as you were there.

MARGOT: (*Agitated.*) Really? (*She picks up a paper.*)

LORD GRENHAM: He's a charming fellow, and, as I say, I think you'll like him. (*He pauses.*) His name, Margot, is Willocks!

(*MARGOT controls her agitation, pretending to read the paper.*)

By the way, you didn't by any chance when you were out in Egypt meet a lady by the name of Margaret Spalding, did you?

MARGOT: (*Very agitated.*) I – I – why should I?

LORD GRENHAM: I was only wondering. This young man fell very much in love with her, and, instead of returning direct to Australia, as he told her he was going to do, he is spending a few weeks in England looking for her!

(*There is a pause.*)

Well, I must go! Margot! You never know with these young men, but possibly when I return I shouldn't be a bit surprised to hear he hadn't come by the four fifty-five.

(*He goes out again. MARGOT, very excited and agitated, throws down the paper. She rings the bell violently and gets her hat.*

ROBERTS enters.)

MARGOT: (*To him, quickly.*) Has the car gone to meet the four fifty-five yet?

ROBERTS: Just going, madam.

MARGOT: Quickly, stop him. Don't stand looking at me, stop him. Tell him I'm coming to the station with him!

(*ROBERTS exits.*

MARGOT goes up to the garden windows, looking off. ANGELA enters.)

ANGELA: I wonder after dinner if you would sing to us that –

MARGOT: (*Excitedly.*) I shall never sing again. (*She exits hurriedly, banging the door after her.*)

(*ANGELA is amazed at her demeanour, then sees the paper WILLIE had previously thrown on the floor, picks it up, straightens it out and puts it on a table.*

ROBERTS enters.)

ANGELA: Roberts, please remove that table.

(*As ROBERTS exits with the tea-table, the VICAR enters.*)

VICAR: What on earth has happened to our dear Margot? She's gone off in the car without even a coat.

ANGELA: Stupid child, she'll catch her death of cold.

VICAR: I can't help feeling your brother has been worrying her again.

ANGELA: Ernest, I am glad we are going home on Monday.

VICAR: So am I, my dear! It's a most comfortable house to stay in, and the food is excellent, excellent, but each year I come here I realise there is no place like home! Your brother knows we haven't to be back for another week!

ANGELA: I have hinted it several times, but it appears not to interest him.

VICAR: Well, it's just as well. I shall be glad to be home again.

ANGELA: I am going to write to Miss Summers; have you any message for her?

VICAR: Tell her we are coming home on Monday, and I will attend the meeting on Thursday, and in the event of our changing our minds and staying on here another week I will let her know.

ANGELA: Very well! (*She exits.*)

(*The VICAR, humming a few bars of the hymn 'Come, all ye faithful people, come', picks up 'The Times'.*
WILLIE enters.)

VICAR: Do you want *The Times*, Willie?

WILLIE: No! Where is Margot? Do you know?

VICAR: She went out a moment ago in a manner that can only be described as one of great unhappiness.

WILLIE: Which way did she go?

VICAR: It's no use going after her; she went in the car.

WILLIE: In the car? But the car's gone to the station to meet the four fifty-five.

VICAR: Well, she went in it.

WILLIE: I suppose my father has been upsetting her again.

VICAR: (*Looking at him.*) Someone has, Willie! Someone has! If anyone wants me I will be in the morning-room.

WILLIE: It's unlikely you will be disturbed!

(*The VICAR exits.*
ROBERTS enters.)

ROBERTS: (*Carrying tray with a card on it.*) I am unable to find his lordship, sir, and the gentleman has just arrived.

WILLIE: (*Picking up the card and looking at it.*) Oh, I know! Show him in here.

(*ROBERTS goes off.*
WILLIE reads out the name on the card, 'Mr. John Willocks,' and throws it on a small table. ROBERTS returns, followed by JOHN WILLOCKS, a good-looking man about thirty and smartly dressed.)

ROBERTS: Mr. Willocks, sir!

(*ROBERTS exits.*)

WILLIE: (*Putting out his hand.*) How do you do?

WILLOCKS: How do you do? You're Mr. Tatham?

WILLIE: That's right.

WILLOCKS: Very glad to meet you.

WILLIE: Thank you.

WILLOCKS: You probably know I am staying the weekend with you.

WILLIE: Yes! I'm glad. My father has had to go out and see an old friend of his, but he won't be long. Do sit down.

WILLOCKS: Thank you. I was coming by train, but it was such a perfect afternoon, and as I want to see as much of your English country as possible, I came by car.

WILLIE: You don't live in England, then?

WILLOCKS: No, I'm an Australian.

WILLIE: Oh! I'll ring for some tea for you.

WILLOCKS: Thank you. I had it on the way down.

WILLIE: Whisky and soda?

WILLOCKS: No, many thanks. What a delightful place this is!

WILLIE: It is rather. I'm glad you like it.

WILLOCKS:. I do immensely! It is exceedingly kind of your father, to whom I am more or less a stranger, to ask me down to stay with you.

WILLIE: Not at all.

WILLOCKS: Oh, it is. I little thought when I wrote him that letter, I should meet anyone quite as kind as he has been to me.

WILLIE: What letter was that, Mr. Willocks?

WILLOCKS: He hasn't told you?

WILLIE: No!

WILLOCKS: Then you don't know how I met your father, Mr. Tatham?

WILLIE: No.

WILLOCKS: My introduction to your father came about in a most curious way.

WILLIE: Indeed!

WILLOCKS: (*Pointing to whisky and soda.*) May I change my mind and have a whisky and soda?

WILLIE: Please, do. (*He rises to pour out the drink.*)

WILLOCKS: Would it bore you if I told you?

WILLIE: Not at all.

WILLOCKS: (*Laughing a little sadly.*) It's the only thought that's in my mind. When I was abroad, I met accidentally at my hotel a lady who also was staying there alone!
(*WILLIE brings down the drink and gives it to WILLOCKS.*)
Thanks.

WILLIE: That's alright.

WILLOCKS: When I met her it was my intention to return home that Saturday, but she attracted me, and I liked her so much, I postponed it for a week to be with her.
(*Lifting his glass.*) Good luck!

WILLIE: Good luck! (*Taking out his case.*) Cigarette?

WILLOCKS: No, thanks. We saw a great deal of each other, and became very friendly; it was inevitable from the beginning. I soon realised I was in love with her, and although your father differs, I shall always believe she was in love with me.

WILLIE: Well?

WILLOCKS: One morning I looked for her. She was nowhere to be found. I inquired of the manager of the hotel if he knew where she was; without a word, not a message, she had left that morning for England!

WILLIE: Extraordinary! But how does my father come
into it?

WILLOCKS: Because in talking one day she mentioned his
name. She appeared to know him well, so as soon as I
got to London I wrote to him and asked him if he could
help me by telling me where I could find her.

WILLIE: And did my father know her?

WILLOCKS: Very well.

WILLIE: (*Rather bored.*) Well, that's alright, then.

WILLOCKS: Not quite! He has written to her and asked
her for her permission to tell me where she is before
giving me the address.

WILLIE: And she will give it, of course.

WILLOCKS: I believe she will, and I hope she will!

WILLIE: Of course she will! You had no quarrel with her?

WILLOCKS: Quarrel with her? The last night I saw her,
I shall never forget. It's difficult to describe to you. But
if you could imagine the most perfect garden of scent
and beauty! Facing us, the reflection of a perfect moon
shining on the water.

WILLIE: This wasn't Egypt, by any chance?

WILLOCKS: It was.

WILLIE: Go on.

WILLOCKS: A violin fellow, and how he could play, my
word, how he could play, playing in the distance
marvellously! (*He stretches his arms out.*) It was the most
exquisite night I shall ever know, and as I gazed at her
lying in my arms, I realised everything was in sympathy
with us, everything was wonderful. And as I watched her
going up the steps to her hotel, I little thought it would
be the last time I would ever see her!
(*He pauses – WILLIE never taking his eyes off him.*)
The next morning, when I found she had gone, I decided
to let her go, and return home. But as the day went on,
I couldn't. I realised I couldn't live without her, so
I decided to come to England to find her. Immediately
on my arrival I wrote to your father. I don't know why
I should bore you with all this!

WILLIE: Not at all, I may be able to help you. Was she dark?

WILLOCKS: Fair.

WILLIE: Grey eyes?

WILLOCKs. Perfect blue!

WILLIE: (*After a pause.*) What makes you think she was in love with you?

WILLOCKS: A woman of her type would never kiss a man if she wasn't.

WILLIE: She kissed you?

WILLOCKS: Of course! I don't care what your father says, I know she was in love with me, but I don't know why she ran away from me.

WILLIE: You needn't despair, Mr. Willocks. You will in time!

WILLOCKS: I hope so.

WILLIE: (*Rising, he rings the bell.*) In the meantime, I'm sure you would like to be shown to your room.

WILLOCKS: Thank you, I would. (*Rises.*)

(*ROBERTS enters.*)

WILLIE: Show Mr. Willocks to his room, Roberts!

ROBERTS: Yes, sir. (*He goes to the door.*)

WILLOCKS: I'll see you later on.

WILLIE: You will!

(*WILLOCKS exits and ROBERTS follows, closing the door. WILLIE sees through the window that MARGOT is approaching; he sits and starts to read. MARGOT enters, hat in hand. She stands and looks at WILLIE for a moment, then round the room; she is obviously in great anxiety.*)

MARGOT: Hullo!

WILLIE: (*Looking at her.*) Hullo!

MARGOT: Haven't you been out?

WILLIE: No! I have been sitting here the whole time.

MARGOT: Shame! It's too wonderful.

WILLIE: I had nothing to go out for.

MARGOT: I hadn't either, but I went.

WILLIE: Is the car going alright again?

MARGOT: I think so. I only went a little way in it.

(*There is a pause. She watches him, hoping to find out his attitude.*)

Have you a cigarette, by any chance?

WILLIE: I think so. (*He puts the paper down, offers her one, strikes a match and lights her cigarette and returns to his reading.*)

MARGOT: Thanks. Oh! By the way, where's the young man who was coming for the weekend?

WILLIE: The young – oh! He's not coming.

MARGOT: Not coming? (*Endeavouring to appear natural.*) Why not?

WILLIE: I don't know! He telephoned and asked a message to be given the Governor, something about having to sail for Australia tomorrow. I really didn't take much notice of what he said. However, he's writing!

MARGOT: (*With great relief.*) What a pity! Your father will be disappointed.

WILLIE: He may not be! (*He picks up the paper again.*)

MARGOT: Willie!

WILLIE: (*Affecting indifference.*) Yes?

MARGOT: Whilst I have been out, I have been thinking.

WILLIE: Interesting.

MARGOT: You're indifferent.

WILLIE: Not at all, I am most interested.

MARGOT: I was thinking of the last words your father said to me before I went away.

WILLIE: (*Bitterly.*) I remember he didn't want you to go.

MARGOT: I know. He said, it was a mistake when two young and attractive people were married to each other, for either of them to go too far or be too long away from home.

WILLIE: In this case he was certainly right.

MARGOT: I was thinking what a pity it was I didn't take his advice.

WILLIE: It's a little late to trouble about that now!

MARGOT: You're not being very helpful, Willie.

WILLIE: I'm sorry. I mean to be.

MARGOT: What I want to say to you, and you're making it terribly difficult, is – (*Her eye falls on the card lying on the small table; she almost utters a cry.*)

WILLIE: Well? Well?

MARGOT: Oh, nothing! Some other time when you are in a less indifferent frame of mind.

WILLIE: (*Putting the paper down.*) I should like to know what you were going to say.

MARGOT: (*Appearing to be thinking.*) Nothing! (*She goes over to a desk, and seating herself, begins to write while she is speaking.*) Nothing at all really! I wonder if I have time to write a note to mother before the post goes.

WILLIE: Plenty.

MARGOT: What date is Monday?

WILLIE: The third! You might tell me what you were going to say.

MARGOT: I was going to say, what a pity it was, under the circumstances, I didn't do what you did whilst I was away, because if I had, it would have helped me to understand and forgive you so much quicker.

WILLIE: Was that all?

MARGOT: That was all!

(*LADY FRINTON enters.*)

Walk to the post with me in a minute?

LADY FRINTON: Love to! Mix me a cocktail, Willie dear.

WILLIE: I've got to go out for a moment. (*He goes to the door.*) You don't mind waiting until I come back?

LADY FRINTON: As long as you are not too long. I have been talking to the Vicar for the last quarter of an hour, so I need alcoholic sustenance.

WILLIE: I won't be long! (*He exits.*)

(*MARGOT rushes to the door to see that he has gone, comes back to LADY FRINTON, letter in hand.*)

LADY FRINTON: Margot darling, what's the matter?

MARGOT: Listen. Quickly! Quickly! Give this note, unknown to anyone, to a man, someone you don't know, a stranger! He's somewhere in the house.

LADY FRINTON: What do you mean?

MARGOT: Oh, I can't explain, but he must get that note before I see him. Don't you understand? It's someone I knew in Egypt.

LADY FRINTON: Oh, my darling, what memories you bring back to me.

MARGOT: Please! Please!

LADY FRINTON: Where shall I find him?

MARGOT: They have put him in the end spare room, for certain; he may be there now! Please, I'm ruined if he doesn't get it.

LADY FRINTON: (*Crossing over to the door.*) What terrible things we women have to put up with. I'll find the brute now. Don't worry, darling. (*She exits.*)

(*MARGOT goes over to the window, looking out. LORD GRENHAM enters and puts his hat and stick on a chair.*)

LORD GRENHAM: Well, Margot, my dear, how are you?

MARGOT: In excellent health, helped considerably by my excellent spirits.

LORD GRENHAM: (*Sits down on settee.*) That's splendid!

MARGOT: You're tired. A cigarette? (*She offers him the box on the table.*)

LORD GRENHAM: (*Taking one.*) Thank you, my dear. (*He half rises to get a match.*)

MARGOT: Don't get up. I'll get you a match! (*He watches her with an amused smile. She gets a match from the box on the table and strikes it.*)

LORD GRENHAM: You're very thoughtful, Margot dear.

MARGOT: (*Holding the match for him.*) One always is, to people one likes.

LORD GRENHAM: True! True! What a wonderful day!

MARGOT: Too perfect!

LORD GRENHAM: And what have you been doing this afternoon?

MARGOT: I went for a little drive in the car, and then came back and wrote a letter.

LORD GRENHAM: Splendid! By the way, did our young friend arrive?

MARGOT: (*Pretending not to understand.*) Our young friend? Oh! The young Australian you expected?

LORD GRENHAM: That's the fellow.

MARGOT: No, he hasn't arrived; he's not coming!

LORD GRENHAM: Not coming?

MARGOT: (*Sitting by LORD GRENHAM.*) So Willie tells me! Willie spoke to him on the telephone. It appears he has had a cable calling him home, and he has to leave for Australia tomorrow.

LORD GRENHAM: (*Smiling.*) Now isn't that splendid?

MARGOT: Why? Didn't you want him to come?

LORD GRENHAM: Very much! But I much prefer that he should go back to Australia.

MARGOT: Then why ask him here?

LORD GRENHAM: (*Looking at her.*) You know why I asked him here?

MARGOT: (*With a look of astonishment.*) I know? How should I know?

LORD GRENHAM: My dear Margot, you can afford to be generous. I never had the slightest intention of Willie knowing.

MARGOT: Of Willie knowing what? What on earth are you talking about?

LORD GRENHAM: Very well. I asked Mr. Willocks here for two reasons: one, I thought his presence might restore your sense of humour as regards Willie; and two, I preferred that he should meet you on the station platform by the four fifty-five instead of in a public building possibly accompanied by your husband! I knew if you met him by the four fifty-five he would immediately return to London again by the five twenty.

MARGOT: May I ask you something?

LORD GRENHAM: Please.

MARGOT: Are you mad, or doesn't drink affect your legs?

LORD GRENHAM: (*Laughing.*) As you like! Mr. Willocks has gone to Australia, and the incident is closed.

MARGOT: You'll pardon me, it isn't. I wish to know in what way I am concerned with Mr. Williams, or whatever his name is?

LORD GRENHAM: (*Smiling.*) Mr. Willocks!

MARGOT: Well? Tell me.

LORD GRENHAM: As he has gone back to Australia, is it necessary?

MARGOT: Absolutely.

LORD GRENHAM: Very well. Mr. Willocks met in Egypt while you were there a widow by the name of Margaret

Spalding; he fell in love with her. Realising it, and having behaved rather, shall we say, stupidly, and not being in love with him, but with her husband, she ran away from him.

MARGOT: But you said she was a widow.

LORD GRENHAM: I didn't. It was she who said she was a widow.

MARGOT: But how extraordinary.

LORD GRENHAM: As you say, how extraordinary! It appears she acknowledged being a personal friend of mine, and loving her dearly, instead of returning to Australia, as he told her he was going to do, he came to England to try and find her. On arrival, the first thing he did was to write to me and ask me if I knew Margaret Spalding and would I help him to find her.

MARGOT: And did you know her?

LORD GRENHAM: Yes, but not by that name.

MARGOT: But how thrilling, how did you find out you knew her?

LORD GRENHAM: Only when he described to me the garden in which they spent their last evening together, and when he described the lady to me.

MARGOT: I shan't repeat it, who was she?

LORD GRENHAM: Are you serious?

MARGOT: Of course, it's most thrilling.

LORD GRENHAM: (*After a pause.*) Margot Tatham!
(*There is another pause.*)

MARGOT: Are you serious?

LORD GRENHAM: Perfectly!

MARGOT: Would you ring the bell?

LORD GRENHAM: What for?

MARGOT: I want you to tell this story to Willie.

LORD GRENHAM: (*Rising and moving towards the bell as if to ring but turns back to her.*) Margot, don't be absurd, you wouldn't be taking this attitude if this man hadn't gone back.

MARGOT: The only regret I have is this young man has gone back! Please ring the bell.
(*WILLIE enters.*)

Here is Willie! Will you please tell him what you were telling me.

LORD GRENHAM: Later on, my dear. So I hear, Willie, this young friend of mine couldn't come, after all; gone back to Australia, eh?

(*WILLIE doesn't answer.*)

You spoke to him on the telephone, didn't you?

WILLIE: No, I didn't really.

MARGOT: But you told me you did.

WILLIE: I had a reason for saying so. He's here!

LORD GRENHAM: (*Starting.*) Here?

WILLIE: He'll be down in a minute.

MARGOT: You say he's here?

WILLIE: I do.

MARGOT: What was your object in telling me he had gone back to Australia when he was here the whole time? Would you be good enough to tell me what you were suggesting?

WILLIE: This! It will be interesting to watch the reunion of you and this man in whose arms you were lying as the dawn broke in that garden of scent and beauty.

MARGOT: In whose arms I!

WILLIE: And who saw you for the last time as you walked up the steps of your hotel. You don't deny it?

MARGOT: I already have to your father, but he doesn't believe me, so I shan't risk it with you. I leave it now to Mr. Wilcox, or whatever his name is. Would you be good enough to send for him?

(*WILLIE does not move. There is a pause. They look at her.*)

Amongst other qualities you lack, must one include deafness?

(*LADY FRINTON enters and goes to MARGOT.*)

LADY FRINTON: I posted your letter, darling; in fact, I gave it to the postman himself, curious man, never said thank you, yes or no, or anything. Just stared at me.
I hope the fool understood what posting a letter means! Where's my cocktail, Willie?

WILLIE: I'll make it in a moment.

LADY FRINTON: (*Looking at them.*) What is the matter with you all?

LORD GRENHAM: Nothing, my dear Mary, nothing at all! You would do us a great service if you would keep the Vicar and my sister away from this room for a few moments.

MARGOT: You will do nothing of the sort. I should like them to be here.

LADY FRINTON: What is it all about?

MARGOT: It appears there is a man in this house at the moment who, while in Egypt, carried on with some woman in a way, as it is told to me, that can only be described as disgraceful!

LADY FRINTON: But what has it to do with you?

MARGOT: Only that my father-in-law and my husband accuse me of being that woman!

LADY FRINTON: (*To LORD GRENHAM and WILLIE, advancing on them.*) You shameful, shameful creatures! I doubt if I can ever speak to either of you again. (*Taking MARGOT's arm.*) Darling, take no notice of them; they know no better. (*Whispering.*) Courage, he had very little on, but what one could see of him he looked a gentleman. (*WILLOCKS' voice is heard off.*)

WILLOCKS: (*Off.*) Where is Lord Grenham?

LADY FRINTON: Courage, darling, courage!
(*WILLOCKS enters, and seeing LORD GRENHAM, goes up to him and shakes hands.*)

WILLOCKS: How are you, Lord Grenham?
(*WILLIE takes him by the arm and brings him forward to MARGOT.*)

WILLIE: I don't think I need introduce you. I think you have already met the lady.

WILLOCKS: (*Looks at MARGOT, hesitates a second or two.*) Unhappily, I have never had that pleasure.

MARGOT: How do you do, Mr Wilcox?

WILLOCKS: (*Looking her full in the face and shaking hands.*) Willocks.
(*WILLIE and LORD GRENHAM gaze at each other in astonishment.*)

End of Act Two.

ACT THREE

Next morning.

ANGELA is knitting. The VICAR enters.

ANGELA: Had your breakfast?

VICAR: I could eat no breakfast.

ANGELA: I'm sorry! Why was that?

VICAR: That distressing scene which I unhappily witnessed last night between Margot and Willie upset me very much. Further, it has completely disorganised my digestive organs.

ANGELA: Still, you wouldn't have missed it, would you, Ernest?

VICAR: I would have given a great deal to have missed it.

ANGELA: Well, why didn't you? You only had to leave the room.

VICAR: It was my duty to stay. I felt my presence might have a conciliatory effect.

ANGELA: Though I trembled with indignation at the infamous accusation Willie made against that sweet girl, I stayed, because I enjoyed every minute of it.

VICAR: My dear! My dear!

ANGELA: And for the same reason you stayed.

VICAR: I deny that.

ANGELA: Very well.

VICAR: I have never spent a more unpleasant evening in my life, and so long as I live I shall never forget, in answer to a simple remark I made, the name your brother called me.

ANGELA: That's the third time you have told me that. What did my brother call you?

VICAR: A name I should be sorry to use in the presence of any woman! (*Going to a sideboard.*) I wonder if there is any bisurated magnesia in the house?

ANGELA: Not in this house. They deal with your complaint much more effectively. (*Pointing to the brandy and soda.*) You'll find plenty of brandy and soda and, unknown to any of your parishioners, I should have one if I were you.

VICAR: I drink a brandy and soda this time in the morning! What do you mean?

ANGELA: I mean your stomach trouble this morning can be accounted for by the state of alcoholic imbecility in which you came to bed last night.

VICAR: I deny that.

ANGELA: If you like! Nevertheless, you would still be trying to get into the legs of your pyjamas if I hadn't got out of bed to direct you!

VICAR: Angela, you grossly exaggerate. I admit I did probably overstep my usual allowance, as I was unhappy and upset at the name your brother called me.

ANGELA: What did he call you?

VICAR: (*Pauses.*) It wasn't damn fool!

ANGELA: (*Smiling.*) Darling Grenham, he's consistently called a spade by its proper name since the age of four.

VICAR: Do you mean he was right to call me by that name?

ANGELA: I meant the other one, darling.

VICAR: For many reasons, Angela, I shall be glad to get you home again, and if it were not that one might be of service to this dear girl, I should leave today.

ANGELA: Yes, Ernest! (*She looks up from her knitting.*) I suppose there is no possible chance that, after all, Margot was the girl?

VICAR: Angela! Do you realise what you are saying?

ANGELA: Sorry, darling, I was only asking for information. (*She smiles.*) You know more about these things than I do.

VICAR: A girl incapable of even thinking such a thought!

ANGELA: Yes. (*Pause.*) In a way, I am sorry it isn't her.

VICAR: You are sorry that – ? (*She looks at him.*) You're indeed a very strange person this morning!

ANGELA: I have become honest in the night.

VICAR: Explain yourself, please.

ANGELA: (*Putting her knitting down.*) I mean when you reach my age, knitting, without one memory, is a dull, dull business.

VICAR: But you have me, Angela.

ANGELA: (*Looking at him.*) I know, darling! But that doesn't make me knit any faster.

VICAR: You are not regretting, Angela, having been a good woman?

ANGELA: I refused the only opportunity I had that would have made me anything else.

VICAR: What do you mean?

ANGELA: Do you remember Mr Tuke?

VICAR: Archdeacon Tuke?

ANGELA: Yes, but when he was Mr Tuke, your curate?

VICAR: Yes! Well?

ANGELA: Years ago when you were out one day visiting the poor, he called and told me how much his mother would have loved me had she known me.

VICAR: Well?

ANGELA: The following week when you were again visiting the poor, he called and told me how much his sister would have loved me had she known me.

VICAR: Go on!

ANGELA: The following week, he called and told me – (*Pauses – she looks at him.*) how much he loved me.

VICAR: (*Aghast.*) Tuke did?

ANGELA: Tuke did.

VICAR: What did you say to him?

ANGELA: All my inclinations were to say – (*Short pause.*) take a seat and tell me more!

VICAR: Angela!

ANGELA: But as I lacked courage, which so often is the only thing which divides good women from bad, I opened the door for him.

VICAR: I trust you told him exactly what you thought of him?

ANGELA: I did! I said, 'Goodbye, Mr Tuke; you'll be an archdeacon some day!' (*She shakes her head.*) And you see, I was right!

VICAR: Thank God no such incident has ever happened in my life.

ANGELA: From a remark you made last night you are more fortunate than I am; yours are yet to come.

VICAR: What remark do you refer to?

ANGELA: When falling violently into bed, you turned to me and asked me, in the most aggressive manner, if it were necessary for all Sunday School teachers to be plain.

VICAR: I meant nothing, Angela.

ANGELA: Nothing, Ernest! Nevertheless, you will find me more companionable in the years to come than you have ever found me in the years that are past.

(*LORD GRENHAM enters and takes ANGELA's hand.*)

LORD GRENHAM: 'Morning, Angela dear. What sort of night, Vicar?

VICAR: Not good, Grenham.

LORD GRENHAM: (*Smiles.*) Ha! Sorry! I have some excellent ginger ale downstairs bottled by the firm of Clicquot. I would advise a glass.

VICAR: Thank you, no!

ANGELA: It would do you good, Ernest.

VICAR: Thank you, no.

LORD GRENHAM: By the way, do either of you happen to know if today is Mary Frinton's birthday?

ANGELA: Does she still have a birthday?

LORD GRENHAM: I imagine she must. Telegram after telegram is arriving for her.

ANGELA: What is happening between Willie and Margot this morning, Grenham?

LORD GRENHAM: Margot is singing in her bath, and Willie, on reflection, is not quite so sure she is all the things he accuses her of.

ANGELA: Do you still believe she was the woman?

LORD GRENHAM: (*Shaking his head.*) It will remain to my everlasting shame that I ever believed it.

(*ROBERTS enters. He is carrying a bunch of flowers.*)

LORD GRENHAM: I can only look for forgiveness elsewhere.

VICAR: I cannot understand you ever believing it.

LORD GRENHAM: I cannot understand myself!

ROBERTS: (*Crossing to LORD GRENHAM.*) From Lady Frinton, my lord, with her love and happiness.

LORD GRENHAM: (*Looks at him perplexed, takes them from him.*) Thank her ladyship very much.

ROBERTS: I will, my lord. (*He exits.*)

ANGELA: What does that mean?

LORD GRENHAM: (*Shaking his head.*) No idea.

ANGELA: How extraordinary! Do you know what it means, Ernest?

VICAR: I know nothing. I am defeated by everything. I only know I shall be glad to be home again. Mentally and physically, I don't feel at all myself.

ANGELA: I insist on your having a glass of champagne, Ernest .

VICAR: No, thank you, Angela.

ANGELA: I insist!

VICAR: (*Rising and moving towards the door.*) Very well – where is it – Oh, perhaps Roberts can tell me. (*He goes, calling to ROBERTS.*) Lord Grenham says I'm to have a glass of champagne! (*They both watch him going out, turn and smile at each other.*)

ANGELA: If Ernest could only humbug others as he does himself, I would be a bishop's wife today.

LORD GRENHAM: (*Kissing her hand, laughing.*) Bless you. (*He puts the flowers on a table and sits.*)

ANGELA: Grenham! Was Margot the woman?

LORD GRENHAM: I wish I could convince myself she wasn't with the ease I have convinced Willie. I'm terribly, terribly worried.

ANGELA: But why? If she were the woman, it is quite evident Mr Willocks is prepared to behave like a gentleman.

LORD GRENHAM: I admit so far his behaviour has been magnificent, but I can't help feeling Mr Willocks is an angry man with a grievance. First, against Margot for having, he sincerely believes, fooled him, and then

against me for asking him here under the pretence
that I liked him, and once or twice at dinner last night
I could see Margot shared that feeling with me.

ANGELA: I'm sure you're wrong.

LORD GRENHAM: I'm rather afraid I'm not. Mr Willocks
unhappily doesn't understand us. I hate to say it, but he
looks upon us as rather useless people; from his point of
view, it would only be a proper thing to show us up and,
unless I am very much mistaken, he proposes to do that
through Margot.

ANGELA: Well, the most he could do would be to tell
Willie.

LORD GRENHAM: And then?

ANGELA: Well, I suppose –

LORD GRENHAM: If she was the woman, you and I know
she meant nothing; she proved that by running away, but
will Willie believe it was merely an innocent thing? No,
my dear, he wouldn't. And Margot has too much
character to live with suspicion! It should never be in the
power of any man to be able to make so much trouble
for a woman as Willocks can!

ANGELA: What made you ask him here?

LORD GRENHAM: I thought it was being clever!
I intended him to arrive by one train, Margot to meet
him, and send him back by the next! He came by car!

WILLOCKS: (*Off.*) Good morning, Roberts.

LORD GRENHAM: Here he comes. You might leave me.
(*WILLOCKS enters. ANGELA rises and moves away.*)

LORD GRENHAM: Morning, my dear fellow. I hope you
slept well and were comfortable.

WILLOCKS: Many thanks, I slept splendidly. (*He goes to
ANGELA.*) Morning, Mrs Lynton!

ANGELA: (*Smiling at him.*) Good morning! Did you see my
husband as you came in?

WILLOCKS: He's sitting out on the lawn having a glass of
ginger ale.

ANGELA: Did he tell you it was ginger ale?

WILLOCKS: Yes.

ANGELA: Dear Ernest.

(*She exits.*)

WILLOCKS: You have a very delightful place here, Lord Grenham.

LORD GRENHAM: Stay and enjoy it as long as you like, my boy.

WILLOCKS: I'd like to very much, but I have decided to return to Australia immediately.

LORD GRENHAM: You are not leaving us at once?

WILLOCKS: If you won't think me rude, this morning.

LORD GRENHAM: Ah! I'm sorry, very sorry!

WILLOCKS: (*Speaking with meaning.*) In its best sense I appreciate your kindness in asking me down. I shall carry back to Australia with me only the tenderest recollections of English hospitality.

LORD GRENHAM: And we shall always think very kindly of you.

WILLOCKS: (*Smiling.*) I wish I could think that! Tell me, Lord Grenham, did you ever have any leanings towards diplomacy?

LORD GRENHAM: Never, my boy! A life devoted to agriculture and women!

WILLOCKS: (*Laughing.*) I see!

LORD GRENHAM: Why do you ask?

WILLOCKS: Because I was wondering why you asked me down.

LORD GRENHAM: For two reasons: One (*Lightly.*) you're a gentleman.

WILLOCKS: And the other?

LORD GRENHAM: (*More sincerely.*) You're a gentleman!

WILLOCKS: (*Smiling.*) It must be quite refreshing to you to sometimes fail to get your own way, Lord Grenham.

LORD GRENHAM: Meaning?

WILLOCKS: Only what I said. By the way, I understand from your son, I shall have the pleasure of his companionship to London with me.

LORD GRENHAM: Willie is going to London, is he?

WILLOCKS: Yes! As a man should, who is married to a wonderful woman like his wife, he appreciates the monstrous accusation he made against her last night, and recognises only time may help her to forgive him. Incidentally, he offered me a most generous apology.

LORD GRENHAM: And you accepted it?

WILLOCKS: (*Pauses.*) I sympathise with it. You see, I hate being fooled even more than he will.

LORD GRENHAM: (*Looking at him.*) I understand perfectly, Mr Willocks.

WILLOCKS: You needn't look at me like that. You would feel the same in my place.

LORD GRENHAM: I never could be in your place.

WILLOCKS: Indeed!

LORD GRENHAM: If a lady innocently philandered with me, and, realising I was taking her seriously, ran away from me, I should have the good grace to leave her alone.

WILLOCKS: Let me tell you –

(*WILLIE enters.*)

WILLIE: (*Nervously.*) Father.

LORD GRENHAM: Yes, my dear fellow!

WILLIE: Mr Willocks has kindly offered to drive me up to town; under the circumstances I think I'll go.

LORD GRENHAM: (*Patting him on the arm.*) Hating losing you as I do, I understand.

WILLIE: I knew you would.

(*The VICAR enters, ANGELA follows.*)

VICAR: (*Walking to LORD GRENHAM, putting out his hand.*) It is my duty, Grenham, my duty, to congratulate you! (*LORD GRENHAM looks at him, then takes his hand, evidently having no idea what he is talking about. He looks at the others to see if they understand.*)

ANGELA: (*Walking to LORD GRENHAM and kissing him.*) You know best, darling, and I can only hope you will be very happy. (*LORD GRENHAM looks more perplexed.*) (*LADY FRINTON enters with a copy of 'The Times' in her hand. She comes to LORD GRENHAM.*)

LADY FRINTON: (*Putting her arms round him and kissing him.*) You darling! And to have done it in such a perfectly sweet way! (*Turning to the others.*) I give you my word of honour I hadn't the slightest idea until I read it in *The Times* this morning.

LORD GRENHAM: Hadn't you, Mary? May I see *The Times*?

LADY FRINTON: There! (*Putting her finger on a paragraph.*) You angel!

LORD GRENHAM: (*Reading.*) 'A marriage has been arranged and will – '

(*As he is reading MARGOT enters.*)

' – shortly take place between Lord Grenham of Grenham Court, and Mary Frinton, widow of the late Sir John Frinton'! (*For a moment he looks at the notice, then he raises his eyes and looks fixedly at MARGOT, whose face is expressionless.*)

MARGOT: I congratulate you with all my heart; you have done a very wise thing.

LORD GRENHAM: Thank you, Margot.

LADY FRINTON: Why did you do it in that divine way?

LORD GRENHAM: I didn't want to take the risk of being refused, and I realised the moment it was published in the papers there was no way out of it for either of us!

LADY FRINTON: I never wanted any way out of it, darling! Oh! I'm too happy! I have already had the most charming telegrams. (*Going a step towards ANGELA.*) Do come and let me read them to you. You can as well, Vicar; now that you're going to be my brother-in-law, you can come into my bedroom just when you like! (*The VICAR looks shocked.*) Come along. (*She goes off.*)

ANGELA: (*To the VICAR.*) We had better, I suppose. (*She follows LADY FRINTON off.*)

(*The VICAR follows, looking very prim, smiles for a second as he passes MARGOT, then becomes serious and goes off.*)

LORD GRENHAM: I notice you haven't congratulated me, Willie?

WILLIE: Frankly, I don't know why you've done it. I thought you were perfectly happy.

LORD GRENHAM: Evidently, I wasn't. (*He puts 'The Times' on the table.*)

WILLIE: There's no reason why you should have another son, is there?

LORD GRENHAM: I can't think of any, Willie.

WILLIE: (*Crossing to LORD GRENHAM and shaking hands.*) Then I hope that you'll be very happy. (*Turning to MARGOT.*) I should like to see you before I go.

MARGOT: That's quite certain, Willie.

WILLIE: Thanks! (*WILLIE exits.*)

LORD GRENHAM: (*Shaking his head.*) A strange world, a very strange world! Well! Well! Well!

MARGOT: Darling!

LORD GRENHAM: Yes.

MARGOT: I rather think Mr Willocks is anxious to discuss English life with me from an Australian point of view.

LORD GRENHAM: Ha! I see! Very well! (*LORD GRENHAM leaves. There is a pause. MARGOT and WILLOCKS look at each other.*)

MARGOT: Well?

WILLOCKS: Well?

MARGOT: Do smoke.

WILLOCKS: No, many thanks. Perhaps you would like to? (*She shakes her head. There is a pause.*)

MARGOT: We may not be alone long.

WILLOCKS: I realise that.

MARGOT: You don't know how to begin?

WILLOCKS: You're quite right.

MARGOT: Strange! And you've been thinking of nothing else ever since you met me in this room yesterday afternoon.

WILLOCKS: You're very observant.

MARGOT: (*Shaking her head.*) Merely terribly alive to the obvious! (*She smiles at him.*) But there's one thing; you know the end, don't you?

WILLOCKS: Do you?

MARGOT: That, if I may say so, is even more obvious!

WILLOCKS: Do you agree with it?

MARGOT: I don't complain! I realise, from your point of
view, I treated you very badly.

WILLOCKS: From any point of view, can you defend it?
You deliberately set out to do it.
(*She shakes her head.*)
Then why Margaret Spalding?

MARGOT: Because as Margot Tatham it would appear
I have a reputation as a singer. Each hotel I arrived at,
I found letters from different people who had heard I was
coming, asking me to sing for their various charities.
I hated refusing. It became so intolerable, ill and tired
I left the town suddenly, leaving no address, and went to
your hotel, and for peace and quietness adopted the
name Margaret Spalding.
(*He laughs.*)
Then why do you think I did it?

WILLOCKS: For the amusement of making some man a
bigger fool than he already was.

MARGOT: You have a much greater opinion of yourself
and other men than I have, Mr Willocks.

WILLOCKS: Then, when you got to know me, why didn't
you tell me?

MARGOT: There we meet on common ground. I should
have. I was frightened to. Do you imagine for a moment
when I first knew you I meant to compromise myself as
I have done? It started as all these ridiculous things do.
It was amusing to be singled out for your attentions in
preference to all the other women in the hotel! It was
flattering to be told all the things about oneself that one
knew were not true, but always hoped were! From a
depressed being, I once again became in conceit with
myself.

WILLOCKS: I meant every word I said to you.

MARGOT: Of course you did, that's why I grew to like you.

WILLOCKS: Like me? You saw me falling more and more
in love with you, and you encouraged me.

MARGOT: You're perfectly right.

WILLOCKS: Why did you?

MARGOT: Mr Willocks! How few people use the power they have over others in the right way?

WILLOCKS: And then, when it amused you no longer, laughing at me, you ran away to your husband.

MARGOT: That isn't quite correct.

WILLOCKS: Then why did you run away?

MARGOT: Will you be generous?

WILLOCKS: Well?

MARGOT: I wanted to remain. I ran away because I was frightened to stay.

WILLOCKS: You ran away because you were frightened to stay?

MARGOT: You who read the papers must realise a great many women don't.

WILLOCKS: And now?

MARGOT: Now is quite different. I'm not frightened any longer. I only wonder why I ever was.

WILLOCKS: You're frank, at all events.

MARGOT: The sincerest form of repentance! Don't you understand, it was never real, the circumstances, the atmosphere, the loneliness, *it* was all so compelling. The moment I got on the boat to come home I realised it, so much so I meant to tell my husband everything!

WILLOCKS: Then why didn't you?

MARGOT: Because, as I entered the room, I found him doing the same thing. I was so angry, I entirely forgot I had done it.

WILLOCKS: And what prevents you telling him now?

MARGOT: Too late.

WILLOCKS: Why?

MARGOT: He'd never like me again. And to stop him liking me would be the cruellest thing I could do to him.

WILLOCKS: Or I could do to him?

MARGOT: For you to tell him would be the cruellest thing you could do to me, and that is all that should matter to you! (*He smiles.*) Why do you smile?

WILLOCKS: I don't know; it's amusing! First of all, I liked you because you liked me, and then I hated you because you didn't, and now I'm beginning to like you all over again because you like your husband.

MARGOT: I'm glad you said that.

WILLOCKS: Why?

MARGOT: It was nice! It gives me an excuse for having liked you too much! Forgive me.

WILLOCKS: Easier than I can myself. I meant to tell everything.

MARGOT: But I did treat you very badly.

WILLOCKS: You didn't, and even if you had that's no reason; but I was angry. I thought, like so many other women, you'd used me as something merely to pass the time.

MARGOT: Oh, no!

WILLOCKS: I know that now.

MARGOT: I want you to tell me something; it's difficult. I do hope I haven't hurt you very badly.

WILLOCKS: (*Taking her hand, kissing it.*) It couldn't hurt any man very much to have loved a woman as nice as you; I shall always be very grateful that I did.

MARGOT: (*Looking at him, smiling.*) I am sure I was right to run away.

(*LORD GRENHAM enters.*)

LORD GRENHAM: I hope I don't interrupt.

WILLOCKS: The opposite. I was just going to look for you to say goodbye. Oh! by the way, you might also say goodbye to your son for me, will you? Mrs Tatham has been telling me she doesn't want him to go to London today. And I agree.

LORD GRENHAM: My dear fellow! I forgot there was another reason why I asked you down here.

WILLOCKS: Was there? What was it?

LORD GRENHAM: I knew you were a gentleman!

(*WILLOCKS laughs, crosses to LORD GRENHAM.*)

WILLOCKS: Thank you, Lord Grenham! (*Putting out his hand.*) Goodbye!

LORD GRENHAM: Goodbye, my dear boy, goodbye!

WILLOCKS: (*Goes to MARGOT.*) Goodbye, Mrs Tatham. (*Shakes hands.*) I am so glad to have met you – meeting you has helped me so much to forget Margaret Spalding! Goodbye! (*She looks at him – doesn't answer.*) Goodbye!

LORD GRENHAM: Not goodbye, I shall see you again. (*WILLOCKS exits.*)

Ah, well! Nice fellow, I like him! As a matter of fact, I could forgive any woman for liking that man. Tell me, now that our young friend has departed, what do you propose to do?

MARGOT: Forgive Willie for ever having doubted me! Oh, this is the part of it I hate so much! The lying! The deceit! Oh, it's dreadful! I want to tell him everything!

LORD GRENHAM: If you love him, for Heaven's sake I implore you not to.

MARGOT: Oh, I'm not going to! But I wish I could! But I shall one day.

LORD GRENHAM: When?

MARGOT: When I'm old and no longer attractive! When he's old enough for understanding to have taken the place of vanity!

LORD GRENHAM: I remember the day so well. When humour takes the place of anger! When tolerance takes the place of disappointment. The young call it old age. Ah, well! I'm glad it's alright, Margot. I'm right in saying it was you who put the announcement of my forthcoming marriage in *The Times*?

MARGOT: Yes.

LORD GRENHAM: A severe punishment, if I may say so.

MARGOT: You gave me away, so I gave you away. You should have told me you knew him, not bring him down here as you did.

LORD GRENHAM: I should have, but still the sentence is severe.

MARGOT: I owed it to Mary. She saved me, and the only way I could repay her was to give you to her, who for some reason she adores.

LORD GRENHAM: (*Sighing.*) And I had planned so many interesting things to do in the next five years.

MARGOT: But you like her?

LORD GRENHAM: Enormously, but I don't want to marry her. I hate the idea of marrying anyone. I'm so used to freedom! I love it so! And married to Mary, there's going to be no more freedom! But I forgive you. But if ever you tell her that it was you who put that notice in the paper and not me, then I'll never forgive you. (*LADY FRINTON enters.*)

LADY FRINTON: Grenham dear, the *Daily Mirror* have just rung up to ask if we would allow their photographers to take our photographs. I said with pleasure. You don't mind, do you, darling?

LORD GRENHAM: If it will please you, I know of nothing that could give me more pleasure.

LADY FRINTON: (*To MARGOT.*) Isn't he too wonderful?

MARGOT: He's a dear. (*Kissing her.*) I hope, and I know you will be very happy. (*MARGOT goes through the French windows.*)

LADY FRINTON: A sweet, sweet creature.

LORD GRENHAM: And a great friend of yours.

LADY FRINTON: (*Going to LORD GRENHAM and pressing his shoulders.*) I know! Grenham, you don't know how happy you have made me.

LORD GRENHAM: You flatter me, Mary dear.
(*LADY FRINTON sits on the settee, LORD GRENHAM beside her.*)

LADY FRINTON: And I was beginning to give up all hope. I was beginning to think I should never get you! What made you do it so suddenly?

LORD GRENHAM: Not suddenly, my dear; after much considered thought. When a man reaches my age, he needs companionship. Living alone, not knowing what to do, becomes unbearable. I couldn't stand it any longer. And in the whole world there was only one person whose companionship I would care to share, so I advertised the fact in *The Times*, and believing you felt the same way as I did, I took the liberty of including your name with mine!

LADY FRINTON: I know I shall cry.

LORD GRENHAM: It would considerably add to my happiness if you didn't, Mary dear.

LADY FRINTON: (*Moving closer to him.*) I won't, then. Tell me, when do you propose we should be married, Grenham?

LORD GRENHAM: That's for you to decide.

LADY FRINTON: Is a month's time too soon?

LORD GRENHAM: Will that give you sufficient time to arrange everything?

LADY FRINTON: More than enough.

LORD GRENHAM: Very well! And while you're fixing up everything, so as not to be in your way, I'll just run over to Paris for that time.

LADY FRINTON: Do!

LORD GRENHAM: (*Appears surprised.*) You don't mind?

LADY FRINTON: I'd like you to. And I hope, when we are married, you'll often do it.

LORD GRENHAM: Go without you, you mean?

LADY FRINTON: Of course! Whenever you want to.

LORD GRENHAM: You're being very generous, Mary dear.

LADY FRINTON: No, my dear, I'm only being very clever. Gradually it will be the cause of your staying at home, or better still, wanting to take me with you.

LORD GRENHAM: (*Laughing.*) I believe you're right!
Mary, there is one thing about you I have always adored.

LADY FRINTON: What?

LORD GRENHAM: You make me laugh.
(*LADY FRINTON laughs.*)
Surely two married people can't ask for much more, can they?

LADY FRINTON: They shouldn't.
(*LORD GRENHAM is just bending over her as ROBERTS enters. They move apart.*)

ROBERTS: Mr Willocks is just leaving, my lord.

LORD GRENHAM: Alright. I'll be there in a moment.
(*ROBERTS leaves. LADY FRINTON and LORD GRENHAM rise, he takes her arm and they move to the door.*)
Come along, we'll go and say goodbye to him together. My age is forty-eight. How old are you, Mary dear?

(*They both stop, and she whispers audibly to him 'Twenty-two', and, laughing, they both go off.*
MARGOT enters through the windows and stands there waving off. The car is leaving in the distance. WILLIE enters. He watches MARGOT at the window. She is unaware that WILLIE is in the room.)

WILLIE: Margot!

MARGOT: (*Starting.*) What a fright you gave me!

WILLIE: What were you looking at?

MARGOT: I was watching Mr Willocks going off in his car.

WILLIE: But I was going with him.

MARGOT: Apparently he's forgotten that!

WILLIE: It doesn't matter. I'll go by train.

MARGOT: I'm going by the four thirty.

WILLIE: To London?

MARGOT: To London!

WILLIE: We might travel together?

MARGOT: If we are going by the same train, it would be ridiculous if we didn't! There is no reason to let everyone know your opinion of me.

WILLIE: I have no opinion of you other than I have always had. I detest myself for ever having had any other!

MARGOT: You mean, you are sorry for all the horrid things you said to me last night?

WILLIE: As long as I live I shall never cease to regret the things I said to you. The only excuse I can find for myself is that I adore you. I was jealous of you to utter madness. But I can find no reason why you should ever forgive me!

MARGOT: And you're convinced I was not that woman?

WILLIE: I'm sure you were!

MARGOT: You're sure – (*Angrily.*) How dare you!

WILLIE: I should have never mentioned it if you hadn't!

MARGOT: Really! How interesting – how terribly interesting! (*Satirically.*) It's sweet of you to be so nice about it.

WILLIE: Not at all; experience has taught me understanding.

MARGOT: Really! Really!

WILLIE: And something else.

MARGOT: Being?

WILLIE: If I had been out in Egypt and met Miss Lake,
I should have returned to you – but I don't think
I should have run away.

MARGOT: Meaning?

WILLIE: (*Coming closer to her.*) He was as attractive as Miss
Lake, and you did?

MARGOT: Yes!

WILLIE: (*Taking her hand.*) And you could have stayed and
I should never have known! And it was because of me
you didn't!

MARGOT: Yes!

WILLIE: All people are as human as you are, but few as good!

MARGOT: Are you really being as nice to me as you
appear, Willie?

WILLIE: I can never be nice enough to you. (*He takes her in
his arms and kisses her.*) What were those words my father
said to you before you went away?

MARGOT: When two young and attractive people are
married to each other, it's a mistake for either of them to
go too far, or be too long away from home!

WILLIE: Only the unattractive ones would refuse to agree
with him! Anyway, I'll take precious good care you
never go away again.

MARGOT: So will I, Willie dear!

WILLIE: We'll never get a carriage to ourselves – let's go
by car, shall we?

MARGOT: Oh yes, let us!

WILLIE: I'll go and order it! (*He kisses her.*) Darling! (*He
goes to leave. LORD GRENHAM enters.*)

MARGOT: Willie!

WILLIE: Yes?

MARGOT: I'm so glad you know!

WILLIE: Don't I know you are!

(*He blows her a kiss. He leaves by the windows. She stands
watching him go off. LORD GRENHAM picks up 'The
Times'.*)

LORD GRENHAM: Willocks has gone. Willie has gone
mad, and I'm going to be married! All very strange.

MARGOT: Willie and I are just going to London.

LORD GRENHAM: That's good, very good; I'm delighted.

MARGOT: I know you are! I may not see you again, so I'll say goodbye. (*Kissing him.*) You ought to be very happy.

LORD GRENHAM: Why particularly, Margot?

MARGOT: Because I'm terribly fond of you. I adore your future wife, and I love your son! Goodbye! (*She leaves by the windows.*)

LORD GRENHAM: It's all very strange. Very strange! (*He sits to read the paper.*)
(*The VICAR enters, looking very upset; he pauses at the door.*)
Come in, old friend! How are you feeling?

VICAR: Very much the same. I laid on my bed, but I was unable to sleep.

LORD GRENHAM: Bad luck!

VICAR: Grenham, my mind is greatly disturbed. I must speak to you.

LORD GRENHAM: But do, my dear fellow. Come and sit down.

VICAR: I feel I cannot eat another mouthful of bread in your house, bearing the resentment I do against you, without telling you.

LORD GRENHAM: Against me, but why?

VICAR: Have you forgotten the name you called me last night?

LORD GRENHAM: Name? I don't remember calling you any name. What was it?

VICAR: If you have forgotten, I prefer not to remind you.

LORD GRENHAM: But I insist! You hear, I insist! What was it?

VICAR: (*Looking round the room to see if anyone is about – he whispers.*) In answer to a simple remark I made last night, Grenham, you called me a bloody old fool!
(*Puts his head in his hands as if crying.*)

LORD GRENHAM: (*Putting his arm round his shoulder.*) But aren't we all, old friend?

The End.

THE LAST OF MRS CHEYNEY

The ladies read Lord Elton's opinion of them: " **My God! 'A fallen woman!'** " May Whitty, Ellis Jeffreys, and Dawson Milward.

Characters

CHARLES
a butler

WILLIAM
a footman

GEORGE
a footman

LADY JOAN HOUGHTON

LADY MARY SINDLAY

HON. WILLIE WYNTON

LADY MARIA FRINTON

HON. MRS KITTY WYNTON

LORD ARTHUR DILLING

LORD ELTON

MRS CHEYNEY

MRS SYBIL EBLEY

JIM
a chauffeur

ROBERTS
Mrs Ebley's butler

Act I: Drawing-room in Mrs Cheyney's house
at Goring. A summer afternoon

Act II: Scene i. A room in Mrs Ebley's
country house. Ten days later.
Scene ii. Mrs Ebley's bedroom. Early next morning.

Act III: Loggia of Mrs Ebley's house. A few hours later.

The Last of Mrs Cheyney was first performed at the St. James's Theatre, London, on 22 September 1925, with the following cast:

CHARLES, Ronald Squire

WILLIAM, Guy Fletcher

GEORGE, Frank Lawton

JOAN, Gladys Gray

MARY, Violet Campbell

WILLIE, Basil Loder

MARIA, Ellis Jeffreys

MRS WYNTON, Mabel Sealby

ARTHUR, Gerald du Maurier

ELTON, Dawson Milward

MRS CHEYNEY, Gladys Cooper

MRS EBLEY, May Whitty

JIM, E. H. Patterson

ROBERTS, A. Harding Steerman

Following its initial success in London (and New York) the play has been often revived in the West End. A notable production in 1944 by Tyrone Guthrie with Coral Browne as Mrs Cheyney inspired *The Times*:

> Lonsdale's work here has the artifice, the polish and not a little of the epigrammatic wit that marks, say, *The Importance of Being Earnest.*

This was praise indeed, for Lonsdale was frequently criticised for having something in common with Congreve, Wycherley, Wilde, Shaw, Maugham, Pinero and Coward – but not enough! He was not, apparently, unduly bothered, and quoted a passage in the *Meditations of Marcus Aurelius*:

How strangely men act! They will not praise those who are living at the same time and living as themselves. But to be themselves praised by posterity, by those whom they have never seen nor will ever see – this they set much value on.

A fascinating but sometimes confusing aspect of Lonsdale's dramaturgy is his attachment to certain names. There is a Lady Frinton in *The Last Days of Mrs Cheyney* and there is another one in *Aren't We All?*, written only two years before. They are clearly different characters although even their Christian names are very close: Mary Frinton and Maria Frinton. I wonder if Ellis Jeffreys, who played both rôles, questioned Lonsdale about this. I expect he would have replied that he liked the sound of – Frinton! (A coincidence, of course, that his house at Birchington on the Kent coast faced directly opposite Frinton on the Essex coast.)

Both plays also have a 'Willie' – Willie Tatham in *Aren't We All?* and Willie Lynton in *The Last Days of Mrs Cheyney*. Another real-life 'Willie' whom Lonsdale adored was W. Somerset Maugham, who once wrote him a note after a Lonsdale play had received bad notices: 'Dear Freddy, Always remember that the English hate wit. Yours, Willie.'

Lonsdale also had a penchant for a particular title – that of Duke! The assorted Dukes of Tadcaster, Warrington and Hampshire each appear in a single play, but his favourite lineage was that of Bristol. Of course, there are no Bristol dukes in the *Oxford Dictionary of National Biography!*

*Ronald Squire as a butler
sans peur, but not sans
reproche.*

ACT ONE

*A room at MRS CHEYNEY's house at Goring. It is afternoon.
French windows lead to the gardens where an unseen singer has
reached the last verse of 'A May Morning'. CHARLES, at the window,
listens a second, then rings the bell. WILLIAM, a footman, enters
carrying two plates of sandwiches; he places them on the table which
is already laid with cakes in dishes and stands, chocolate eclairs and
biscuits and a dish of fruit. A decanter of 'Kirsch' stands by the fruit.
GEORGE follows the other footman. He is carrying a large silver
tray containing a decanter of whisky, a decanter of sherry, jug with
lemonade, syphon, four large glasses and four cocktail glasses. The
syphon is lying on its side, and the tray is generally slovenly arranged.*

GEORGE: Where shall I put these?

CHARLES: (*Pointing to the table.*) I suggest there.

GEORGE: My word, some of those singers out there have
    got 'orrible voices.

CHARLES: A charity concert, without 'orrible voices
    would not be a charity concert, George! By the way, it's a
    small matter, but there is an 'h' in 'orrible!

GEORGE: Where I come from there ain't!

CHARLES: Quite! And I dare say it does quite well
    without it!

    (*WILLIAM exits.*)

GEORGE: Anyway, I never believed I would see a garden
    so full of swells as I have today. I've called everybody
    'my lord' and I ain't been contradicted once!

CHARLES: The English middle-classes are much too
    well-bred to argue!

GEORGE: Who was the old bloke who spoke at the
    beginning?

CHARLES: The old bloke was His Grace the Duke of
    Bristol!

GEORGE: That's funny! If you didn't know he was, and saw
    his picture in a Sunday paper, you'd say, 'There's them
    Bolshies at it again!'

CHARLES: You would!

Nevertheless, we have with us today what may be known as the social goods! Lady Mary Sindlay, one of our leading hostesses: rich, charming, and modest. In fact, one might almost describe her as a lady! Lady Joan Houghton, twenty-three, courageous and beautiful, a woman who calls a spade a bloody spade and means it!

GEORGE: I like her! She said to me out there just now, 'Willie, 'and me a match!'

CHARLES: She was born with a natural desire to please every one! And then we have Mrs Wynton, the honourable of such, young, attractive, and a person. She married one of the most stupid of God's creatures; but rumour has it she has remained faithful to him! She is either a very good woman, George, or very nervous.

GEORGE: I like the old party they call Maria!

CHARLES: In her way, George, she's a darling! Her business in life has been to find people; she has a habit of finding them on Tuesday and serving them up on a gold salver on Wednesday, but should they fail her by being unamusing, it is she who closes the drain on them as they go down it on the Thursday! It was she who found your mistress!

GEORGE: The old one with the painted face and the pearls – I don't think much of her!

CHARLES: She is Mrs Ebley. It is said of her that, seated in her chair one day looking into her glass, she spied a double chin; at that moment her last of many lovers called to pay his respects; looking into that glass and without flinching, she said, 'I am not at home!'

GEORGE: Good for 'er!

CHARLES: With the knowledge that given suitable conditions even a Bishop's eyesight can be affected, she kept to her pearls, but became respectable! Her house today is the most exclusive of all our English homes!

GEORGE: I must say I like 'em when they get away with it! They all didn't make half a fuss of that tall bloke when he came in.

CHARLES: That tall bloke was Lord Elton – a rich, eligible bachelor, an intimate friend of royalty, and a man of considerable importance. Dukes open their doors personally when he calls upon them; the aspirants to the higher life leave theirs open, in the hope that it might rain and he might be driven in for shelter.

GEORGE: He sounds great.

CHARLES: To have got him here today. George, is a triumph; he so seldom goes anywhere!

GEORGE: What do you think brought him here?

CHARLES: You've heard the singing at this charity concert, so the intelligent assumption is, he finds your mistress a very attractive young lady.

GEORGE: She's a knock out. The feller who couldn't do the card trick – I like him – he makes me laugh. Who was he?

CHARLES: He? He's quite of another kind! He is my Lord Dilling. Young, rich, attractive and clever! Had he been born a poor man, he might have died a great one! But he has allowed life to spoil him! He has a reputation with women that is extremely bad, consequently, as hope is a quality possessed of all women, women ask him everywhere! I would describe him as a man who has kept more husbands at home than any other man of modern times.

GEORGE: Do you like him?

CHARLES: Personally. I hate him. Besides, he's too clever, George, for any man to like very much! And too unscrupulous for any woman not to love very much!

GEORGE: 'As he got an eye to my mistress?

CHARLES: He has got two eyes to your mistress!

GEORGE: She don't like him?

CHARLES: Not in the way that he would like her to, George. Unless I am very much mistaken, she is a young lady with two eyes to herself!
(*LADY JOAN enters through the windows, with cigarette in long holder.*)

JOAN: Do something with that for me, Charles, please!

CHARLES: Yes, my lady! (*He takes the cigarette out of the holder and hands it to GEORGE.*)

(*GEORGE takes the cigarette from CHARLES and exits, closing the door.*)

JOAN: Charles, who the devil told those women out there that they can sing?

CHARLES: Their music teacher, my lady, when she found they had the money to pay for lessons in advance!

JOAN: I like that. May I use it as my own?

CHARLES: With pleasure, my lady!

JOAN: By the way, are your ears burning?

CHARLES: No, my lady!

JOAN: They should be; we've been talking about you for the last quarter of an hour; we are intrigued, Charles! Tell me, have you always been a butler?

CHARLES: I never remember allowing myself the privilege of forgetting it once, my lady.

JOAN: Oh! Likely to?

CHARLES: I shouldn't know how to, my lady! (*He is about to go off, having opened the door.*)

(*LADY MARY enters through the windows.*)

MARY: Oh! Charles, may I have some tea, please?

CHARLES: It will be here in a moment!

(*CHARLES exits, closing the door.*)

JOAN: Isn't he divine?

MARY: Who? Oh, Charles! Don't be absurd, Joan.

JOAN: Every time I see that man I realize how dreadfully our family is in need of a drop of new blood!

MARY: How very attractive Mrs Cheyney has made this house!

JOAN: Terribly! What a darling she is, Mary!

MARY: I like her enormously! By the way, don't you think it's rather amusing that the pompous Elton, who never goes anywhere, should be always here?

JOAN: I know! You don't think that sweet Mrs Cheyney would marry that prig, do you?

MARY: Being Lady Elton would have certain advantages?

JOAN: Heavens! Think of waking up in the morning and finding Elton alongside of one.

MARY: One wouldn't!

JOAN: That's true!

MARY: Well, it's all very amusing! Elton at a charity concert, and of all people in the world, Arthur Dilling!

JOAN: I have been watching Mrs Cheyney, and she appears not to be the least impressed by Arthur!

MARY: I know. It's frightfully good for him; poor darling, he can't understand it. It's something that has never happened to him before.

JOAN: Well, I can't understand any woman preferring Elton to Arthur.

MARY: If a woman has ideas of marriage, there wouldn't be much reason to waste time on Arthur.

(*WILLIE WYNTON enters through the windows.*)

WILLIE: Ah, there you are! The first part of the concert is over: and if the second part isn't better than the first, the garden will be strewn with bodies.

MARY: Don't grumble, Willie; it's sweet of Mrs Cheyney to have lent her garden, and we must help her.

WILLIE: I'm not grumbling; I'm just a poor, disappointed fellow who hardly ever finds anything right! (*Catching sight of himself in the framed mirror on the piano.*) Oh! Lord, how I hate my face!

JOAN: Supposing you had to live with it, like your wife has.

WILLIE: I never thought of that. I'll give her a present.

(*WILLIAM enters with teapot on salver. He places the teapot on the table and exits.*)

MARY: Hurrah! (*To JOAN.*) Tea, darling?

(*She rises and pours out tea.*)

WILLIE: (*Finding the whisky and soda and helping himself.*) I say, apparently our Mrs Cheyney is a rich woman.

MARY: Obviously!

WILLIE: Who actually is Mrs Cheyney, Mary?

MARY: Mrs Cheyney is the widow of a rich Australian; meaning to stay in England only a little, she liked us all so much, she has decided to settle amongst us!

WILLIE: Settle Elton seems to me to be more accurate.

MARY: Give that to Joan. (*She holds out a cup.*)

WILLIE: Right-o!

JOAN: You think he is in love with her?

WILLIE: I'm positive! I'll tell you another bloke who isn't far off it, too!

JOAN: Arthur?

WILLIE: That's right. (*Hands cup of tea to JOAN.*) But she's heard too much about him; she's not having any. My word, I wish I had a quarter of that fellow's brains!

MARY: What would you do with them if you had, Willie?

WILLIE: Well, I wouldn't waste time like he's doing; it's a crime to see that feller dissipating himself to pieces like he is doing! Thirty thousand a year and no occupation has done him in all right!

JOAN: He enjoys life.

WILLIE: Not he. He's exhausted nearly everything that there is in this life for him.

(*MARY has poured out a cup of tea for herself.*)

MARY: Some one said the other day he's drinking, rather. Is that true?

WILLIE: I'm afraid it is! Pity, because with all his faults he's such a damn good fellow!

JOAN: I adore him!

(*LADY MARIA FRINTON and MRS KITTY WYNTON enter through the windows.*)

MARIA: Tea! Divine! Enjoying the concert, Willie?

(*MRS WYNTON goes and pours out tea.*)

WILLIE: Like hell!

MARIA: Darling! And we got it up for you! It's charming. Don't you like the dear, fat, sweet creature who played the violin?

WILLIE: In the days of my early ancestors they would have thrown stones at her?

MARIA: And how right they would have been! The beast, I thought she was never going to stop!

WILLIE: Have some tea, darling?

MARIA: Tea. Yes, please.

MRS WYNTON: The one amusing thing was when Arthur suggested to Elton he should play his little piece.

JOAN: How pompous Elton looked when he said it!

WILLIE: (*Crossing to MARIA with the tea.*) That's what I like about Arthur. We're all such snobs about Elton, and he simply doesn't care a damn about him.

MRS WYNTON: You're swearing rather a lot today, Willie.

WILLIE: Sorry, darling, but I've been sitting next to Joan all the afternoon!

MARIA: I wish I knew for certain whether Elton hates Arthur more than Arthur despises Elton?
(*LORD ARTHUR DILLING enters through the windows.*)
Tea, Arthur?

ARTHUR: A whisky and soda! Give me one, Willie!

WILLIE: I will!

ARTHUR: (*Going to MRS WYNTON, lifts her pearls.*) Imitation of the opulent Sybil?

MRS WYNTON: What do you mean?

ARTHUR: You have got them all on.

MRS WYNTON: Naturally one wears the pearls given one by one's husband!

MARIA: And Willie likes her to wear them; they advertise you, don't they, Willie?

WILLIE: In what way? (*Giving ARTHUR the whisky and soda.*)

MARIA: A trap for other women, darling! If a man is prepared to give the woman he married such divine pearls, what would he be prepared to give the woman he loves?

WILLIE: Nothing of the sort! I'm much too mean to be unfaithful!

ARTHUR: (*Laughing.*) I like that, Willie!
(*ARTHUR puts more whisky into his glass from the decanter.*)

MARIA: What brings you to a charity concert, Arthur?

ARTHUR: A misjudged 'Kruschen' feeling. (*Examines the decanter of whisky.*)

MARY: Is that what brought Elton here?

ARTHUR: Elton, I take it, finds Mrs Cheyney very entertaining.

MARIA: Do you think he means to marry her?

ARTHUR: With the consent of his solicitor and his mother, he may in time propose to her!

JOAN: Why don't you marry her, Arthur?

ARTHUR: She wouldn't have me!

MARIA: You should ask her!

ARTHUR: As I could never make any woman happy for more than a year, I wouldn't be so impertinent!

MRS WYNTON: You should try!

ARTHUR: I have! And miserably failed! My maximum so far has been eight months. The last two of those months I shall never forget! I should hate any woman again to watch me suffering as that poor creature did!

JOAN: (*Laughing.*) I heard you described the other evening as a dishonourable man with thirty thousand a year!

MARIA: No man with thirty thousand a year who can write his name could ever be dishonourable!

ARTHUR: Quite right, Maria!

(*WILLIE laughs.*)

MRS WYNTON: (*To WILLIE.*) What are you making those curious noises for?

WILLIE: I'm laughing! I'm such an ass myself, I love anyone who isn't!

(*CHARLES enters. He crosses to the windows.*)

ARTHUR: Charles, you might put that down for me, please.

CHARLES: (*Taking ARTHUR's glass.*) Yes, m'lord. (*He puts the glass on the table.*)

MARIE: Ever tried tea, Arthur?

ARTHUR: Tea, what for?

(*As CHARLES is going off.*)

Charles! Been able to remember where we have met before?

CHARLES: Unfortunately I have not, my lord!

ARTHUR: (*Smiling.*) You might try!

CHARLES: I am, my lord.

(*CHARLES exits through the windows.*)

MARIA: What does that odd conversation mean?

ARTHUR: Where I have seen that feller before? I don't know, but I have seen him, and I'd give a devil of a lot to know where.

MRS WYNTON: Does it worry you, then?

ARTHUR: It's interesting to know why a gentleman should be a butler, that's all!

MARIA: Not really! Does anyone know where Elton and Mrs Cheyney are?

ARTHUR: I left Elton patronizing the tea that Mrs Cheyney was giving the villagers!

JOAN: I do wish he would marry Mrs Cheyney. It would be such fun.

(*LORD ELTON enters through the windows and puts his hat on the piano.*)

MARIA: My dear! Some tea?

ELTON: Many thanks, but I have had some!

ARTHUR: A whisky and soda, Elton?

ELTON: Thank you, no!

ARTHUR: We were just discussing marriage, Elton!

ELTON: And have you come to any conclusion?

ARTHUR: We have! We have decided you should!

ELTON: Indeed! For you to take such an interest in me is flattering!

ARTHUR: Not at all! Society needs a Lady Elton; the world more strong men like yourself!

ELTON: Having such strong convictions as regards marriage, I wonder you remain single!

MARIA: Yes, why do you?

ARTHUR: Ah, that's my affair! Mrs Cheyney is rather an attractive woman, if I dare say so, Elton?

ELTON: Forgive me, but perhaps it's because I am not modern, but I prefer the word likeable to attractive.

ARTHUR: Perhaps it's because I am too modern, but I differ! To accuse a beautiful woman of being liked by one is suggestive that her underclothes are made of linoleum.

(*Everyone laughs except ELTON, who looks displeased and astonished.*)

But to suggest that she is attractive betrays a meaning that, with encouragement, you have more and better things to say to her.

MARIA: Angel!

(*WILLIE laughs.*)

MRS WYNTON: (*To WILLIE.*) Do stop that silly noise!

ELTON: (*Ignores ARTHUR.*) The concert seems to be quite a success.

MARY: Terribly good, isn't it?

ELTON: The tall lady who played the violin; is she a professional?

ARTHUR: She is – but not at violin playing.

(*MRS CHEYNEY enters through the windows, carrying a parasol, followed by MRS SYBIL EBLEY.*)

MRS CHEYNEY: Have you all had tea?

MARIA: (*Rising.*) Of course! I insist on your sitting down and resting; you'll be worn out!

MRS CHEYNEY: (*Putting MARIA into her seat again.*) Nonsense. Mrs Ebley has been an angel; she's helped me to entertain all those dozens of people in the garden!

MRS EBLEY: Nonsense! I did nothing! This child, Maria, is a perfect marvel; you don't know how they adore her out there!

MARIA: Thank heaven we have something in common with them in here.

ARTHUR: A sentiment to which I heartily subscribe!

MRS CHEYNEY: (*Curtseys.*) Thank you, my lord! Have you had some tea?

ARTHUR: I had a whisky and soda.

MRS CHEYNEY: I've got some good news for you; one more item, then Lord Elton has promised to make a little speech – the collection – and after that you can all go home!

MARIA: You have been an angel to have taken all this trouble today!

ELTON: Most kind!

MRS CHEYNEY: It's kind of you all to have come; I'm afraid you have hated it!

MARIA: (*Taking MRS CHEYNEY's hand.*) We adore you, my dear, and that makes it perfect!

MRS EBLEY: I have made her promise to come to me on Friday week, when you all come!

MARIA: That's wonderful!

ARTHUR: I'll bring you!

MRS CHEYNEY: Lord Elton has very kindly offered to drive me from London.

ARTHUR: Splendid! Then I'll get Elton to give me a lift in his car.

MARIA: And don't forget, young woman, I am giving a dinner for you on Tuesday!

ARTHUR: Tuesday? I'll remember.

MRS CHEYNEY: I won't forget! You know, you're all too kind to me. I don't know why you are; I'm not the least amusing or modern; I don't drink; I don't smoke, and I don't swear – I'm really terribly dull!

JOAN: You're an angel, and I swear enough for both of us.

MRS CHEYNEY: I'm terribly sorry; but I'm going to push you all back to that concert – we are being rather rude to the singers.

MARIA: Not nearly as rude as the singers have been to us.

JOAN: If that fat woman plays the violin again I shall hiss her body off the stage.

(*MRS EBLEY, WILLIE and MRS WYNTON exit through the windows.*)

MARIA: My dear! She's a joke compared with the woman who sings like the bath water running away.

MRS CHEYNEY: You must go, my dears!

MARIA: The moment Elton has made his little speech I'll go; so, in case I don't see you again, goodbye and don't forget you are dining with me on Tuesday.

MARY: Give me a lift and I'll come with you.

MARIA: Certainly. Can I give you a lift, Elton?

ELTON: Many thanks, I have my own car.

MARIA: Thank God! I hope he always has it.

(*MARIA and MARY exit through the windows.*)

JOAN: Are you going my way, Arthur?

ARTHUR: Which is your way?

JOAN: Grosvenor Square.

ARTHUR: Sorry; mine's the other way. Besides, I too have a car, and why not, indeed?

JOAN: (*Going up to MRS CHEYNEY and shaking hands.*)
Goodbye, Mrs Cheyney – I'm going to face that foul
violin-player. (*She exits through the windows.*)

ARTHUR: You poor dear, I'll come with you. Well, thank
heaven, we have your speech to look forward to, Elton.
(*To MRS CHEYNEY.*) And, thank heaven, you have my
speech to look forward to, young woman. (*He goes out.*)

ELTON: Can I give you some tea?

MRS CHEYNEY: You don't like Lord Dilling?

ELTON: How did you know that? (*Pouring out tea.*)

MRS CHEYNEY: Instinct!

ELTON: If you hadn't mentioned it, I should have said
nothing, but as you have, I don't like him! (*Handing her a
cup of tea.*)

MRS CHEYNEY: He's very young.

ELTON: (*Going to the table for the plate of cakes.*) All women
make that excuse for him!

MRS CHEYNEY: And a good many women who have
known him made that excuse for themselves, I suppose?
(*ELTON offers cakes.*)
No, thanks.

ELTON: Yes!

MRS CHEYNEY: Odd creatures, women, aren't they?

ELTON: Frankly, I have to confess I know very little about
women.

MRS CHEYNEY: So they tell me!

ELTON: May I ask what they tell you?

MRS CHEYNEY: You don't like women! But I hope I am
an exception! I should hate you not to like me.

ELTON: I do, very much.

MRS CHEYNEY: I'm glad!

ELTON: (*Nervously.*) And I only hope it is mutual!

MRS CHEYNEY: It is! I like you very much!

ELTON: Thank you, I'm glad. By the way, my mother is
writing you today with the hope that you will be able to
come and stay with us for a little! I'm afraid it will be a
little dull, but we would both be very grateful if you
would come!

MRS CHEYNEY: It's most kind of your mother, and I shall write and tell her so, and how pleased I will be to come!

ELTON: I'm pleased, very pleased!

MRS CHEYNEY: I shall see you again before we meet at Mrs Ebley's?

ELTON: I trust so!

MRS CHEYNEY: I suppose it's a very lovely house.

ELTON: Do you know, I've never been there!

MRS CHEYNEY: You are going that weekend?

ELTON: Yes, if you are going.

MRS CHEYNEY: Don't you like them?

ELTON: (*Choosing his words.*) Oh, yes, very much – but – er – we live in rather a different world. Quite frankly, I don't understand these sort of people, and at my age it would be ridiculous to start and try.

MRS CHEYNEY: A young man of your age should start to try almost anything.

ELTON: It's very kind of you to say so, but I fear not.

MRS CHEYNEY: Nonsense! I'm an optimist.

(*CHARLES enters through the windows.*)

CHARLES: Lord Dilling has asked me, my lord, to tell you the audience are eagerly awaiting your speech, and also, my lord, he is the most eager of them all!

ELTON: Thank you!

MRS CHEYNEY: Shall we go?

(*MRS CHEYNEY rises picking up her parasol.*)

ELTON: Please! (*Takes his hat from piano.*)

(*MRS CHEYNEY and ELTON exit through the windows. CHARLES smiles. WILLIAM enters, followed by GEORGE. WILLIAM commences to clear up tea things and pack them on to the tray. GEORGE is making as if to go into the garden. CHARLES stops him, snapping his fingers.*)

GEORGE: Can't I go and hear that bloke speak?

CHARLES: There is so much dullness coming to you in your life that cannot be avoided, George, that I am not prepared to allow you to add what can! Clear these things!

GEORGE: Right ho! I must say I'm surprised because I never thought I would, but I like the toffs!

CHARLES: They have qualities, George!

GEORGE: I always 'eard them talked about as being stupid!

CHARLES: All the climbers in the world who fail in their ambition to know them, apologize for themselves by describing them as stupid or decadent.

(*WILLIAM has packed his tray.*)

GEORGE: Our Member down our way, he says the most terrible things about them!

CHARLES: And I dare say he is right. But the day one of them invites him to dinner he'll even have a bath!

The snobbishness of the upper classes, George, is only excelled by the snobbishness of the middle and the lower!

(*GEORGE opens the door for WILLIAM, who exits with tray.*)

GEORGE: I wish I could be 'Sir Georgie', I wouldn't 'alf come it over them down my way.

(*ARTHUR enters.*)

ARTHUR: Give me a whisky and soda, please.

CHARLES: Yes, my lord!

ARTHUR: Here! (*He offers some money to GEORGE.*)

GEORGE: (*Taking the money.*) What's this for, my lord?

ARTHUR: For you. (*With an inclination of his head towards CHARLES.*) I haven't the courage to give it to him!

GEORGE: Thank you, my lord.

(*GEORGE exits, closing the door.*
CHARLES is holding the whisky and soda. The two men look at each other.)

ARTHUR: I can't remember! (*Smiling.*) Can you?

CHARLES: What, my lord?

ARTHUR: Where we have met.

CHARLES: We have never met, my lord!

ARTHUR: I assure you we have! I was educated – I mean, I was at Oxford!

CHARLES: I once passed through Oxford in the train, my lord.

ARTHUR: Your manner suggests to me you might have got out and stayed there for a few years.

CHARLES: I had no idea Oxford had a school for butlers, my lord!

ARTHUR: Hadn't you? Tell me, how long have you been with Mrs Cheyney?

CHARLES: Mrs Cheyney engaged me six months ago next Tuesday in a registry office, in an adjoining street near Brook Street, to be her butler, my lord!

ARTHUR: Many thanks for the details! So you were not with Mrs Cheyney in Australia?

CHARLES: Has Mrs Cheyney ever been to Australia, my lord?

ARTHUR: Didn't you know Mrs Cheyney came from Australia?

CHARLES: How should I, my lord? Mrs Cheyney would never think of discussing her affairs with servants!

ARTHUR: (*Smiling.*) I accept the rebuke! (*He takes the glass from CHARLES.*)

CHARLES: There was none meant, my lord!
(**MRS CHEYNEY enters through the windows.**)

MRS CHEYNEY: Hello! I thought you had gone.

ARTHUR: Why?

MRS CHEYNEY: All the others have!

ARTHUR: I'm waiting for my man with my car.

CHARLES: (*Bowing and indicating outside windows.*) Your man has been waiting for some time, my lord!

ARTHUR: Has he? Well, it's a lovely afternoon, tell him to wait a little longer!

CHARLES: Yes, my lord! (*He bows and exits through the windows.*)

ARTHUR: I like that fellow.

MRS CHEYNEY: You mean my butler?

ARTHUR: Yes!

MRS CHEYNEY: Why do you like him?

ARTHUR: I like his insolence!

MRS CHEYNEY: He was rude to you?

ARTHUR: The reverse. I have often been told to go to hell, but never so pleasantly as he told me to, a moment ago!

MRS CHEYNEY: I shall dismiss him for that!

ARTHUR: Please, I ask you not to!

MRS CHEYNEY: I shall! (*Smiling.*) He should have known
  you had already gone!

ARTHUR: But I haven't! Who told you I had?

MRS CHEYNEY: Some of the women who went part of the
  way with you.

ARTHUR: (*Laughing.*) I'd go the whole way for a woman
  who said a thing like that!

MRS CHEYNEY: What a pity it is, then, that I've chosen
  the other direction!

ARTHUR: With Elton as your companion?

MRS CHEYNEY: At all events, he would know the way.

ARTHUR: He would! I want to ask you something. When
  you were in London staying at the Ritz last week I rang
  you up five times, and each time I was told you were
  out!

MRS CHEYNEY: What a shame!

ARTHUR: Were you out?

MRS CHEYNEY: No! Each time I was in!

ARTHUR: I thought so!

MRS CHEYNEY: Twice I answered it myself and told you
  I was out!

ARTHUR: May I ask why?

MRS CHEYNEY: Certainly! I don't care to be alone with
  you even on the telephone!

ARTHUR: Why not?

MRS CHEYNEY: It's my only way of paying tribute to
  your reputation!

ARTHUR: Thank goodness! For a moment, I thought you
  were going to embarrass me by saying you were nervous
  of me!

MRS CHEYNEY: My dear Lord Dilling – if I allow you to
  call me Fay, may I call you Arthur?

ARTHUR: I have always wanted you to, Fay!

MRS CHEYNEY: Thank you, Arthur!

ARTHUR: You were saying something?

MRS CHEYNEY: Oh yes! You have the great distinction,
  Arthur dear, of being one of the few men in the world
  I am not nervous of, and I feel I ought to be.

ARTHUR: Modestly, may I ask why?

MRS CHEYNEY: Well! You're not bad looking, exquisitely indifferent, even rude to people, a great sense of humour, brilliant – and –

ARTHUR: What else?

MRS CHEYNEY: That's the trouble! Nothing else!

ARTHUR: I am what is commonly termed – one of those who don't attract you?

MRS CHEYNEY: Isn't it odd?

ARTHUR: It's disappointing!

MRS CHEYNEY: I feel that, too.

ARTHUR: Tell me, did you learn the art of rebuking people so charmingly from your butler, or did he learn it from you?

MRS CHEYNEY: Neither! I expect Charles feels the same as I do – if there are to be insults, let us get them in first!

ARTHUR: I wonder if you would tell me what you mean by that?

MRS CHEYNEY: I want to very much! During the short time you have known me, Arthur dear, you have made me practically every proposal that a man can make a woman with the exception of one – marriage!

ARTHUR: I am not aware that I have ever made a suggestion to you that could not be spoken from any pulpit in any church! This is all pure imagination on your part!

MRS CHEYNEY: How disappointing!

ARTHUR: What do you mean?

MRS CHEYNEY: I mean, I hate you to use the stock remark of all men when they fail with a woman.

ARTHUR: You're quite wrong, but I see your point, because I suppose if a woman comes from Australia to England with the deliberate intention of marrying a –

MRS CHEYNEY: Arthur dear, ring the bell, will you?

ARTHUR: What for?

MRS CHEYNEY: Charles knows where your hat is!

ARTHUR: I didn't intend to be rude, I –

MRS CHEYNEY: You weren't rude, I assure you; you were only just a little feminine!

ARTHUR: (*Embarrassed.*) Feminine! Really! Well, I –
(*He turns to the table, picks up his glass and drinks.*)

MRS CHEYNEY: You don't drink alcohol with your meals, do you?

ARTHUR: I do. Why do you ask?

MRS CHEYNEY: Because you drink so much between them!

ARTHUR: (*Angrily.*) Do I? (*Puts his glass down.*)
(*MRS CHEYNEY laughs and he faces her.*)
May I ask what there is to laugh at?

MRS CHEYNEY: Because I'm enjoying myself so much! It's so amusing to have put you once in the position of embarrassment that you must have so often succeeded with women by putting them in!

ARTHUR: If I may say so, you appear to have rather a low opinion of me!

MRS CHEYNEY: It would be more civil of me to put it another way – I haven't a very high one of you!

ARTHUR: Really?

MRS CHEYNEY: Have you of yourself?

ARTHUR: Not at the moment!

MRS CHEYNEY: Then there's hope.

ARTHUR: Thank you! I suppose you would despise me even more if I were to finish that?
(*Indicates the whisky.*)

MRS CHEYNEY: Not at all! I should like you more if you didn't, that is all!

ARTHUR: I should hate you not to like me! Perhaps there is something else I could do for you?

MRS CHEYNEY: Heaps!

ARTHUR: As, for instance?

MRS CHEYNEY: One: live up to the reputation you have for possessing a sense of humour!

ARTHUR: Ah! Ah! Anything else?

MRS CHEYNEY: Stop living on the glory of your ancestors!

ARTHUR: What do you mean by that?

MRS CHEYNEY: What I say, Arthur dear!

ARTHUR: I am not aware that I do!

MRS CHEYNEY: Then I'm wrong, and I'm sorry – but you might tell me one thing you do that proves I am!
(*He looks at her; there is a pause.*)
Don't hurry. I am not dining until half-past eight!

ARTHUR: Why should I tell you?

MRS CHEYNEY: No reason at all! I'm only suggesting you should contradict what other people tell me!

ARTHUR: And what do you suppose gives you the right to ask me questions like this?

MRS CHEYNEY: The same right that has entitled you to ask me some of the questions you have! But as you can't answer, I'll answer for you! You've done nothing! Your epitaph at this moment is only this: 'He was a good fellow; metaphorically he lived on the dole; his only success was women.'

ARTHUR: I resent very much being talked to in this manner!

MRS CHEYNEY: One always hates a thing one is not used to!

ARTHUR: And you have no right to!

MRS CHEYNEY: No, really! I resent equally as much being treated by you as a –

ARTHUR: What?

MRS CHEYNEY: (*Waving her hand.*) Well, there are various names for that particular type of woman; when I have never given you the slightest encouragement which would give you the right to. (*A pause.*) You must see my point, Arthur dear.

ARTHUR: If anything I have done suggested that – yes.
(*A pause.*)

MRS CHEYNEY: Will you be an angel and tell me exactly what was in your mind to say to me when you came back here after the others had gone?
(*ARTHUR looks at her.*)
Go on, pretend you're in a hunting field, and you have to be a sportsman!

ARTHUR: (*Laughing.*) I follow!

MRS CHEYNEY: Go on.

ARTHUR: Very well. I meant to tell you, you were the most attractive woman I have ever known!

MRS CHEYNEY: We are about to take another fence! Was I?

ARTHUR: I hadn't considered whether you were or not!

MRS CHEYNEY: Splendid! Then?

ARTHUR: If that went well, I proposed to suggest a little dinner in my flat!

MRS CHEYNEY: And if that went well?

ARTHUR: Then I am experienced enough not to have said another word till after the dessert!

MRS CHEYNEY: Oh! (*She laughs.*) What was it your friends – divine! And now?

ARTHUR: I realize I had no right to, I was wrong. I beg your pardon; and in future I should never dream of asking you to dine with me without a couple of bishops. You didn't mean all those things you said to me just now?

MRS CHEYNEY: I like you so much, every one!

ARTHUR: Am I really as bad as that?

MRS CHEYNEY: Really!

ARTHUR: Good God! I may be a teetotaller tomorrow, but I feel I shall be very drunk tonight!

MRS CHEYNEY: But why?

ARTHUR: You've depressed me! I don't feel I'm half the hell of a feller I thought I was, and it's a bore!

MRS CHEYNEY: You are a hell of a feller, if you only knew it!

ARTHUR: I don't propose to agree with anything you say – I am not!

MRS CHEYNEY: Have a whisky and soda?

ARTHUR: Thank you, I don't drink!

MRS CHEYNEY: Angry with me?

ARTHUR: I'm something with you, but I don't know what it is! My lords, I rise with certain diffidence not in support of the motion before the House, but –

MRS CHEYNEY: What are you talking about?

ARTHUR: I feel I ought to be in the House of Lords speaking on behalf of some one who is down and out, or something or other!

MRS CHEYNEY: May I come and hear you, the day you do?

ARTHUR: I would insist. In my peroration, I will point to you and say, 'There is the good woman that pointed the way!'

MRS CHEYNEY: It almost makes one resolve to be a good woman!

ARTHUR: Resolve? Aren't you a good woman?

MRS CHEYNEY: Not very!

ARTHUR: Well, what the devil do you mean by talking to me as you have tonight?

MRS CHEYNEY: There is more than one way of not being a good woman, Arthur dear!

ARTHUR: There is more than – explain that!

MRS CHEYNEY: Don't be so absurdly serious; besides, it would take too long! Look at the time!

ARTHUR: But –

MRS CHEYNEY: I am dining at half-past eight!

ARTHUR: I insist on knowing whether you are a good woman or not!

MRS CHEYNEY: Why do you want to know?

ARTHUR: Because I should feel such a fool if you weren't!

MRS CHEYNEY: (*Putting out her hand.*) I am!

ARTHUR: Thank God!

(*ARTHUR takes her hand, is going to kiss it, changes his mind and takes the hem of her dress and kisses it.*)

There! Could anything be more respectable than that?

MRS CHEYNEY: Nothing!

ARTHUR: And, in addition, it's the one thing in my life I have never done before.

MRS CHEYNEY: (*Laughing.*) Mrs Wynton has asked me to lunch with her tomorrow.

ARTHUR: She hasn't asked me, but I shall be there, nevertheless!

(*He exits by the windows.*

MRS CHEYNEY watches him go, shrugs her shoulders, picks up a cigarette, lights it, and throws it down.)

MRS CHEYNEY: Damn! (*She takes up ARTHUR's glass; smells the whisky, pulls a face and puts it down, gazing into space, evidently thinking and her mind distracted, turns to the piano and commences to play.*

She plays an excerpt from 'Scriabine' Op. No. 9, Nocturne II, for the left hand.

WILLIAM enters. He closes the door and switches on the lights.

He then goes up to the windows, looks out, closes all the windows, fastens them and draws the curtains. He takes a packet of cigarettes from his trousers pocket and lights a cigarette from matches he finds in his pocket. He sits and takes a paper from his pocket and reads. GEORGE enters; he carries the 'Evening News,' opened at a crossword puzzle. He sits on the table.

JIM enters. He is a chauffeur and in his uniform, carrying his hat. He looks round and decides to sit on the settee.

CHARLES enters. He closes the door. He is smoking a cigar and takes a look at them all. He goes up to windows, looks outside through the curtains and stands behind MRS CHEYNEY by the piano stool.)

CHARLES: Charming! Charming! Scriabine.

JIM: Scriber – what?

WILLIAM: Bean.

JIM: (*To MRS CHEYNEY.*) Play us that tune, 'I want to be 'appy!'

(*MRS CHEYNEY stops playing and looks at them all.*)

MRS CHEYNEY: (*Starting to play something else.*) What a pretty lot of pets you look, don't you?

CHARLES: Thank you, darling!

MRS CHEYNEY: Well! (*She plays a scale on the piano, rises.*) I've got the invitation.

CHARLES: When?

MRS CHEYNEY: I am asked to stay with Mrs Ebley as an honoured guest on Friday week!

JIM: Great!

CHARLES: Wonderful! The pearls she was wearing this afternoon struck me as being worth, say, as a venture, twenty thousand!

JIM: Here! I hope she has got better ones than that at home.

CHARLES: Much.

WILLIAM: Then if we bring this off there isn't any reason why we shouldn't retire, should we be so inclined!

CHARLES: None! It will put us in the happy position of only doing the things, and those, we want to!

JIM: Charlie, this was a great idea of yours.

CHARLES: Not too bad, if I may say so, old friend!

WILLIAM: Wonderful! You're a master, Charles!

JIM: It's great, that's what it is!

MRS CHEYNEY: I should have added, I haven't definitely accepted the invitation.

CHARLES: Why not?

WILLIAM: You ain't thinking of refusing it, are you?

MRS CHEYNEY: I am!

(*There is a pause. They all look alarmed.*)

CHARLES: Jane, my dear, I –

MRS CHEYNEY: I have changed it to Fay!

CHARLES: Fay! Delightful! I prefer it! May I ask why you are in doubt?

MRS CHEYNEY: Certainly! I happen to like all these people very much; and in consequence, at the moment I am finding it rather distasteful to take Mrs Ebley's pearls from her!

JIM: Oh, chuck all that!

MRS CHEYNEY: (*Pointing at JIM.*) Very little of that, Charles dear, will decide me definitely not to do it!

CHARLES: Quite! I see Jane's – Fay's point perfectly!

MRS CHEYNEY: The idea of persuading perfectly charming people into inviting you to their house for the purpose of robbing them isn't pleasing me at all!

JIM: Here! You have had none of these scruples before?

MRS CHEYNEY: No! But during my adopted career I have never before come in contact with the people I have had to carry on my profession with, as it were!

CHARLES: No.

JIM: And you ain't going to do it?

MRS CHEYNEY: I am in grave doubt, Jim darling! (*Goes up to window and looks out into the night.*)

JIM: (*To CHARLES.*) Here, can't you do anything?

CHARLES: I? What can I do?

JIM: Can't you tell her to stop behaving like a fool?

CHARLES: I can't, because I know so well how she feels! I remember on one occasion practically having got a pocket-book containing a large sum from the pocket of a client, when I heard him say something rather kind and attractive to the person he was with; it was very wrong of me; but, do you know, I was so touched, I put it back!

JIM: Oh, for God's sake, let us sing Hymn 225 and have done with it!

WILLIAM: So you've fallen for the swells, have you?

MRS CHEYNEY: I suppose that describes it; they are charming, and I like them.

WILLIAM: Perhaps you have ideas of being Lady Elton?

MRS CHEYNEY: I have a suspicion I will refuse that!

WILLIAM: Well, the other feller ain't a marrying sort, you know!

MRS CHEYNEY: So he tells me!

CHARLES: (*Indifferently.*) Do you like him, Fay?

MRS CHEYNEY: Terribly! But don't be alarmed, I'm going to refuse him, too!

CHARLES: I'm relieved.

WILLIAM: Do you mind telling me what we've been giving you lessons for every day this week?

MRS CHEYNEY: I'm sorry; but I didn't quite realize, when I adopted this profession, that the people I would have to take things from would be quite so nice.

CHARLES: Quite!

WILLIAM: So we've spent months planning this, teaching her all we know, dressed up as butlers, she pretending to be an Australian widow, and on the verge of the greatest coup that has ever been made, she turns sentimental and refuses to do it.

CHARLES: I have rather enjoyed it! I'm not trying to persuade you, my sweet, but there is this to be remembered: the pearls we want from Mrs Ebley were taken by that lady, without a scruple, from the wives of the men who gave them to her!

MRS CHEYNEY: I know that!

CHARLES: And if you got them, there is this to be said, you would be in a position to say farewell to your profession, should you care to.

MRS CHEYNEY: That I have thought of, too.

CHARLES: Quite! But you feel a little sentimental about it?

MRS CHEYNEY: Yes!

CHARLES: That, I feel, is a little wrong! If that principle were generally adopted, the world would stop! For instance, supposing a woman went to a doctor without appendicitis, but with a hundred pounds, and he became sentimental and told her her appendix was as pure as the driven snow, how many honourable men would there be in the medical profession, I ask you? Supposing a man went to a lawyer with a bad case, but the money to pay for a good one, and that lawyer became sentimental and told him the truth – he was sure to lose – how many honourable lawyers would there be in the world, I ask you?

MRS CHEYNEY: I've no idea! I only know I'm sorry I took on this particular thing!

CHARLES: I feel for you, because I am on the side of all repentant people, but I have a leaning towards the wise ones who make certain their repentance is going to be spent in comfort – I would quote Mrs Ebley as an instance!

MRS CHEYNEY: That's true!

WILLIAM: 'I don't want to do it!' I have never heard such damned nonsense in my life!

CHARLES: Not at all. (*He winks at WILLIAM.*) I am full of sympathy for her!

(*MRS CHEYNEY turns to the piano, sits and plays softly.*)

MRS CHEYNEY: And, after all, if she had been sentimental, she would have never taken the pearls herself, would she?

CHARLES: She certainly would not!

MRS CHEYNEY: That's true! Jim, old dear, what was the name of that tune you wanted me to play?

JIM: 'I want to be 'appy!'

MRS CHEYNEY: So do I!

> (*MRS CHEYNEY plays a chorus of 'I want to be happy'. All the gang look at each other – they realize she has decided to steal the pearls – JIM, WILLIAM and GEORGE do 'thumbs up' – and begin to dance comically.*)

End of Act One.

ACT TWO

Scene 1

*A room in MRS EBLEY's country house. Ten days later. Two doors,
French windows, a fireplace.*

*After dinner on a warm summer evening. The French windows are
open.*

*MRS EBLEY seated in an arm-chair is doing needlework. MARY is
at the piano left, playing. JOAN is at the back doing jazz movements
to the accompaniment of the piano. ARTHUR, MARIA, WILLIE
and MRS WYNTON are sitting round a card table, playing bridge.
A rubber is almost over. ARTHUR, who is 'dummy', is sitting on a
stool below the card table, his back to the audience. MARIA is at the
top of the table facing the audience. MARIA has a good hand; there
are also good cards in the 'dummy'. She has six tricks at her left;
WILLIE two. Each player has five cards.*

*MARY is playing 'Poor Little Rich Girl' forte. ARTHUR rises; he is
smoking a cigarette, and goes to the table and stands watching the
game between MARIA and WILLIE.*

MARIA: Girls, girls, must you make that noise? Please.
　　(*MARY continues to play; JOAN goes over to ARTHUR; they
　　commence to dance at the back. MARIA leads a card. MRS
　　WYNTON and WILLIE follow. MARIA collects up the trick.*)
　　Arthur! Arthur!
　　(*MARY stops playing. ARTHUR and JOAN continue to dance,
　　singing 'Ta-ra-ra-ra-ra' to the time of the tune.*)
　　Oh, do stop that ta-ra-ra. It's impossible to play.
　　(*They stop dancing. JOAN goes over to MARY and sits against
　　her on the piano stool.*)
ARTHUR: Sorry, darling, sorry.
　　(*MARIA pauses a long time before playing her next card; she
　　tries to have a look at MRS WYNTON's hand; who hides her
　　cards. MARIA then deliberately drops her handkerchief at
　　her right. WILLIE bends down to pick it up; as he does so*)

MARIA takes a good look at his cards which he has in his right hand; he quickly hides his hand over his shoulder.)

WILLIE: (*Handing MARIA the handkerchief.*) Allow me.

MARIA: That's very civil of you, Willie.

WILLIE: Not at all. I just didn't want you to look over my hand.

MRS WYNTON: Willie!

ARTHUR: Bravo, Willie!

MARIA: Am I to assume that you think I would cheat?

ARTHUR: You are to assume that I am sure you would cheat. If you remember, at the ninth hole this morning, you turned to my caddy and said, 'Is Lord Dilling looking?' He said, 'No, m'lady'. Whereupon, you said, 'Well, kick my ball on to the pritty.'

MARIA: The boy's a liar! I told him to kick yours into the rough.

(*They play another round.*)

(*Playing.*) Give me that queen; the rest are mine.

WILLIE: Blast!

MARIA: Four honours in one hand, seventy-two.

WILLIE: Four honours in one hand, sixty-four.

(*MRS WYNTON gathers the cards.*)

MARIA: And score above.

ARTHUR: And the date is September 3rd, 1925, but there is no reason to count that in.

MARIA: Shut up! I make four hundred and seventy-two at five shillings a hundred is twenty-five shillings.

WILLIE: At half-a-crown a hundred is twelve and six, and we carry it forward.

(*ARTHUR picks up the bridge marker.*)

JOAN: (*Going up to the windows.*) What a divine night! How I would love to be out in that exquisite garden, being told by someone I was the most beautiful thing he had ever seen.

MARY: Who would you like to be told that by in particular?

JOAN: Shouldn't care a damn, darling, as long as it was a man and I was told it! Doing anything for a few minutes, Arthur?

ARTHUR: (*Writing on the score card.*) I am! But Willie isn't.

JOAN: Come and make love to me in the garden, Willie?

WILLIE: I'd rather sit here and smoke!

JOAN: Pig!

MARIA: Any signs of the young lovers?

JOAN: Not a sign – not a sound!

MRS WYNTON: And they have been out there for at least half an hour.

MARIA: I'm so excited I can't bear it; does this mean that Mrs Cheyney comes back into this room the future Lady Elton? (*Bangs table.*) Answer, some one.

ARTHUR: Does it necessarily follow because two people stay out in a garden alone for half an hour that they should return engaged to be married?

MARIA: No two people ever stayed alone in a beautiful garden on a beautiful night like this alone without something happening, and as it is Elton, I say that it is marriage!

ARTHUR: I disagree! Unless he has very much altered, I suggest he is describing to her in detail the History of England!

MARIA: If he is, I hope she tells him she is not that sort of woman and smacks his face!

MRS EBLEY: I should have thought you knew more about the geography of gardens than Elton, Arthur!

ARTHUR: I suggested that to her, myself!

MRS WYNTON: And what did she say?

ARTHUR: She said I knew too much about them!

MARIA: Arthur darling, I'm going to ask you a question.

ARTHUR: Am I in love with Mrs Cheyney.

MARIA: How did you know?

ARTHUR: Because it has been evident that you have been going to, ever since we arrived in this house two days ago!

MARY: And are you?

ARTHUR: As every one is expected to contribute something to a week-end party, my contribution is this: I think I am!

JOAN: You think you are! Oh, divine.

MARIA: To what extent?

ARTHUR: That I don't know, myself?

MARIA: Stuff and nonsense! What are the symptoms?

ARTHUR: I have suddenly discovered a liking for little children.

MARIA: That sounds like the real thing!

(*WILLIE laughs.*)

MRS WYNTON: If you can't stop that noise, Willie, I will send you to bed! Go on, Arthur!

ARTHUR: During the time I have known her, I have also discovered that in the past one has eaten too much; that one only needs a little food!

JOAN: Go on, darling!

ARTHUR: Sleep, I find, is not essential!

MARIA: The man is really in love – but this is marvellous.

MARY: What else, Arthur?

ARTHUR: It's the first time in my life I have been seriously obsessed by any woman.

JOAN: Do you like it?

ARTHUR: I do, rather! You must admit it's generous of me to tell you all this, particularly as she may, at any moment, return into the room affianced to another!

MARIA: It's divine of you, and it's the first thrill I have had since that horrid man tried to be familiar with me in a railway carriage.

(*They all laugh.*)

MRS EBLEY: Curious, how you have never been able to forget that!

MARIA: My dear, it was two years ago, and each day I grow older I feel the only literature I care for is railway time tables.

(*They all laugh.*)

MRS WYNTON: Arthur dear, having admitted all this, I can't understand why you doubt that you are in love with her?

ARTHUR: She won't have anything to do with me; she prefers to me, what I have always considered the world's prize ass; it may be that I am piqued!

MARY: I wonder if she is doing it on purpose?

ARTHUR: What do you mean by that?

MARIA: She may be merely encouraging Elton to encourage you!

ARTHUR: If she is, then she isn't a bit what I think she is!

MARIA: Good lord, the man has got it so badly he thinks her different from any other woman.

ARTHUR: I do!

MARIA: It's an extraordinary thing, but when an old man or a bad man falls in love, God help them!

(*ELTON with MRS CHEYNEY on his hand, enter from the garden.*)

MRS CHEYNEY: Playing bridge on a divine night like this! Shame.

ARTHUR: To have gone out would have been sacrilege to your divine night!

MRS CHEYNEY: Why?

ARTHUR: We all know each other too well.

MRS CHEYNEY: (*Laughing.*) Really?

ELTON: (*To MRS EBLEY.*) Mrs Cheyney has a very bad headache.

ARTHUR: Who shall blame her?

(*All the others snigger and suppress ill-mannered laughter.*)

ELTON: I have been trying to persuade her to take something for it!

MRS EBLEY: (*Rising and going to the bell below the fireplace, putting her work in work-bag.*) But, of course, there's some aspirin in my room.

MRS CHEYNEY: Please don't, it may pass off!

MRS EBLEY: But, my dear, I –

MRS CHEYNEY: Please! I get them so often that I'm trying to get rid of them without taking anything; but if it gets worse I'll come in to you for them, may I?

(*ELTON takes up a paper and reads it.*)

MRS EBLEY: I insist that you do!

MRS CHEYNEY: Thank you so much!

(*MRS EBLEY catches ARTHUR's eye. He makes a sign to her to get the others out of the room.*)

MRS EBLEY: Well, I suggest an early bed – perhaps just another rubber.

(*ARTHUR signs 'No more. Get them all into another room.'*)

(*To MARIA quietly.*) Say 'It's hot.'

MARIA: What?

MRS EBLEY: Hot.

ARTHUR: H – O – T.

MARIA: What's hot?

MRS EBLEY: The room.

MARIA: But it isn't – it's beautifully cool.

MRS EBLEY: Maria, be bright.

(*MRS EBLEY nudges MARIA, who sees ARTHUR signing to her – she at last understands and rises.*)

MARIA: Oh yes, of course. This room is insufferably hot. Can't we go and play in the er – bathroom – er I mean, the next room?

MRS EBLEY: (*To MRS CHEYNEY.*) You would rather not play, my dear?

MRS CHEYNEY: I won't, if you don't mind.

MARIA: You'll play, Arthur?

ARTHUR: I've got a headache, too.

MRS EBLEY: Well, come along! Come along, everybody – come along, Willie.

(*MRS EBLEY exits, followed by WILLIE.*

JOAN begins to play Patience.)

MARIA: Mary – Mary dear, we shall want you.

MARY: Oh, sorry. (*She exits.*)

MARIA: We've got six already, but it can't be helped. Kitty, Kitty dear.

(*MRS WYNTON crosses to MARIA who whispers in her ear, indicating MRS CHEYNEY and ELTON. MRS CHEYNEY is standing warming her feet at the fire. ELTON is absorbed in an evening paper.*)

What do you think?

MRS WYNTON: Not a notion.

MARIA: I'm doubtful. Arthur, do come and play.

(*MRS WYNTON exits.*)

ARTHUR: I'm sorry – I can't – I'm in terrible pain.

MARIA: Elton, will you kindly make us up?

ELTON: Certainly, if you want me to.

(*ELTON puts down the paper, and crosses to door.*)

MRS CHEYNEY: (*Turning to ELTON as he is crossing to the door.*) If you leave the door open, and you would like me to, I'll play to you!

ELTON: Thank you very much – that would be delightful!

(*ELTON exits. MARIA pulls a face at ARTHUR and exits, following ELTON.*

MRS CHEYNEY sits at the piano. JOAN remains at the table, playing Patience; she doesn't notice the others go. ARTHUR coughs; she takes no notice; he rises.)

ARTHUR: (*To JOAN.*) You are wanted on the telephone!

(*MRS CHEYNEY begins to play.*)

JOAN: (*Eagerly.*) I am! Who wants?

(*ARTHUR puts his cigarette out on the ash-tray on the card table.*)

Oh, damn funny, aren't you? (*She exits.*)

ARTHUR: Engaged?

MRS CHEYNEY: (*Sweetly.*) Talking to me?

ARTHUR: I don't see anybody else!

MRS CHEYNEY: Sorry! I didn't quite catch what you said.

ARTHUR: I asked if you were engaged?

(*She stops playing.*)

MRS CHEYNEY: Tell me all that you have been doing since dinner? (*She resumes playing the same piece.*)

ARTHUR: Explaining my symptoms.

MRS CHEYNEY: Aren't you well?

ARTHUR: No! Are you sorry?

MRS CHEYNEY: Terribly! What's the matter with you?

ARTHUR: Loss of appetite – loss of sleep!

MRS CHEYNEY: You should take something for it.

ARTHUR: I agree; but you give me no encouragement.

MRS CHEYNEY: Any particular thing you would like me to play you?

ARTHUR: No!

(*ARTHUR walks up to the window.*)

MRS CHEYNEY: You have no idea what a perfect night it is out there!

ARTHUR: Let us go out and see if you exaggerate.

MRS CHEYNEY: I have such a headache!

ARTHUR: Isn't piano playing rather bad for it!

MRS CHEYNEY: The reverse; it soothes it!

ARTHUR: And Elton?

MRS CHEYNEY: What do you mean by that?

ARTHUR: If you are playing the piano, it's obvious to him that you are doing nothing else!

MRS CHEYNEY: (*Smiling.*) That's clever of you.

ARTHUR: I'm terribly well up in all these things!

MRS CHEYNEY: Amuse me by telling me some of your past!

ARTHUR: Each of my pasts only convinced me that there might be a wonderful future!

MRS CHEYNEY: Too deep.

ARTHUR: I realize how marvellous it would all be if I had loved them!

MRS CHEYNEY: But you told them you did!

ARTHUR: I have some regard for good manners!

MRS CHEYNEY: Quite!

(*ARTHUR bends over the piano and pushes her hands off the keys.*)

ARTHUR: Did you accept Elton?

MRS CHEYNEY: What makes you think I had the opportunity to?

ARTHUR: Did you refuse him?

MRS CHEYNEY: I did not.

ARTHUR: You asked for time to think it over?

MRS CHEYNEY: You know so much, tell me a little more.

ARTHUR: In the end you will refuse him!

MRS CHEYNEY: Why?

ARTHUR: That man's wealth and position can never compensate you for all his stupidity and blab – (*He makes a grimace in imitation of ELTON.*)

MRS CHEYNEY: I disagree! Assuming all this is correct, the love of a good man stands for something.

ARTHUR: Not at all! That is proved by the fact that it is always a bad man who is the co-respondent.

MRS CHEYNEY: (*Laughing.*) Tell me why you are so interested in my marrying Lord Elton?

ARTHUR: Obvious! I am in love with you myself!

MRS CHEYNEY: From anyone else that would suggest a proposal of marriage.

ARTHUR: If you like!

MRS CHEYNEY: Don't look like that, Arthur, otherwise I'll believe you.

ARTHUR: You can!

MRS CHEYNEY: You seriously mean to tell me you want to marry me?

ARTHUR: I wouldn't say that!

MRS CHEYNEY: Ho!

(*They both laugh.*)

ARTHUR: Don't misunderstand! To me, the idea of marriage has always been the death and burial of all romance in one's life! And God knows I have done all I can to persuade you that that is so, but you don't agree! Very well, as I like you so much –

MRS CHEYNEY: (*Correcting.*) As I attract you so much!

ARTHUR: If you like! I am prepared to be at any church you like to name at eleven o'clock tomorrow morning!

MRS CHEYNEY: I must attract you very much, Arthur!

ARTHUR: More than I care to acknowledge, even to myself! For the first time, I don't understand myself; I'm unhappy when I'm not with you; I'm unhappy when I am! I can see nothing but you when you are present, and nothing but you when you are not; your voice is the only one I ever hear; in fact, let us face it, I've got it worse than any of God's creatures have ever had it before!

MRS CHEYNEY: There are three reasons why I should like to marry you, Arthur!

ARTHUR: Being?

MRS CHEYNEY: One, I like you terribly!

ARTHUR: Are the other two important?

MRS CHEYNEY: Two! It would be such fun to go to tea with all the women you haven't married!

ARTHUR: Oh, shut up! And the third?

MRS CHEYNEY: I should be some sort of widow again within a year!

ARTHUR: There's always a chance of that, but I think it is worth it!

(*MRS CHEYNEY shakes her head.*)

You don't agree. Why?

MRS CHEYNEY: I know too much about you, and you know too little about me.

ARTHUR: Is there anything more to know about you than I do?

MRS CHEYNEY: Three volumes closely printed!

ARTHUR: I'd give a great deal to understand what there is I don't understand about you, Fay.

MRS CHEYNEY: It might amuse you.

ARTHUR: Might it?

MRS CHEYNEY: I hope so.

ARTHUR: I see! I take it, my first and only offer of marriage is rejected?

(*She nods her head.*)

Have you been laughing at me, by any chance?

MRS CHEYNEY: What makes you think so?

ARTHUR: I don't know; you look so strange! By God, I should be angry if you were! Are you laughing at me?

MRS CHEYNEY: The reverse; it's the first time in my life I remember not laughing at myself.

ARTHUR: What do you mean by that?

MRS CHEYNEY: Just that.

ARTHUR: You're an odd creature!

MRS CHEYNEY: I wish I weren't!

ARTHUR: There's some reason why you can't marry me?

MRS CHEYNEY: No!

ARTHUR: You just don't like me?

MRS CHEYNEY: I like being single!

ARTHUR: Can I ask you one other question?

MRS CHEYNEY: Yes.

ARTHUR: Are you all that I think of you, as a woman?

MRS CHEYNEY: In what way do you think of me as a woman?

ARTHUR: All the things that a man demands from a woman he is going to marry.

MRS CHEYNEY: I'm every one of the things you mean.

ARTHUR: I know you are! You're an angel.

MRS CHEYNEY: (*Rising.*) I really have got a headache!

ARTHUR: I'm sorry! Why go into the garden in such thin shoes? Let me get you some aspirin!

MRS CHEYNEY: No, thanks! I think I'll go to bed!

ARTHUR: Fay, may I be allowed a platitude?

MRS CHEYNEY: Yes?

ARTHUR: (*Humorously.*) Perhaps in time?

MRS CHEYNEY: (*Shaking her head.*) No!

ARTHUR: Just friends?

MRS CHEYNEY: That's right!

ARTHUR: I understand! (*He turns away and picks up a newspaper.*) I think Centaur will win the big race on Tuesday!

MRS CHEYNEY: Inglesby!

ARTHUR: Know anything?

MRS CHEYNEY: Just an instinct!

ARTHUR: I'll back it! I believe in you! The only woman I ever have!

(*JOAN enters shrieking with laughter.*)

The woman's in wine.

(*MARIA enters.*)

MARIA: Shut up, Joan! My advice to any man, woman or child who likes bridge is, not to marry Elton!

MRS CHEYNEY: What has he done?

MARIA: Done? He's done every conceivable thing that doesn't appear in the book of rules. I'm afraid I was very rude to him. Oh dear! I'm always putting my foot in it!

JOAN: He's pompous even when he revokes. What a colossal ass he is!

MRS CHEYNEY: I like him!

ARTHUR: Oh dear, oh dear!

JOAN: Sorry, darling! (*She puts out her hand to MRS CHEYNEY.*)

ARTHUR: This young woman has a bad headache!

MRS CHEYNEY: I have, rather! I'm going to bed!

MARIA: So am I, my dear! It's the only place I'm sure of not getting into trouble!

ARTHUR: Oh, come, come!

MARIA: I'll come with you!

MRS CHEYNEY: (*Looking at ARTHUR.*) Good night!

ARTHUR: Good night, Fay dear! I'm going to back Inglesby!

MRS CHEYNEY: It's a risk! Good night, Lady Joan!

JOAN: Good night, darling, hope you will be all right in the morning!

(*MRS CHEYNEY exits.*)

MARIA: Good night, Arthur! Good night, Joan!

JOAN: Good night, darling; sleep well!

(*MARIA exits, closing the door.*)

Sorry she has a headache!

ARTHUR: Yes. (*He puts down his paper on the piano with a sigh.*) Joan! Now, think before you speak. Supposing, only supposing, I asked you to be my wife, what would you say?

JOAN: I'll be ready in five minutes!

ARTHUR: What!

JOAN: Well, four.

ARTHUR: Good! Why?

JOAN: Heaps of reasons!

ARTHUR: I give it up! (*He starts to walk away towards the door.*)

JOAN: Don't leave me; you're being so interesting; where are you going?

ARTHUR: I'm about to resume my ordinary life! The whisky, I take it, is kept in the other room? Tell me something I can say that will annoy Elton!

JOAN: Tell him – tell him – I know, ask him which room Mrs Cheyney is sleeping in?

ARTHUR: Excellent! (*He is about to go.*)

JOAN: Hi! Come back and tell me how he died!

ARTHUR: I will! And I'll bring my whisky and soda and drink it here – (*He kisses her on the head.*) you are more amusing! (*He exits.*)

(*JOAN takes lipstick and powder from her little bag. ROBERTS enters. He sees only JOAN. He goes to the windows to look into the garden.*)

JOAN: What is it, Roberts?

ROBERTS: Do you know where Mrs Cheyney is, my lady?

JOAN: Gone to bed. Who wants her?

ROBERTS: A cable came for her this evening, and Charles, her butler, thinking it might be important, has brought it over, my lady!

JOAN: Is Charles out there?

ROBERTS: Yes, my lady!

JOAN: Show him in.

ROBERTS: Yes, my lady!

(*ROBERTS exits through the windows.*
JOAN quickly applies lipstick and powder. ROBERTS shows
CHARLES in, and goes out again closing the door.)

CHARLES: Good evening, my lady!

JOAN: Charles, I'm delighted!

CHARLES: You are, my lady?

JOAN: Ever since I have known you, I have always said to myself: 'Ah! but what does he look like in ordinary clothes?'

CHARLES: And, my lady?

JOAN: I had no right to doubt you!

CHARLES: My late master, who left us some time ago, and of whose destination I am only suspicious, I am sure would be glad to hear how much you approve of the clothes that he left me, my lady, before he left us!

JOAN: I suppose clothes do make the man, Charles?

CHARLES: Many a bride has been disappointed when they have taken them off, my lady!

JOAN: (*Laughing.*) I never meet you, Charles, without something to say at dinner the next evening!

CHARLES: My mistress, I understand, has gone to bed, my lady?

(*ARTHUR appears in the garden with a glass of whisky. He is about to pass when, through the window, he sees CHARLES and stops; quietly he stands back watching him the whole time.*)

JOAN: Yes! Do you want her particularly?

CHARLES: No, my lady! A cable came for her, and as I heard her say she expected an important one, I thought

I had better bring it over; I have also enclosed some letters that have come for her, in the parcel, my lady!

JOAN: I'll give it to her!

CHARLES: (*Giving the parcel to JOAN.*) If you would be so kind, my lady! Good night, my lady! (*He walks away towards door.*)

(*ARTHUR, drawing back, shows that he has recognized and remembered CHARLES.*)

JOAN: (*Speaking after CHARLES has got to the door.*) Good night, Charles!

CHARLES: (*Giving her a look.*) Good night, my lady! (*He exits, closing the door.*)

(*Pause. JOAN laughs. ARTHUR enters from the garden.*)

ARTHUR: Well, I've come back to talk to you!

JOAN: Who do you think has been here since you left?

ARTHUR: Not a notion.

JOAN: My divine Charles!

ARTHUR: Charles? Charles who?

JOAN: Mrs Cheyney's butler!

ARTHUR: No! Really? What did he want?

JOAN: Brought her some cables or something!

ARTHUR: I see!

JOAN: Arthur, I'm going to ask you a question; do clothes make the man? Because I've a splendid answer!

ARTHUR: I don't know. Clothes can alter a man.

JOAN: How?

ARTHUR: I'll tell you. Some years ago, quite a number, there was a crook fellow living at the same hotel in Monte Carlo that I was; no one knew he was a crook, and we all liked him because he was rather amusing; one day he was, as it were, caught in the act; everybody started to chase him, and as I could run faster than the rest, it amused me to run in the opposite direction to my crook friend, with the result they all followed me and he got away!

JOAN: What has that got to do with clothes?

ARTHUR: Nothing; only, years later, he was dressed differently and I didn't recognize him!

JOAN: Which I call a damn dull story!

ARTHUR: Quite!

JOAN: I'm going to bed; I'll take that up to Mrs Cheyney on my way!

(*She is about to take the parcel when ARTHUR puts his hand on it across the table.*)

ARTHUR: No, go and talk to her for a minute, and I'll bring it up, which will give me a chance to say good night to her!

JOAN: You haven't half got it, dearie. (*She kisses ARTHUR.*) But I'm a sport; but don't be too long!

ARTHUR: I won't!

(*JOAN exits.*

ARTHUR looks at the parcel, examines it, appears very serious. He shakes it, turns it over in his hand, looks round to see if anyone is about and opens the parcel, which contains an empty 100 cigarette box. Turning it about to see what is inside, he sees written on the lid 'Courage, my sweet!' He reads it aloud.)

'Courage, my sweet!'

(*He shakes his head and repeats it, then puts the box back in the parcel and closes it up. He whistles a tune.*

MRS EBLEY and ELTON enter from the garden.)

ELTON: Many thanks for a very pleasant evening! Good night! (*Shaking hands.*)

MRS EBLEY: Wouldn't you like something before you go to bed?

ELTON: No, many thanks! Good night!

(*MARY enters from the garden.*)

Good night, Dilling.

ARTHUR: Good night Elton, and again good night!

(*ELTON exits.*)

MARY: (*Sighing.*) Ho! what a dull man.

(*MRS WYNTON enters from the garden.*)

MRS WYNTON: (*Speaking behind her as she enters.*) Willie, get me a glass of barley water! Arthur, were you really serious tonight when you told us you were really in love?

ARTHUR: My dear! It was my odd way of being amusing!

MRS EBLEY: I do wish you would marry, Arthur!

ARTHUR: I wanted to once!

MARY: Why didn't you?

ARTHUR: One; she refused me! Two; I have an idea she was everything I thought she wasn't!

MRS WYNTON: (*Laughing.*) How tragic!

MARY: Tell us about her!

ARTHUR: I have told you all that I know.

(*WILLIE enters by the door with a glass of barley water; he gives it to MRS WYNTON and then goes to MARY; they talk at the fireplace.*)

MRS WYNTON: I am going to bed! (*She kisses MRS EBLEY.*)

MRS EBLEY: Don't forget. Breakfast at ten.

MRS WYNTON: (*Turning on her way to the door.*) Oh! Can't I have mine in my bedroom?

MRS EBLEY: Lazy girl – of course you may.

MRS WYNTON: Well, good night, darling, and ever so many thanks for a perfect week-end!

MRS EBLEY: So glad you have liked it, darling!

MRS WYNTON: I have.

ARTHUR: Oh, Kitty! Give this to Mrs Cheyney, would you, on your way up? Her butler brought it – you might tell her that.

(*He has taken up the parcel and turns to MRS WYNTON.*)

MRS WYNTON: (*As she takes the parcel and opens the door she sees WILLIE talking to MARY.*) Willie!

WILLIE: Going to bed, Arthur?

ARTHUR: I? Not for years!

(*MRS WYNTON goes out.*)

WILLIE: (*Turning to ARTHUR.*) I'll come back and have a cigarette with you, (*In ARTHUR's ear.*) as soon as I can get away!

(*WILLIE follows MRS WYNTON out.*)

ARTHUR: (*To MARY.*) Say good night to the pretty lady and hop it!

MARY: Are you talking to me?

ARTHUR: Yes, lovely!

MARY: (*To MRS EBLEY.*) Do you mind being left alone with him?

MRS EBLEY: I'll take the risk.

MARY: Very well; good night, darling; and, by the way, you have got me until after lunch.

MRS EBLEY: Splendid!

MARY: (*Taking a book from table and going to the door.*) Good night, Arthur!

ARTHUR: Good night.

(*MARY exits.*

There is a pause.)

MRS EBLEY: What's the matter, Arthur? You look so worried!

ARTHUR: I? I'm not a bit; a little tired!

MRS EBLEY: So am I!

ARTHUR: It's been a particularly happy weekend!

MRS EBLEY: I have loved having you all.

ARTHUR: If I may say so, our little friend, Mrs Cheyney, has considerably contributed to the pleasure of it.

MRS EBLEY: I simply adore her; that is a sweet woman, Arthur.

ARTHUR: Very! By the way, where did Maria find her, do you know?

MRS EBLEY: She met her first, I believe, at the tables at Cannes.

ARTHUR: Ha!

MRS EBLEY: Then, by some accident, on the way home, they found they were staying at the same hotel in Paris, and Maria, with that love she has of finding new people, took her up, and showed her the sights, as it were!

ARTHUR: I envy her! That's a job I would have enjoyed!

MRS EBLEY: I'm sure you would!

ARTHUR: By the way, was her butler, the immaculate Charles, with her at the time?

MRS EBLEY: Fortunately he was, because Maria lost some valuable things and Charles was instrumental in getting some of the things she valued most returned to her.

ARTHUR: Did he, by George? That was decent of him. (*He goes over to the window.*)

MRS EBLEY: Mighty useful for Maria.

ARTHUR: What a divine night. (*He turns to MRS EBLEY.*)

MRS EBLEY: Yes, isn't it?

ARTHUR: (*Looking at MRS EBLEY's pearls, which he takes in his hands.*) Those are pretty good, if I may say so, Sybil.

MRS EBLEY: They are more than pretty good, if I may say so, Arthur.

ARTHUR: Insured?

MRS EBLEY: To be vulgar, for fifty thousand.

ARTHUR: Where do you keep them at night?

MRS EBLEY: Oh, I don't know. Alongside my bed.

ARTHUR: I'd like to sleep with fifty thousand pounds alongside my bed.

MRS EBLEY: Don't be ridiculous.

ARTHUR: (*Putting his hands to his head.*) Oh dear, oh dear!

MRS EBLEY: What's the matter, Arthur? You look terribly tired.

ARTHUR: So would you if you hadn't slept for three nights.

MRS EBLEY: Not slept for three nights – why?

ARTHUR: Sybil, may I be a perfect pig?

MRS EBLEY: Well!

ARTHUR: I hate that infernal room you've given me.

MRS EBLEY: Why, what's the matter with it, Arthur?

ARTHUR: Well, the walls are covered with ivy and it's full of sparrows – I can't sleep a wink.

MRS EBLEY: Arthur, why didn't you tell me this before?

ARTHUR: Because I have a beautiful and unselfish nature.

MRS EBLEY: Rubbish!

ARTHUR: Why did you give Elton my room?

MRS EBLEY: Well, he's never stayed here before, and it seemed only civil to give him that room.

ARTHUR: It seems a pity I should lose my life on account of Elton.

MRS EBLEY: Oh, Arthur!

ARTHUR: Can't Roberts make me up a room somewhere else?

MRS EBLEY: I'm afraid it's impossible. The house is full. Now, what can I do?

ARTHUR: Don't worry; it doesn't matter.

MRS EBLEY: My dear, I shouldn't sleep a wink, knowing you weren't comfortable. I'm miserable. What can I do?

ARTHUR: Nothing.

MRS EBLEY: Arthur, would you like my room?

ARTHUR: Good heavens, no!

MRS EBLEY: Why not? It doesn't make the slightest difference where I sleep – I certainly shouldn't sleep a wink if I thought you weren't comfortable.

ARTHUR: I wouldn't dream of such a thing.

MRS EBLEY: Don't be ridiculous, Arthur! (*With a friendly little shake of his shoulder.*) Besides, I've spoilt you ever since you were born; there's not much reason in my not going on with it.

ARTHUR: On your oath, you swear you don't mind?

MRS EBLEY: Of course not. What difference does it make? I've often slept in that room. I'll get my maid to move your things, then you'll get a decent night's rest. (*She turns to the door.*)

ARTHUR: The difference between you and me is, that I'm a selfish swine and you're an angel.

MRS EBLEY: Nonsense! You're nothing of the sort.

ARTHUR: Oh! and, Sybil, you might do something else for me.

MRS EBLEY: What?

ARTHUR: If you see any of the others, don't mention it to them; they'd think me such a fool.

MRS EBLEY: Of course not. And, Arthur, as you're not sleeping I'll have some hot milk sent up to your room.

ARTHUR: No – I don't think I'll risk that – but you might get Roberts to send me up some sandwiches and a pint of champagne.

MRS EBLEY: Why, is champagne good for not sleeping?

ARTHUR: My dear, champagne is good for everything.

MRS EBLEY: Oh, all right!

ARTHUR: Oh! and, Sybil – (*He advances and takes hold of the pearls.*) look! Just for a lark, let me – er – er – no, don't bother; (*He drops the pearls and turns from her a little.*) it doesn't matter; I'll come and kiss you good night on the way up.

MRS EBLEY: Well, don't be long – I shall be asleep in two winks – I don't mind the sparrows and the ivy. (*She exits and closes the door and immediately is heard speaking outside.*) Yes! I've loved having you, Willie.

(*WILLIE enters.*)

WILLIE: (*As he closes the door.*) Good! Glad you are here! Can I pour you out a whisky and soda?

ARTHUR: You can! A large one.

(*WILLIE crosses to get whisky and soda. ARTHUR quickly turns up stage and looks round outside the windows; he returns.*)

WILLIE: Been a devilish amusing week-end, Arthur!

ARTHUR: Devilish!

WILLIE: I've enjoyed it! (*Giving ARTHUR his drink.*) Great fun! Sorry it's over! What a darling that little Cheyney woman is!

ARTHUR: You like her?

WILLIE: Enormously! She has all the qualities men like in a woman.

ARTHUR: Quite! I often wonder what a feller does when, by accident, he finds out that a woman he admires hasn't any of the qualities he thought she had!

WILLIE: I don't know. I suppose he'd be a little disappointed, wouldn't he?

ARTHUR: Are you asking me?

WILLIE: Yes!

ARTHUR: Speaking for myself, I should be damned angry!

Scene 2

MRS EBLEY's Bedroom. ARTHUR is sitting by the day-bed, leaning back reading a book. He is wearing a dressing-jacket. The fire is lighted. After a moment the clock over the mantel strikes three. He continues reading for a few seconds, then puts down his book, rises, stretches himself and turning round opens the door a little and stands listening, then closes it again. He crosses over to the dressing-table and looks in the mirror. He examines his face rather critically, pulling down his lower eyelids and moving his head from side to side as he endeavours to get a good light on his eyes. He stands back a little to get a more general survey of his face. He takes off his wrist watch and puts it on the table. Turning to the bed he takes his pyjamas which are on the pillows and lays them out on the bed – turns the bed down, arranges the pillows, looks at and fingers the lace trimming. He is just about to take off his dressing-jacket when he hears a sound. He stands motionless for a moment looking over to the door. Then, quickly, he re-buttons his jacket and crosses on tiptoe to the door. Putting his ear to it, he listens. He goes up to the door of the dressing-room and looks in, shuts the door again and is moving to the bedroom door when he appears certain that he hears someone coming – he steps back quickly and switches off the lights. The flicker of the fire is just sufficient to show MRS CHEYNEY opening the bedroom door. She does so very quietly and comes into the room. She whispers 'Mrs Ebley! Mrs Ebley!' She crosses to the bed. She pauses there a moment and then goes slowly to the dressing-table. As she approaches it ARTHUR switches on the lights, locks the bedroom door and puts the key in his pocket.

ARTHUR: (*Smiling at her.*) Do you know, I had a feeling that you would come.

MRS CHEYNEY: What do you mean?

ARTHUR: Champagne! (*He points to the bottle on the table.*) And sandwiches! Could anyone, I ask you, be more thoughtful?

MRS CHEYNEY: I – I – I – thought this was Mrs Ebley's room, and I came to ask her for some aspirin for my head.

ARTHUR: As a host, I'm superb, really I am. I even thought to borrow that, too, here they are! (*Takes pearls out of his pocket, holds them up to her.*)

MRS CHEYNEY: I – I – don't know what you mean! Why are you in this room?

ARTHUR: As I have said, I had an idea you were coming in to it, and as I like you so much, I tricked Sybil into changing rooms with me.

MRS CHEYNEY: (*Quickly crossing to the door.*) Let me out of this room, do you hear?

ARTHUR: I will let you out when the penalty of coming into it has been paid.

MRS CHEYNEY: What do you mean?

ARTHUR: What I say!

MRS CHEYNEY: Unlock this door.

(*ARTHUR smiles at her.*)

Do you hear? Unlock this door, or I will break it down.

ARTHUR: Well, why don't you?

(*She stares at him.*)

But if you want them to know who you really are, and, believe me, when they do they will have considerably less sympathy for you than I have, there is a night bell (*With a jerk of his head he indicates the bell-push by the bed-head.*) ring it, and rouse the butler.

(*Pause. They look at each other.*)

I do hope you will believe me when I tell you I sympathize with you very much!

MRS CHEYNEY: You mean, at being locked in a room with you alone?

ARTHUR: On that, my inclinations are to congratulate you. I mean, you nearly made such fools of us all, it seems a pity not to have allowed you to complete it! (*Shows her the pearls; coming to the table he places the pearls upon it.*)

MRS CHEYNEY: (*Looking at them.*) Beautiful, aren't they? (*She takes a cigarette from the box on the table.*)

ARTHUR: Want a light, darling? Please! (*Lights a match for her.*)

MRS CHEYNEY: (*Lighting her cigarette at the match ARTHUR is holding.*) Thank you! (*Looking at him.*) I –

ARTHUR: You were going to say something?

MRS CHEYNEY: (*Looking at his dressing-jacket.*) Why the fancy dress?

ARTHUR: (*Looking at her coloured pyjama costume.*) Well, I didn't want to feel out of it.

(*She picks up the pearls, hands them to ARTHUR, and sits.*)

MRS CHEYNEY: How did you find out, Arthur?

ARTHUR: I recognized your – what is Charles to you by the way?

MRS CHEYNEY: My butler!

ARTHUR: Yes! I meant in his spare time?

MRS CHEYNEY: My butler! How did you recognize him?

ARTHUR: I saved him from gaol once before!

MRS CHEYNEY: You couldn't see your way to making a habit of it?

ARTHUR: I have always had a horror of doing the same thing twice.

MRS CHEYNEY: I sympathize!

ARTHUR: By the way, where is Charles at the moment?

MRS CHEYNEY: Underneath that window with a very bad headache, waiting for the aspirin! (*Indicating the pearls in ARTHUR's hand.*)

ARTHUR: (*Smiling.*) Forgive me being inquisitive, but are you married to him?

MRS CHEYNEY: I'm nothing to him – except that we are in business together! (*Blows smoke to ceiling.*) What terribly nice cigarettes!

ARTHUR: I'll send you some!

MRS CHEYNEY: That's sweet of you! I'll give you my address tomorrow – when I know it!

ARTHUR: Why? Are you thinking of changing your present one?

MRS CHEYNEY: I have an idea that you may make it difficult for me to keep it!

ARTHUR: Ah! one always expects to pay a little more for a thing one wants enough!

MRS CHEYNEY: Quite! But I don't think I want it enough to pay your price!

ARTHUR: (*Putting the pearls in his left-hand pocket.*) But I have never mentioned it!

MRS CHEYNEY: Haven't you?

ARTHUR: I confess I have been wanting to spend an evening with you like this ever since I knew you! I even offered you marriage.

MRS CHEYNEY: But I refused!

ARTHUR: (*Kneeling.*) You did! (*He puts his hand on her knee; she pushes it away.*) But surely the assumption is, you have changed your mind?

MRS CHEYNEY: How clever of you! So, if I understand you rightly, if I agree to stay you say nothing!

ARTHUR: Nothing! Of course, I shan't!

MRS CHEYNEY: And if I don't?

ARTHUR: Oh, come, come, you wouldn't be so ungenial. What's the matter, Fay? (*He rises.*)

MRS CHEYNEY: (*Laughing.*) That's an original way of punishing a crook! And only another crook could have thought of it!

ARTHUR: Yes! It amuses you?

MRS CHEYNEY: Immensely, but of course I know it shouldn't! In fact, I realize if I were really a nice woman I should hate you, but I don't; I feel rather flattered! There's something rather attractive in being locked in a room with a man, alone, even if it's against your will!

ARTHUR: I hate you to say that! Because the only reason I have locked the door is to prevent anyone coming into it, thereby saving you from explaining why you ever came into it!

MRS CHEYNEY: Quite! As crooks go, do you know the difference between Charles and you?

ARTHUR: No?

MRS CHEYNEY: Well, Charles robs with a charm of manner, and you rob with violence!

ARTHUR: That's not fair. I feel I am behaving more generously!

(*Pause.*)

MRS CHEYNEY: Would you mind my sending a message to Charles?

ARTHUR: How do you propose to do that?

MRS CHEYNEY: The lights have told him Mrs Ebley is awake. All that he is waiting to know now is if I'm all right, or if I am discovered. The manner in which I pull those curtains is the signal.

ARTHUR: Which of the messages do you propose to send him?

MRS CHEYNEY: I'm going to send him a message that I'm quite all right!
(*She goes to the window and pulls the curtains slightly.*)
There! Now the poor darling can go home quite happy! Open the bottle, Arthur dear! Let us all be happy!

ARTHUR: A good idea! (*He reaches for the bottle and starts to open it.*)

MRS CHEYNEY: Don't let it pop, for heaven's sake! Elton loves me so much he's not sleeping well, and he might think it a revolver shot and rush to my room to rescue me.

ARTHUR: Do you love Elton?

MRS CHEYNEY: With only that bell to ring, would I be here with you if I did?

ARTHUR: True! (*The bottle opens quietly.*) Could anything be more quiet than that?

MRS CHEYNEY: Nothing, but I expected it! You do everything marvellously, Arthur!

ARTHUR: Thank you, Fay.

MRS CHEYNEY: Ever so little for me.

ARTHUR: (*Filling the glass.*) Even with the knowledge of who you are, I still adore you!

MRS CHEYNEY: (*Taking up the glass.*) Is that an offer of marriage, or are you just being broadminded?

ARTHUR: You know how often I have told you how I hate marriage!

MRS CHEYNEY: True; and I must be content that you still adore me?

ARTHUR: Yes.

MRS CHEYNEY: I should like to think, though, that you are a little disappointed in me!

ARTHUR: (*Shrugging his shoulders.*) Your life is your own.

MRS CHEYNEY: But how indifferent! If I refused to stay here tonight, what would you do?

ARTHUR: I shan't let you go!

MRS CHEYNEY: Now isn't that flattering. As you paid me the great compliment of asking me to be your wife,

I wonder if it would interest you to know that as a
woman who has done nearly everything there is to do
in this world – this is one of the things I have never
done.

(*He laughs.*)

Why do you laugh?

ARTHUR: I thought we had done with posing!

MRS CHEYNEY: You don't believe me?

ARTHUR: What a fool you would think me if I did!

MRS CHEYNEY: But it happens to be true!

(*He laughs.*)

Why should I say so if it weren't?

ARTHUR: Merely a trick to make me sentimental and open
that door, that you may make a fool of me again! I'm
sorry, Fay.

MRS CHEYNEY: To refuse to be your wife surely wasn't
making a fool of you!

ARTHUR: You couldn't very well accept that!

MRS CHEYNEY: I suppose not! You won't believe me
when I tell you I have never done a thing of this sort
before?

ARTHUR: Fay, my dear, why this stupidity?

MRS CHEYNEY: I can quite understand your not
believing me. But I wish I could make you, though.
I wonder how I can prove it to you?

ARTHUR: You couldn't, it's too difficult!

MRS CHEYNEY: I suppose it is! (*Looking into her glass.*)
Look, isn't that lucky, I haven't drunk it all!

ARTHUR: Why lucky?

MRS CHEYNEY: Because –

(*She throws the wine into his face. She retreats, frightened.
He follows her threateningly.*)

ARTHUR: (*Angrily but controlling himself.*) And what does
that mean?

MRS CHEYNEY: That means, if you don't believe that
I have never done this before, you will at all events
believe I am not going to do it now!

ARTHUR: (*Angrily.*) Just as you like!

MRS CHEYNEY: Ring that bell and tell Mrs Ebley who I am, or unlock that door and let me go!

ARTHUR: I shall do neither!

MRS CHEYNEY: You can't keep me here against my will!

ARTHUR: I intend to.

MRS CHEYNEY: Do you? Well, I prefer a million times that they should know what is true about me than you should believe what isn't! Open that door! (*She crosses to the door.*) Open this door!

ARTHUR: Nothing in the world would induce me to! (*MRS CHEYNEY runs to the bed.*) What are you going to do? Are you trying to persuade me you are going to ring the bell?

MRS CHEYNEY: Unless you open the door!

ARTHUR: Why the bluff, Fay dear? It doesn't impress me in the slightest! (*He sits on the bed and laughs at her.*) You're much too sensible to take the risk of being the guest at Holloway, probably for five years.

MRS CHEYNEY: You're wrong. Five years in Holloway wouldn't be nearly as long as one night with you! Give me that key! (*She reaches out to him.*) (*He laughs, takes hold of her hand and tries to pull her to him. She struggles and releases herself.*) Very well then. (*She rings the bell at top of bed, which is heard ringing loudly outside the room.*)

ARTHUR: (*Amazed, but without raising his voice and remaining seated.*) My God! Do you realize what you have done?

MRS CHEYNEY: Perfectly!

ARTHUR: Don't you understand, in a minute from now they will all come rushing into this room?

MRS CHEYNEY: I do! (*She stops ringing the bell.*)

ARTHUR: What did you do it for?

MRS CHEYNEY: To give you an opportunity to tell them only the truth about me.

ARTHUR: You fool!

MRS CHEYNEY: Evidently I had to be, in some form or other – I prefer this one.

(*There is a knock at the door.*)

ROBERTS: (*Outside.*) It's Roberts, ma'am.

ARTHUR: (*Rising and pointing to the dressing-room door.*) Go in there quickly – I'll get rid of him.

MRS EBLEY: (*Heard off.*) What is the matter, Roberts?

ROBERTS: (*Off.*) My bell rang, madam.

MRS EBLEY: (*Knocking on the door.*) Arthur, Arthur, open the door at once.

ARTHUR: (*Going nearer to the door.*) It's all right my dear. Go back to your room; I'll come to you in a minute.

MRS EBLEY: (*Speaking off.*) I insist on your opening that door at once. Oh! Lord Elton.

ELTON: (*Off.*) What's the matter?

MRS EBLEY: (*Off.*) Arthur's sleeping in my room. The bell rang – I can't think what's the matter.

MRS CHEYNEY: (*Calling.*) Mrs Ebley!

MRS EBLEY: (*Off.*) Mrs Cheyney?

MRS CHEYNEY: (*Calling.*) Lord Elton!

(*ARTHUR turns and looks at her.*)

ELTON: (*Outside.*) Open this door at once, Dilling.

(*ARTHUR moves to MRS CHEYNEY and looks at her.*)

ARTHUR: This is for remembrance!

(*He gives her a slap on the face. Then he unlocks the door and opens it. MRS CHEYNEY goes to the dressing-table, crying. ELTON and MRS EBLEY enter.*)

MRS EBLEY: (*Pausing a second at the door with a rapid glance at ARTHUR, she looks across and sees MRS CHEYNEY.*) What is the explanation of all this?

ELTON: (*Looking from MRS CHEYNEY to ARTHUR.*) My God!

MRS CHEYNEY: Lord Dilling has something to tell you, Mrs Ebley.

MRS EBLEY: What is it, Arthur?

(*ARTHUR does not answer.*)

ELTON: What is it, do you hear?

MRS CHEYNEY: (*Looking at ARTHUR.*) Would you prefer that I tell them?

MRS EBLEY: Arthur, do you understand? I insist!

ARTHUR: I'll tell you. I – I – persuaded Mrs Cheyney to come into this room by false pretences. In the presence of you both, I humbly tell her I have behaved like a cad.

ELTON: Cad? You're the lowest thing I have ever known.

MRS EBLEY: (*Terribly shocked.*) I don't know what to say to you, Arthur. I had no idea you could ever do a foul thing like this.

ELTON: I was perfectly aware of it. (*To MRS CHEYNEY.*) You will remember, in the letter I wrote to you, I told you the type of man he was.

MRS EBLEY: (*Putting her arm round MRS CHEYNEY.*) So, pretending you couldn't sleep and accepting my offer to change rooms, was merely a trick to get Mrs Cheyney into it?

ARTHUR: Yes.

ELTON: Dilling, I for one will, and I hope every decent person in this world will, cut you.

MRS CHEYNEY: Everybody should – except the Insurance Company. They should love him.

MRS EBLEY: What do you mean?

(*MRS CHEYNEY crosses to ARTHUR, takes the pearls from his dressing jacket pocket and before he realizes what she is going to do returns with them to MRS EBLEY.*)

My pearls! What is the meaning of this?

MRS CHEYNEY: (*Handing MRS EBLEY the pearls.*) It means – I came here – to – I like them as much as you do. (*A pause. MRS EBLEY and ELTON look at her.*)

ELTON: My God! You mean you – were going to – ? (*MRS CHEYNEY nods her head.*)

But there must be some mistake.

MRS CHEYNEY: (*Shakes her head.*) None.

MRS EBLEY: I don't know what to say to you – I am bewildered, horrified! I prefer to deal with you in the morning. Please go.

(*MRS CHEYNEY hesitates, she tries to say something. She turns and walks slowly across to ARTHUR. They face each other. He shakes his head, goes up and opens the door – she exits. ARTHUR closes the door.*)

(*To ELTON.*) I simply cannot believe it.

ELTON: (*To ARTHUR.*) She – there is no mistake? (*ARTHUR shakes his head.*)

MRS EBLEY: It's too awful, too terrible, too horrible Arthur! Did you take these, knowing that she – ? (*ARTHUR takes MRS EBLEY by the arm and leads her towards the door.*)

ARTHUR: Let me advise you to go back to your room. It is so much wiser to discuss all this in the morning. Please; I'm sure I'm right. (*He opens the door for her.*)

MRS EBLEY: (*Turning in the doorway.*) Yes, I suppose so. Good night to you, or good morning, or whatever it is. (*MRS EBLEY exits. ARTHUR closes the door.*)

ARTHUR: You liked her, Elton?

ELTON: Liked her? Good heavens, man! I asked her to be my wife!

ARTHUR: With what result?

ELTON: I don't know yet.

ARTHUR: I sympathize. Sorry I can't offer you a drink, old feller. Oh, yes, I can. (*He pours out champagne.*) Have a drop of our fiancée's.

End of Act Two.

ACT THREE

*The loggia, at MRS EBLEY's house. The next morning. A long
refectory table is laid for breakfast, on the veranda of the loggia.*

*MRS EBLEY and MARIA are seated. ELTON is walking up and
down. ROBERTS is standing by the serving table.*

MRS EBLEY: I give it up – I simply give it up. Elton, what
do you think?

(*ELTON signs to her to send ROBERTS away.*)

All right, Roberts, you needn't wait.

(*ROBERTS exits through the windows.*)

Elton, what do you think?

ELTON: I don't know! I have no idea! I am defeated!

MARIA: We all are! But wouldn't you be wise to sit down?
You'll tire yourself out!

ELTON: When I think of her – the most modest – the most
simple – the – the – the innocence of any knowledge of
the world – n – no – I can't believe it!

MARIA: Nevertheless, the one woman of all the women in
the world that you and Dilling have chosen to be your
wife is a crook!

ELTON: I know! I know!

MRS EBLEY: Do you love her very much?

ELTON: Yes! Yes! No! No! How can one love a woman of
that description very much?

MARIA: I agree! And the way she trapped me into taking
her up! What a fool I am going to look! Not only have
I made the most ridiculous fuss of her, but with pride
I have introduced her to every one I know!

ELTON: The way she has cheated us is too terrible! (*He
bangs the table.*) What are we going to do with her, I ask?

MARIA: Please don't make that noise, Elton! My nerves are
in a dreadful condition already!

ELTON: I'm sorry!

MRS EBLEY: I have been thinking for hours what to do
with her! Her confederate, the man Charles, we will have

159

no trouble with: he expects no sympathy. He arrived here early this morning and gave himself up! It's this woman! Our duty, of course, is to send her to gaol as well!

ELTON: No, no, that is impossible! (*He goes to the serving table and helps himself to food.*)

MARIA: My view is, the man should go to gaol, and she be given the alternative of either going with him, or leaving for Australia by the next steamer! Obviously, she will accept the chance of going to Australia with alacrity, and that way we get rid of her for ever.

(*ELTON comes back to his chair with a plate of food and sits.*)

MRS EBLEY: I am so angry I can only think of gaol for her. (*MRS EBLEY pours coffee for ELTON, which MARIA passes to him.*)

ELTON: Such a thing is out of the question. Think of my position in this matter! President of a hospital, President of the Lifeboat Institution, Chairman of various societies for the protection of unhappy women – director of a bank! Do you realize that is only a few of the public appointments I hold?

MRS EBLEY: I do! I do!

ELTON: A man who has regularly contributed to *The Times* on all questions of social reform, even subjects of religion! If it became known that I asked this woman to be my wife, will you tell me what subjects I will be able to write to *The Times* about?

MARIA: The Lifeboat!

ELTON: Quite!

MRS EBLEY: But, after all, it's only her word against yours, you could deny having asked her to be your wife!

ELTON: The revolting thing of it all is, I cannot.

MARIA: Why?

(*Pause.*)

ELTON: Being inexperienced and unacquainted with the manner one makes a proposal of marriage to a lady, I wrote it!

MRS EBLEY: My dear, how terrible for you!

(*MRS EBLEY and MARIA exchange glances. They are very amused.*)

MARIA: Poor lamb, I see it's going to be very difficult for you, and, who knows, perhaps expensive!

ELTON: It was a letter teeming with affection and sentiment – it took me days to write it! Dilling says the cinema rights of it alone are worth ten thousand pounds!

MARIA: How dreadful! I am sorry for you!

MRS EBLEY: A great pity, a great pity! (*Smothering her laughter.*)

ELTON: And that is not all! It pains me as much to tell you this as it will pain you to hear it; but it is my duty to tell you – (*Pause.*) In that letter I wrote my personal opinion of you all!

(*They look at him.*)

MARIA: You wrote your –

MRS EBLEY: Do I understand that you have put on paper anything which might sound in the least disparaging about me?

MARIA: Or me?

ELTON: As I intended to marry her, she being an Australian, I thought it my duty to point out to her the people I should like her to know or not, as the case might be.

(*MRS EBLEY is about to make a remark, but MARIA anticipates her.*)

MARIA: Am I to understand we are among the 'nots'?

ELTON: Yes!

MRS EBLEY: How dare you!

MARIA: What are you doing in this house now?

ELTON: Unhappily, the answer to that is in the letter, too! I explained – (*He passes his cup for more coffee to MRS EBLEY.*) – to her that I had never visited Mrs Ebley before, and the only reason I was doing so now was because she was going to be there! No, no sugar, please.

MRS EBLEY: I am to sit here and be insulted like this! Can I do nothing? (*She absent-mindedly puts in piece after piece of sugar.*)

ELTON: No – no sugar, please. I do feel for you very much! You don't suppose, had I known this was going to develop, I should have written that letter, do you?

MRS EBLEY: I imagine you capable of anything!

MARIA: You shouldn't be president of a hospital, you should be in one!

ELTON: I agree!

MRS EBLEY: How did Arthur Dilling see this letter?

ELTON: We were up late talking last night – fortunately, being a business man, I kept a copy of the letter. (*He takes it out of his pocket.*) It will pain you, but you had better read it!

(*He passes it to MARIA. MARIA offers it to MRS EBLEY.*)

MRS EBLEY: I don't want to read it! (*Takes the letter.*)

ELTON: I insist! It will convince you of the very difficult position we are all in with this woman.

MRS EBLEY: (*After reading, rises.*) How dare you! How dare you write a letter of this sort?

ELTON: Because I had no idea she was a woman of that sort!

MRS EBLEY: (*Standing waving the letter.*) You – you – do you realize, if this woman shows this letter written by you, my position in society is ridiculous and at an end?

ELTON: Perfectly! Dilling says if it were his letter, and he were her – he were she – he wouldn't sell it for twenty-five thousand pounds! We are in an extremely awkward position!

MRS EBLEY: This is too terrible!

MARIA: (*Taking the letter from MRS EBLEY.*) How do I appear in this letter?

ELTON: Not well, I fear! (*Pointing to the place in the letter.*) There is the unhappy paragraph I wrote of you!

MARIA: (*Reading and starting up.*) My God! I'm a fallen woman.

ELTON: No, no, you exaggerate! I only say –

MARIA: That I am in every way an undesirable person for her to know! That I – ho! if this is ever seen, I'm ruined! (*Sinks into her chair again.*)

ELTON: Precisely why I have shown it to you!

MRS EBLEY: You must get the original of this letter back, do you understand?

MARIA: At once!

ELTON: She refuses to give it back!

MRS EBLEY: She refuses?

MARIA: Naturally. Would you in her place? It's worth thousands! (*She continues to read on.*)

ELTON: I went to see her personally, and told her if she returned it to me, I would forgive her everything!

MARIA: What did she say?

ELTON: She said she was keeping it until the rest of you had forgiven her, and her confederate Charles – whom she appears to be very concerned about!

MARIA: Would you tell me the object of telling us this at all? If you possessed the slightest decency you would have bought it back at any price to save our feelings!

ELTON: I would have, but when I explained to Dilling the delicate position I was in, that you were threatening to hand her over, his view was that it would be better for you to read it in your own drawing-room, than have it read to you in a police court!

MARIA: A police court! Understand, Elton, I cannot openly quarrel with you at this moment, but the moment this is settled I will never speak to you again!

MRS EBLEY: Neither shall I! (*She goes through the windows into the house.*)

ELTON: That is perfectly fair!

MARIA: And, for God's sake, stop being pompous!

ELTON: Pompous! I forgive you, because you are unstrung!

MARIA: Unstrung! I could brain you!

ELTON: Dilling prepared me for this! He said this would happen! (*Walks up and down.*)

MARIA: I have always believed, and I was right, that had I been your mother, I would have had you certified on the day of your birth!

(*MRS EBLEY comes through the windows.*)

MRS EBLEY: It seems to me, instead of putting this woman in gaol, where she ought to be, we'll all of us have to go on our knees with thousands of pounds begging her to keep out of it!

(*WILLIE enters through the windows.*)

WILLIE: (*Trying to control himself.*) Elton! What is it Arthur Dilling tells me you've written to Mrs Cheyney about my wife?

ELTON: I'm sorry, Wynton, very sorry! But I must tell you the truth. I said that it was evident to me that she preferred always to be with some other man than her husband, and though I could understand it, I could not condone it – that is all I said!

WILLIE: (*To MARIA, unable to control himself.*) He says that is all he said! And it's a lie! Kitty would rather be with me than any man.

ELTON: I'm sure she would; all I mentioned was, she never was.

WILLIE: I want to tell you this: it's a lucky thing for you it's a lady's honour that is concerned, otherwise I would take you outside and give you a damn good thrashing!

MARIA: I wish you would!

(*JOAN enters through the windows.*)

JOAN: (*To MRS EBLEY.*) Darling, I can't open my mouth without swearing – I'm the foulest-tongued woman in England; Mrs Cheyney would be well advised not to know me; I belong to a small set of people who are making themselves ridiculous all over London! And lots more, darling!

MARIA: That's nothing to the things he has said about others of us!

(*MARY enters through the windows.*)

MARY: 'Morning, every one! (*She kisses MRS EBLEY.*) 'Morning, Elton dear!

ELTON: 'Morning, Mary!

MARIA: Are you in the letter?

MARY: I am!

MARIA: What are you?

MARY: I'm a nice woman – aren't I, Elton darling?

ELTON: That's what I said!

MARY: And quite right, I am.

ELTON: I would like to be believed when I say that had I had the remotest idea there was the least chance of this letter ever being read or seen by anyone but Mrs Cheyney, I would never have written it!

WILLIE: Oh, go to hell!

JOAN: Why be so mild about it? (*To MRS EBLEY who is carrying coffee to MARY.*) Can I tell this bottle of Mellin's Food in my own way how and where he ought to go?

MRS EBLEY: Certainly not!

MARIA: Whether you believed it would be seen or not, are those things you have written in that letter your opinion of us?

WILLIE: Yes! Are you prepared to withdraw the suggestions you have made against us?

ELTON: They are not suggestions; they are facts. What possible comfort could you derive from my withdrawing something all of you know to be true?

MARIA: Help! I'm starting a stroke! (*ARTHUR enters.*)

ARTHUR: 'Morning!

MARIA: What are you?

ARTHUR: (*Very amused.*) I? I have the distinction of being one of the most unmitigated blackguards walking about this earth!

MRS EBLEY: Arthur, this is a dreadful position to be put in by this man!

ARTHUR: As an optimist, I take the gravest view of it!

MARIA: What are we going to do with this woman?

ARTHUR: Let us be accurate! What is this woman going to do with us?

MARIA: How true! How true! (*She picks up a newspaper and throws it at ELTON.*) You beast! It's all through you.

ARTHUR: Steady! Steady!

(*ROBERTS enters.*)

ROBERTS: Can I speak to you a moment, Mr Wynton?

WILLIE: Yes, what is it?

ROBERTS: Your wife's maid wishes me to tell you, sir, nothing she can do will make your wife stop laughing!

ARTHUR: Who wants to stop her? We envy her!

WILLIE: Don't be funny about my wife having hysterics, Dilling! (*To ROBERTS.*) Tell her to try ice!

ROBERTS: Very good, sir!

(*ROBERTS exits.*)

ARTHUR: Let us all try ice!

MRS EBLEY: Can you offer no suggestion, Arthur?

ARTHUR: Certainly I can! There are two alternatives facing us. One, let us be English men and women, and hand her and Charles over to justice – in which case that letter may be read at the Old Bailey!

MRS EBLEY: (*Together.*) No! No!

MARIA: (*Together.*) Out of the question!

ELTON: (*Together.*) Certainly not!

ARTHUR: Carried unanimously! The other: let us throw ourselves upon her mercy, and buy the letter back!

WILLIE: And Elton pays for it!

ARTHUR: All those in favour?

ALL: Yes!

ARTHUR: Carried unanimously! Shall I settle the figure, or will you, Elton?

ELTON: I am not a rich man, Dilling!

ARTHUR: You can't afford to be a poor one, Elton!

MARIA: I say, not one penny should be paid her until she is on the boat that will take her to Australia!

ARTHUR: Why?

MARIA: Because as long as she remains in England we are always at her mercy.

ARTHUR: True! True!

ELTON: May I offer a suggestion?

ARTHUR: The man who pays certainly should!

ELTON: Then my view is this: we should not for a moment let her think that letter important. We should offer her her passage back to Australia, and in consideration of her returning the letter the matter is at an end!

MARIA: Don't keep on being an idiot! Do you think she will accept that?

ELTON: She will – if we tell her the other alternative is we will have her arrested!

ARTHUR: In other words, we put up a bluff that we don't care whether she has the letter or not, that it is unimportant.

ELTON: And, if necessary, I will say I never meant a word of it!

ARTHUR: (*To them all.*) What do you think?

MARIA: There is something in what he says!

MRS EBLEY: And it does save our dignity a little!

MARY: Thank Heaven I'm a nice woman.

MARIA: Don't be vulgar, Mary; the only nice women in the world are the ones who have had no opportunities!

MARY: You assume too much because I am able to keep my mouth shut!

MARIA: Be quiet, and eat your breakfast.

ARTHUR: Business, please! The attitude you suggest we should take is, we are a lot of light-hearted boys and girls who don't care a damn; she either, as it were, coughs up the letter, consents to return to Australia, or we hand her over to justice!

MARIA: That sounds right to me!

MRS EBLEY: It seems to me if we convince her we are determined people, it will have some considerable effect on her attitude!

WILLIE: I say, I've got an idea! Supposing we send for one of those detective – ah! – inspector – er – a – policeman fellers – they can see him and he needn't know why he is here!

MARIA: That's a good idea!

MRS EBLEY: That is an extraordinarily good idea; what do you think, Arthur?

ARTHUR: Yes!

ELTON: I know that's a good idea! It will prove that we are people who are not going to be trifled with!

ARTHUR: All those in favour of the policeman!
(*They all put their hands up.*)
Carried unanimously! Willie, telephone for a policeman!

WILLIE: Right! What shall I say we want him for?

ELTON: Anything but the facts, of course!

WILLIE: You needn't think because you are a damn fool every one else is!

JOAN: Hear! Hear!

ARTHUR: Willie, tell him we don't like the look and are very suspicious of next year's asparagus!

MARIA: Arthur, be serious! (*Irritably.*) Willie – oh, tell him we are suspicious of one of the servants – (*To MRS EBLEY.*) Roberts won't mind!

WILLIE: Right! (*He exits.*)

ARTHUR: What's the next move?

MRS EBLEY: I suppose the next move is to send for these horrid people!

ELTON: Yes!

ARTHUR: Is it your pleasure that I put this proposition to Mrs Cheyney, or would you prefer that Elton should?

JOAN: Good heavens, hasn't he made sufficient mess of it already?

MARIA: I should think so, indeed!

MARY: Joan, dear – Joan!

(*JOAN rises.*)

ARTHUR: Do you approve that I should, Elton?

ELTON: Please!

ARTHUR: Sybil, kindly ring the bell! (*To JOAN and MARY.*) I would ask you two to keep as quiet as possible; and if you would, Elton, I would ask you not for a moment to cease looking an English gentleman!

(*MRS EBLEY rings the bell. WILLIE re-enters.*)

WILLIE: It's all right. The chief inspector is coming himself.

ARTHUR: Good!

(*ROBERTS enters.*)

Roberts, would you kindly ask Mrs Cheyney if she would be good enough to join us here?

ROBERTS: Yes, my lord!

MARIA: (*Whispering to ARTHUR.*) What about the man – Charles – the man?

ARTHUR: Oh yes! Roberts! By the way, you might also tell Charles, who I believe is waiting downstairs, that I would like to speak to him for a moment!

ROBERTS: Yes, my lord! I believe Mrs Cheyney and Charles are in the library, my lord!

MARIA: (*To MRS EBLEY.*) Ah!

(*ROBERTS exits.*)

ARTHUR: That, if I may say so, was rather delicately done! Let us pray!

MARIA: Oh, Arthur! Arthur!

ELTON: You will be firm, Dilling?

ARTHUR: Stand by me – be grateful that I am an unmitigated blackguard!

MRS EBLEY: To me it's too terrible to think that instead of merely handing these people over to the police, we have to be clever with them to save ourselves!

ARTHUR: Ssh!

(*MRS CHEYNEY enters by the windows. She is closely followed by CHARLES. She stands as if in a court of justice, and looks round at them all.*)

MRS CHEYNEY: Guilty!

MARIA: Ah! you admit it!

ARTHUR: Silence! Won't you take a chair?

(*ELTON rises, gives MRS CHEYNEY his chair and stands behind it.*)

MRS CHEYNEY: Thank you! (*She sits down.*) As Charles was born a gentleman, mayn't he sit down as well?

ARTHUR: Of course! Take a seat, Charles.

CHARLES: No, thank you, Dilling!

MRS CHEYNEY: I naturally expected it, but you sent for me?

ARTHUR: Quite! I will be brief, Mrs Cheyney; the position is as follows: you have acknowledged frankly that in accepting Mrs Ebley's invitation to stay here, it was for the purpose of taking Mrs Ebley's pearls!

MRS CHEYNEY: Or anything else that happened to be lying handy about.

ARTHUR: That is very frank! The penalty for such things is considerable!

MARIA: Very considerable!

MRS CHEYNEY: Charles and I think with a charm of manner we may get off with three years.

ARTHUR: That, of course, we don't want to happen to you. Lord Elton feels very strongly that if you have once asked a woman to be your wife, it would be ungenerous to treat her so drastically!

MRS CHEYNEY: Thank you, Lord Elton!

ELTON: Er – er – not at all!

ARTHUR: So this is what we have decided! If you will accept your ticket and a small sum – you did mention the amount – Elton?

ELTON: A hundred pounds!

ARTHUR: Paid to you on the steamer, in return for the letter he wrote you, we are prepared to consider the matter closed.

MRS CHEYNEY: Is it my turn now?

MRS EBLEY: But, Arthur – I should like –

ARTHUR: Please, Sybil! (*He puts his hand up and stops her.*)

MRS CHEYNEY: I am very sorry that I cannot accept Lord Elton's kind offer, but Charles and I have decided we must go to gaol.

CHARLES: We have.

ARTHUR: After all, you did not succeed in getting the pearls!

MRS CHEYNEY: Precisely. We failed, and that is why we should go to gaol. If we had got them we would have succeeded – a crime for which no one ever goes to gaol.

CHARLES: You put it charmingly, Fay dear!

MRS CHEYNEY: Thank you, my sweet!

ARTHUR: You didn't understand me. We don't want you to go to gaol!

MRS CHEYNEY: Then, equally you don't understand us – we do!

ARTHUR: Quite!

(*There is a pause – they all look at each other.*)

MARIA: My good woman, you can't be serious when you say you want to go to gaol?

MRS CHEYNEY: Isn't it sad, Charles, they don't understand us!

CHARLES: Tragic! It makes me blush for them!

MRS CHEYNEY: Charles and I in our humble way have tried to live up to the highest tradition of our profession – a profession in some form or other we are all members of – and that tradition is, never be found out – but if you are, I say if you are, be prepared to pay the price!

ARTHUR: I've got you!

(*ROBERTS enters.*)

ROBERTS: Inspector Wilkinson has arrived, madam, who says you want to speak to him!

MRS EBLEY: Ask him to wait.

ROBERTS: Yes, madam.

(*He exits.*)

MRS EBLEY: You see, Mrs Cheyney, we are terribly serious!

MRS CHEYNEY: It's your duty to be, Mrs Ebley!

MARIA: It seems to me you are a very stupid young woman not to accept such a good offer instead of being taken away by that horrid policeman!

MRS CHEYNEY: Not at all – he may be charming! (*She rises.*) Are you ready, Charles?

CHARLES: Yes, my sweet!

MRS CHEYNEY: Your arm, Charles.

(*CHARLES offers MRS CHEYNEY his arm, which she takes and they move into the window.*)

MRS CHEYNEY: Before we go. I would like you to know how pained Charles and I are at having, through our stupidity, put you to all this trouble. We feel it almost as much as the loss of your pearls, Mrs Ebley.

CHARLES: And they are beautiful pearls, if I dare say so!

MRS CHEYNEY: (*Looking round at every one.*) And as I shall never see any of you again, I would like you to know how much I have enjoyed knowing you all, and how sorry I am to lose such nice friends. Goodbye, Lord Elton. It was sweet of you to ask me to be your wife. (*Suggesting they shall go.*) Charles? (*Turning to MRS EBLEY, who makes a movement.*) Please don't bother to come down – we'll find the policeman. Goodbye!

ELTON: Mrs Cheyney!

MRS CHEYNEY: Yes?

ELTON: I – er – have something to say to you.

MRS CHEYNEY: Yes, Lord Elton?

MARIA: Come and sit down.

MRS EBLEY: Yes, sit down.

MRS CHEYNEY: But the policeman you sent for?

MARIA: Oh, damn the policeman!

MRS CHEYNEY: But isn't it rather bad manners to even keep a policeman waiting?

ELTON: I – er – I wanted to say this –

MRS CHEYNEY: I'm sorry, but I'm afraid I can't listen to anything you have to say, with a policeman waiting.

ELTON: Send that infernal fellow away!

MRS EBLEY: What shall we tell him?

ARTHUR: (*To JOAN.*) Tell the policeman there has been a mistake, and we don't want him.

JOAN: Here, I don't want to miss any of this. Curse it! (*She exits.*)

ARTHUR: Obviously, the bluff is over.

MRS CHEYNEY: (*Sweetly.*) Bluff? Have you been bluffing, Arthur? (*She sits.*)

MARIA: You know perfectly well he has.

MRS CHEYNEY: But why?

MARIA: Oh, do stop trying to be so innocent!

MRS CHEYNEY: Do you know what they mean, Charles?

CHARLES: I'm so young in crime I must be forgiven! I don't!

ARTHUR: Mrs Cheyney, in a moment of impulse, prompted by affection for you, Lord Elton wrote a letter to you asking you to be his wife.

MRS CHEYNEY: A letter which I will always treasure very much.

MARIA: We know that!

ARTHUR: I am authorized by Lord Elton to ask you your charge for the return of that letter.

MRS CHEYNEY: My charge? Please forgive me, but I don't know what you mean!

ARTHUR: The suggestion is, we give you five hundred pounds – (*ELTON looks horrified. ARTHUR dismisses him with a wave of the hand.*) and your passage to Australia.

MARIA: Which I call very generous.

MRS CHEYNEY: Five hundred? Australia? I don't know that I would like Australia.

ELTON: But you came from Australia.

MRS CHEYNEY: Clapham!

(*JOAN re-enters.*)

JOAN: What's happened?

ARTHUR: Ssh! Ssh!

MARIA: Come, come! What will you take?

MRS CHEYNEY: I prize the letter so much that I don't think I would part with it for any money you could offer me.

MARIA: A thousand?

MRS CHEYNEY: But this is amazing!

MARIA: Come, come, young woman! What is your usual charge for the return of letters?

MRS CHEYNEY: Speaking as one fallen woman to another, there never have been any letters; but if there had been, my charge would have depended entirely on the position and the manners of the people mentioned in it. (*She rises.*) And as I don't propose to sit here and be insulted I will, with your permission, say goodbye!

CHARLES: You are perfectly right, Fay darling, and if I had known that they were the type of people they are, I should never have allowed you to come and stay with them!

ELTON: Please, please! I agree; Lady Frinton was very hasty, and I'm sorry. Please sit down.

MRS CHEYNEY: When she has apologized, I will.

CHARLES: Hear! Hear!

MARIA: I'll do nothing of the sort!

MRS CHEYNEY: Very well. (*She starts to go off.*)

MRS EBLEY: Stop, please! (*To MARIA.*) Will you at once say you are sorry?

MARIA: I won't!

ELTON: I insist! You understand!

MARIA: My God! (*To MRS CHEYNEY, swallowing hard.*) I'm sorry!

MRS CHEYNEY: (*Sitting down again.*) Granted.

CHARLES: We'd reached the point where a thousand pounds was bid for the letter.

ARTHUR: Which was refused!

ELTON: Mrs Cheyney, what will you take for it?

CHARLES: I offer five thousand.

ELTON: Be quiet!

CHARLES: I'll do nothing of the sort! My money is as good as yours.

ELTON: Will you please answer my question?

MRS CHEYNEY: If I sell the letter, I will do so not in the sense of blackmail, but more in the spirit of breach of promise, for ten thousand pounds!

CHARLES: It's giving it away!

ELTON: Ten – no, no, I refuse!

MRS CHEYNEY: I'm glad, because I would so much rather have the letter! (*She rises.*)

MRS EBLEY: No, no! Elton, you have no alternative but to pay!

MARIA: And I have no sympathy for you!

ELTON: But, Mrs Cheyney, surely –

MRS CHEYNEY: Ten thousand, Lord Elton!

ELTON: (*Looking at them all.*) It's terrible, terrible!

CHARLES: Terrible be damned! I'll give eleven for it!

(*ELTON hurriedly takes a cheque book out of his pocket, and goes into the house.*)

JOAN: Ten thousand! Phew! (*To CHARLES.*) How much would you charge for a course of twelve lessons?

CHARLES: I never charge, m'lady; I'm a man who just loves his work.

MARIA: I hope you enjoy spending it, young woman.

MRS CHEYNEY: Thank you, I'll do my best. (*To ARTHUR.*) What is your contribution to this, Lord Dilling?

ARTHUR: (*Very depressed.*) I wish to be associated in Lord Elton's cheque for ten thousand pounds.

(*ELTON re-enters with the cheque and goes to MRS CHEYNEY.*)

ELTON: (*Giving her the cheque.*) The letter, please?

MRS CHEYNEY: (*Looking at the cheque, turns to them all.*) We have something in common, after all!

MARIA: Very little, thank heaven!

MRS CHEYNEY: Then why pay this money to keep it a secret what we have?

MRS EBLEY: Kindly give Lord Elton the letter!

MRS CHEYNEY: Oh, yes! (*She tears the cheque into small pieces, and puts the pieces on the table.*)

CHARLES: Fay!

MRS EBLEY: What are you doing?

MRS CHEYNEY: I'm doing what I did with the letter! I had no idea it had any money value until you suggested to me yourself this morning that it had! (*She gives an envelope to ELTON.*) I hope you will find all the pieces there, Lord Elton!

ELTON: (*Taking if from her.*) You –

CHARLES: (*Wiping his eyes with his handkerchief.*) Forgive me! Ten thousand pounds gone down the drain; it's more than I can bear! And I have tried so hard to make her a crook.

ELTON: You've torn the letter up?

MRS CHEYNEY: Wasn't it stupid of me?

ELTON: I think it was very generous –

MARIA: Nonsense. She wouldn't have torn it up if she had known she would have been offered that sum for it!

MRS CHEYNEY: You're never right about anything. I tore it up after Charles told me it was worth twice that sum!

CHARLES: As I watched her tearing it up, I cried for the first time for fifteen years!

MRS CHEYNEY: Poor sweet (*She puts her hand out; CHARLES takes it.*) it was a cruel thing to do!

ARTHUR: Why did you tear it up?

MRS CHEYNEY: I'll tell you. Courage, I was born with plenty; decency, they gave me too much!

MRS EBLEY: Decency, indeed! If Lord Dilling hadn't rung that bell last night, decency wouldn't have prevented you taking my pearls!

ARTHUR: Lord Dilling didn't ring the bell; Mrs Cheyney did!

ELTON: Mrs Cheyney did? What do you mean?

ARTHUR: (*To MRS CHEYNEY.*) Go on, tell them.

MRS CHEYNEY: It will embarrass you!

ARTHUR: An unmitigated scoundrel is never embarrassed!

MRS CHEYNEY: Very well! If it hadn't been for decency I might be wearing your pearls – or others – at this moment, provided by Lord Dilling!

ARTHUR: Charmingly expressed; most touching.

MARIA: You mean to tell me you took the risk of being clapped into gaol, and rang that bell!

ARTHUR: She did!

MARIA: Nonsense, Arthur; it's sweet of you, but not fair to us to defend her like this!

ARTHUR: I give you my word of –

MRS CHEYNEY: It's all right. I can understand her not believing it; I gathered from that letter, she didn't ring the bell – (*General movement.*) – and there was no risk of gaol!

MARIA: How dare you!

CHARLES: You're a grand woman, Fay, a grand woman.

MARIA: Be quiet, you horrid man!

CHARLES: Wrong again! I'm just a simple, tolerant, ordinary sort of feller, who only takes material things that can be replaced. How many of you can say that?

MARIA: Be quiet!

ELTON: There is one question I would like to ask – why are you a crook.

CHARLES: She isn't! But God knows I tried to make her one! I've taught her to take watches – the tie-pins she can remove like – (*Putting his hand to his tie he discovers his pin is not there.*)

MRS CHEYNEY: (*Taking the pin from the lapel of her dress and handing it to CHARLES.*) I took it as we came in.

CHARLES: (*Taking the pin.*) Isn't she divine? She's the greatest expert I have ever known – but there is always a catch in the good things of life – she won't take them from the people she ought to!

MRS CHEYNEY: You mustn't be angry with me, Charles; it's that decency that I'm cursed with that prevents me!

CHARLES: (*Putting his hand on her shoulder.*) I couldn't be angry with you, my sweet!

(*She pats his hand. CHARLES puts the pin in his tie.*)

ELTON: What made you start this life, then?

MRS CHEYNEY: You'll despise me, but I'll tell you! I wanted to improve my social position.

MRS EBLEY: A curious way of doing it!

MRS CHEYNEY: Not nearly so curious or so difficult as it would be by remaining a shop girl!

MARY: You were a shop girl?

CHARLES: In the stocking department!

MRS CHEYNEY: Where he found me.

JOAN: You don't look like one!

MRS CHEYNEY: There's a greater tragedy than that – darlings as they are, I don't think like one! So Charles was good enough to say that I was meant for better things – secretly in my heart I believed I was – but as a shop girl I realized there were no better things; loving beauty, nice people and everything that was attractive, I took the risk – I became a pupil of Charles.

CHARLES: The best I ever had!

MRS CHEYNEY: And evidently I have made even a greater failure of it than I did as the shop girl!

ELTON: If I may say so, you have been very generous, and in – er – er – appreciation of your generosity I should be very happy to start you, if you would allow me to, in some – er – er – shop of your own.

MRS CHEYNEY: You would, Lord Elton?

ELTON: Very!

JOAN: That's divine of you! (*To MRS CHEYNEY.*) I'll be a customer!

MARY: I certainly will!

MRS CHEYNEY: (*To MARIA.*) I would like to think I would have your patronage!

MARIA: You know you've got to have it!

MRS CHEYNEY: (*To ARTHUR.*) I hope you will persuade some of your many lady friends to buy from me?

ARTHUR: I will do more than that! From the moment the shop opens, Elton and I give you our word of honour we will never wear anything but women's underclothes! And quite frankly, I always believed Elton did! I apologize, Elton.

ELTON: (*Smiling a little.*) Mrs Cheyney, you know my address. As soon as you decide please let me know.
I shall be very happy to be of any service to you!

MRS CHEYNEY: I'm very grateful, Lord Elton! (*Offers her hand.*)

ELTON: Please! (*Taking her hand.*) And if I'm not being too modern, I should like to say goodbye. (*He exits.*)

MARIA: If you are going, Elton, you can give me a lift.
(*Puts out her hand to MRS CHEYNEY.*) You don't deserve it, but I'll give you a luncheon party and ask everyone the day the shop opens.

MRS CHEYNEY: You're an angel!

MARIA: (*Turns to CHARLES.*) Occasionally I give little dinners to lawyers, politicians and Members of Parliament. We have a little bridge afterwards – perhaps we might arrange to cut as partners.
(*She offers her hand to CHARLES. They shake hands.
MARIA exits.*)

MARY: I'll be at the luncheon party.

WILLIE: Whenever my wife and I have a row and I have to give her a present, I'll come to your shop for it.

MRS CHEYNEY: I like you so much, I'm glad I'm going to be seeing you every day.

WILLIE: (*Mentally slow.*) Oh – yes – ah, ah! I see.
(*MARY and WILLIE exit.*)

JOAN: I adore crepe-de-chine! Get quantities; the world is full of young men who want to buy me something.

MRS CHEYNEY: You're a terribly nice girl.

JOAN: Say 'Joan', and I'll believe you.

MRS CHEYNEY: Joan.
(*They shake hands.*)

JOAN: (*Turning to CHARLES.*) If ever you want a pupil, Charles, you'll find my number in the telephone book.

CHARLES: I shall never want a pupil, m'lady – but I'm glad I shall find your number in the telephone book.

(*She laughs. They shake hands.*)

JOAN: So long. (*She exits.*)

MRS EBLEY: Well – I must go and see those people off. Arthur – perhaps you had better keep your eye on the spoons.

(*They all laugh.*

MRS EBLEY exits.)

MRS CHEYNEY: Oh! (*To CHARLES, taking off her hat which she puts on the table.*) Nice people, aren't they, Charles?

CHARLES: Most of us are, Fay darling!

ARTHUR: What made you take up this job, Charles? With your brains, it seems a pity you haven't used them to better purposes.

CHARLES: One of His Majesty's judges may use those exact words one of these days. I found out, at an early age, what most men find out in an old one – life is very dull, my lord!

ARTHUR: I agree.

CHARLES: (*To ARTHUR.*) But I have an excuse. When I was thirteen years of age a trustee sent me to Eton, where I remained for five years wondering why I hadn't been sent to Harrow! From there, for another three years I was sent to Oxford, where I remained wondering why I hadn't been sent to Cambridge! With the result that, at the early age of one-and-twenty, I found that life and I were two dull things. So I decided to take it into my two hands: I began it as a blackmailer! But that was too easy – the world is so full of honest people that whenever you said 'I know all', they parted with such alacrity that this became even more dull than the world and myself! So I went for higher and greater things! I hate parting with it, my lord, because being the first I ever took, I treasure it; but there is your gold watch I took from you on Derby Day five years ago! (*He takes a watch from his pocket.*)

ARTHUR: My dear Charles, I've always wanted to meet the man who took it, and I hope you will do me a favour – keep it!

CHARLES: May I?

ARTHUR: I'd like you to!

CHARLES: That is very nice of you – I will! So long, Dilling!

ARTHUR: So long, Charles!

CHARLES: Goodbye, my sweet!

MRS CHEYNEY: What do you mean by goodbye?

CHARLES: What it means is, I have decided to take a little trip round the world!

MRS CHEYNEY: You're not going to leave me, do you understand!

CHARLES: I am, and now.

MRS CHEYNEY: But I don't want you to!

CHARLES: I must!

MRS CHEYNEY: Why?

CHARLES: Whenever you come into a person's life, come into it instantaneously; when you go out of it, go out of it even quicker! Goodbye, my love!

MRS CHEYNEY: Charles, I'm going to cry!

CHARLES: Don't do that! my sweet; but I would be terribly sorry if you didn't want to!

MRS CHEYNEY: Please don't go – come and be my manager.

CHARLES: No use I'd have to be honest, and it would bore me.

ARTHUR: Are you going round the world for pleasure, Charles?

CHARLES: (*Imitating dealing cards.*) Mixed with business, my lord!

(*He looks at MRS CHEYNEY, blows her a kiss, then exits.*)

ARTHUR: Next to going round the world with the woman one loves, I can think of nothing more attractive than going round it with Charles.

MRS CHEYNEY: You would enjoy it – you have so much in common.

ARTHUR: I agree. You liked him?

MRS CHEYNEY: I adored him.

ARTHUR: How much is that?

MRS CHEYNEY: As much as a woman can like a man she is not in love with.

ARTHUR: Like to go with him?

MRS CHEYNEY: I'd hate to.

ARTHUR: I'm going to ask you a question; you needn't answer if you don't want to.

MRS CHEYNEY: I'll answer it with pleasure – if Mrs Ebley had been in the room last night and not you, I should have taken them.

ARTHUR: You mean that?

MRS CHEYNEY: Yes! But of all the women you have ever known, none has ever been so glad to see you in a bedroom as I was last night.

ARTHUR: Thank you, Fay.

MRS CHEYNEY: Not at all – you made an honest woman of me.

ARTHUR: I've always believed that most of the good things done in this life were unintentional.

MRS CHEYNEY: I wonder.

ARTHUR: Fay!

MRS CHEYNEY: Yes, Arthur.

ARTHUR: It's an extraordinary thing, but the most difficult question in the world to ask a woman is a nice one.

MRS CHEYNEY: What sort of question were you going to ask me?

ARTHUR: I was about to describe my hopeful contribution to your future.

MRS CHEYNEY: Please do; I'm interested.

ARTHUR: Well, after you left me last night I couldn't sleep, so very early this morning I dressed myself, got out my car and went to see a friend of mine, who is a bishop, with whom I had breakfast at eight o'clock this morning.

MRS CHEYNEY: How surprised he must have been to see you.

ARTHUR: I described to him in detail a little trouble I was in – he listened so sympathetically – when I had finished, he looked at me and said, 'If you'll give me a cheque for fifty pounds and bring her with you and be here at eleven o'clock this morning, I'll fix it for you.'

MRS CHEYNEY: What was he to fix for you?

ARTHUR: That I could have breakfast with you at eight o'clock tomorrow morning.

MRS CHEYNEY: I never eat any.

ARTHUR: I told him there was a possibility of that.

MRS CHEYNEY: Tell him anything else?

ARTHUR: I loved you.

MRS CHEYNEY: Did he believe you?

ARTHUR: He covered his eyes with tears.

MRS CHEYNEY: He was right to – tell him anything else?

ARTHUR: I told him that when I thought over my past life – the weakness, the dishonesty of it all – I wondered if any really nice woman could ever take tea with me.

MRS CHEYNEY: He agreed?

ARTHUR: Mildly.

MRS CHEYNEY: Did you tell him about me?

ARTHUR: Everything.

MRS CHEYNEY: What did he say?

ARTHUR: He said, 'Get her; you'll never get another like her!'

MRS CHEYNEY: I don't believe even a bishop said that.

ARTHUR: I'll swear.

MRS CHEYNEY: Still, I don't believe you. I've a good mind to come with you and ask him, myself.

ARTHUR: I said we would be there at five minutes to eleven.

MRS CHEYNEY: Oh! Does he think I'll come?

ARTHUR: He's more certain of it than I am.

MRS CHEYNEY: Why?

ARTHUR: He says you love me.

MRS CHEYNEY: Really? I wonder what makes him think that?

ARTHUR: I don't know. He's an idea that you would never have rung the bell last night if you hadn't.

MRS CHEYNEY: What a darling he sounds – I'd rather like to meet him.

ARTHUR: He asked us to be punctual.

MRS CHEYNEY: Do you think he'll like me?

ARTHUR: A bishop is never allowed to leave his wife –
my dear, he'll adore you.

MRS CHEYNEY: Do you?

ARTHUR: Terribly! What is more important, do you?

MRS CHEYNEY: Much more terribly – I wish, though,
that –

ARTHUR: Ssh!

(*He kisses her on the eyes.*)

MRS CHEYNEY: What's that?

ARTHUR: That is the last of Mrs Cheyney.

MRS CHEYNEY: I'm so glad.

(*He embraces her and kisses her on the lips.*)

What's that?

ARTHUR: That's the beginning of Lady Dilling.

MRS CHEYNEY: Beast! You're never happy unless you
make me cry.

The End.

ON APPROVAL

Beware of widows: Ellis Jeffreys as Mrs. Wislack.

Characters

HELEN HAYLE

MRS MARIA WISLACK

RICHARD HALTON

GEORGE
Duke of Bristol

Act I: Helen Hayle's house in Mayfair. August.

Act II: Mrs Wislack's house in Scotland. September.

Act III: The same. Three hours later.

The hawk and the pigeon: Mrs. Wislack and her enslaved admirer, to whom she graciously grants a three weeks' platonic trial. Ellis Jeffreys and Edmond Breon.

On Approval was first performed at the Fortune Theatre, London, on 19 April 1927, with the following cast:

HELEN, Valerie Taylor

MARIA, Ellis Jeffreys

RICHARD, Edmond Breon

DUKE, Ronald Squire

This 'farce in three acts' as it was originally billed was first revived in 1933 at the Strand Theatre 'under the supervision of the *author* – and preceded by Stanley Holloway in selections from his repertoire!' It was again revived at the Aldwych Theatre in 1942, when other shows in war-time London included Edith Evans in John Van Druten's *Old Acquaintance*, Emlyn Williams in his new play *Morning Star*, Vivien Leigh in Shaw's *The Doctor's Dilemma* and Noel Coward's *Blithe Spirit*. It was directed by Peter Hall in 1993, but before this it was staged at the Haymarket in 1975 by Frank Hauser, exactly 21 years after Lonsdale's death. The reviews were delightfully divided, mainly about the performance of the leading lady.

> John Barber: *On Approval* must be the feeblest play in town…yet you must rush to see it. It contains the funniest single performance of the year. The astonishing Geraldine McEwan has transformed herself into a mincing shrew so formidable that the acid in her threatens to burn holes in the carpet… Thin-lipped, Eton-cropped, hands limp, shoulders cramped into an affected droop, avid beak… malicious narrowed eyes…this society harpy is studied to the life. What makes her so comical is that the actress somehow presents her in a state of permanent disadvantage. Squeaking protests, gibbering insults…she can never keep the lid on her bile… A lost evening scooped up and saved by an exquisite performance.

Milton Shulman: Geraldine McEwan...adopts a querulous whine, a stooped walk, a sneering look and a nasal moan...it is an interpretation of such exaggerated mannerisms as to make nonsense of Edward Hardwicke's repeated claims, as Richard, that he has loved her for 20 years.

Felix Barber, who had been so cool to the 1967 production of *Aren't We All?*, was warmly welcoming on this occasion: 'Another revival, and it's got my approval!'

His Grace's enamoured vassal: Valerie Taylor as Helen Hayle.

*" Leave us still our old
nobility "*: *Ronald Squire as
the imperturbable Duke of
Bristol.*

ACT ONE

HELEN HAYLE's house in Mayfair, August. HELEN enters. She turns at the door and looks off stage; voices can be heard arguing. She smiles to herself and goes to pour out coffee.

MRS MARIA WISLACK follows as HELEN reaches her position at the table. MARIA is obviously very angry.

MARIA: (*Slamming the door.*) I – I hope his cigar chokes him.

HELEN: Darling, you take him too seriously.

MARIA: Do I? If he were not a duke, no one would know him. The beast!

HELEN: But what did he do that's annoyed you so much?

MARIA: From the moment we sat down to dinner, his only conversation was women over forty.

HELEN: Then you could never have been in his mind, because he kept saying you were only thirty-eight.

MARIA: I was born on the same day as his stepmother, and that damn woman couldn't keep her mouth shut about anything. Oh, how I dislike him!

HELEN: How ridiculous you are! Liqueur?

MARIA: (*Shaking her head.*) Even as a boy he was unpleasant; if he hadn't been a duke and we hadn't been snobs, not one of us would have even dared to take him on our knee. Hideous child, how I detested him!

HELEN: I'm sorry, because I like him so much.

MARIA: That reminds me. Why is he always dining here?

HELEN: I have told you, I like him so much.

MARIA: You wouldn't marry him?

HELEN: How far is it from here in a taxi to St. George's, Hanover Square?

MARIA: Ten minutes. Why?

HELEN: If he asked me to marry him tonight I'd undertake to run it in five.

MARIA: Helen, you're mad,

HELEN: Am I? It's an attractive complaint.

MARIA: But – but he literally hasn't a penny in the world.

HELEN: My father was a far-seeing man; he bottled some
pickles.

MARIA: Give me some brandy!

(*HELEN half rises.*)

No, no, I don't want any!

(*HELEN sits again.*)

This is terrible, terrible! Will you believe me if I tell you
that he hasn't one penny in the world, and if he married
you it will only be for your money.

HELEN: I can't see that that makes him very terrible. A lot
of women have lived with him for his.

MARIA: Keep silent a moment, I think I'm going to have a
stroke. What do you see in the brute?

HELEN: Everything! He's not bad-looking, has a charming
voice. He's witty, and I adore him.

MARIA: If you married him, in a year you would find he is
none of those things.

HELEN: I should?

MARIA: Nineteen years ago I was asked in a church if
I would take a man to be my wedded husband, and
I answered 'yes'. I looked at him and believed he looked
and was everything that he wasn't; he then drove me
home, for the purpose of proving to me that he was
everything that he was.

HELEN: You needn't be the least bit alarmed. The reason
the Duke of Bristol comes here so often is – he's fond of
my cook, he approves of my champagne, my cigars are
in perfect condition, and my coffee is the only coffee
worth drinking – but to me personally, he is entirely
indifferent – I don't exist.

MARIA: Thank God!

HELEN: That's cruel of you!

MARIA: The reverse, it's kind of me, – a girl of twenty-two,
an orphan, and one of the richest women in England,
you're at the mercy of any man like him.

HELEN: Then even if you loved someone terribly, you
would never marry again?

MARIA: I don't say that; but if I ever do, I shall require to know a great deal more about the next one than I did about the last!

HELEN: I don't see how that can ever be done.

MARIA: It can. I should take him away alone for one month on approval.

HELEN: (*Laughing.*) But Maria darling, supposing at the end of the month you found you didn't like him, what would you do then?

MARIA: Give him his railway fare and send him home again.

HELEN: Wouldn't your position be a little embarrassing?

MARIA: Not in the least. I should give him clearly to understand when we started that I was taking him away only to find out if he loved me for myself alone; if when we were away I found I had not convinced him that was the case, I should then in a subtle way prove to him I was one of the few women in England who could use a revolver accurately.

HELEN: (*Smiling.*) Would your women friends believe that?

MARIA: Ninety-six per cent of my women friends hate revolvers.

HELEN: I wish you would do it, darling. It would be a marvellous precedent for other women if you did.

MARIA: I am thinking very seriously of doing it.

HELEN: You don't mean that?

MARIA: At your table tonight there was a man –

HELEN: Richard!

MARIA: Richard, whom I have known all my life, and who, ever since I have known him, has for causes of shyness or lack of means not been able to quite tell me that he loves me.

HELEN: I have always believed he adores you. And he's one of the nicest men in the world,

MARIA: On the surface he appears everything that is desirable. But married to him, he may be none of those things. That is what I am thinking seriously of finding out.

HELEN: You are going to take him away on approval?

MARIA: I say I may. Of course there – (*Hearing the men approaching.*) Careful!

(*The DUKE OF BRISTOL and RICHARD HALTON enter.*)

DUKE: Well, here we are.

MARIA: Curiously enough, I am able to control my excitement,

DUKE: Splendid!

RICHARD: Sing us something, Helen.

HELEN: I'm sorry, Richard, but I don't sing.

DUKE: I congratulate you; that is a great accomplishment. (*To MARIA.*) I suggest, my dear, our revered old friend Maria dances us the Charleston,

MARIA: I'm neither your dear, nor your revered, or your old friend; and I suggest you try and say something intelligent.

(*HELEN begins to play softly on the piano.*)

DUKE: (*Patting MARIA's hand gently.*) Naughty, naughty! that's the third time you have spoken harshly to me tonight,

MARIA: (*Moving her hand.*) Don't do that! I hate it.

DUKE: (*Listening to HELEN playing.*) Exquisite! I feel rather in the mood tonight to engage a hundred lovely women, all with lovely voices, seated about on lovely divans, to sing to me in a whisper.

MARIA: If you had a little more brain you would be in an asylum.

(*RICHARD laughs rather loudly.*)

DUKE: Richard has either enjoyed your joke immensely or has eaten something indigestible. Ho! Richard, tell them that story you told me at dinner.

RICHARD: (*Nervously.*) What story?

DUKE: You know, the man who said he couldn't sing.

RICHARD I don't remember it,

(*HELEN stops playing.*)

DUKE: Don't be absurd! Of course you do.

RICHARD: I tell you I don't.

MARIA: Do you tell coarse stories, Richard?

RICHARD: Certainly not!

MARIA: Then tell it.

RICHARD: Er – er – it has one word in it that I don't care to use before ladies.

MARIA: Leave out the word.

RICHARD: Then the story has no point.

DUKE: Here, I'll tell it.

RICHARD: You'll do nothing of the sort,

MARIA: Exactly! I thought so. (*To HELEN.*) What I was saying to you just now – what does any woman know about any man?

DUKE: But what is much more to the point is, what does any man know about any woman.

MARIA: Having made the remark of a complete imbecile, perhaps you will tell us the answer.

DUKE: He knows everything about them, and, you nasty old lady, you expected me to say he knew nothing about them. Got you!

MARIA: If you use the word 'old' again to me, I'll throw something at you.

DUKE: Very well, but I pray that when I reach the age of nearly forty-one, I shall not be ashamed. My stepmother, who will be forty-one in August, isn't.

MARIA: Beast! Beast!

(*She walks out of the room into the garden.*)

DUKE: Got her that time!

RICHARD: George, you're a bounder.

DUKE: Funny you should say that. A woman said exactly the same thing to me at dinner last night. I suppose I am. Am I a bounder, Helen?

HELEN: I don't think so. But you have upset Maria terribly.

RICHARD: And if you are a gentleman, you will at once go and tell her you are sorry.

DUKE: A gentleman, Richard, is a man of courage without imagination. Were Maria a lady by nature instead of by birth, I should at once go and tell her I was sorry.

RICHARD: Then I shall go and tell her that I am sorry for you. (*To HELEN.*) Will you forgive me?

(*He goes into the garden.*)

DUKE: There's something terribly attractive about an English gentleman. (*He sighs.*) I wish I'd been born one instead of a duke.

HELEN: (*Laughing.*) Why aren't you one?

DUKE: It's out of the question. If I were, the middle classes and the Americans visiting England would have nothing to talk about. My mood tonight, Helen, is one of singular sadness; I have a grievance against God's creatures; I feel they don't appreciate me. Every morning of my life I expect to be wakened by someone saying 'Come at once, you have been made Governor of the Bank of England,' and the most that ever happens is someone says 'There's a gent downstairs who says the President of the Divorce Court would like to speak to you.'

HELEN: I think that is a great pity.

DUKE: It is, and it's expensive.

HELEN: Have you *no* ambition in life, *no* desire to do anything for anyone?

DUKE: When I think of the miseries of others, my heart bleeds so profusely for them it almost ceases to bleed for the miseries of my own.

HELEN: Instead of thinking about others, mightn't you be happier if you did something for them?

DUKE: My dear! The most that can be expected of any Duke is to think.

HELEN: Then has marriage no attraction for you?

DUKE: It always has had considerable attraction for me; no less than the husbands of three women I have known have threatened me with it.

HELEN: I was meaning some unmarried girl who was fond of you, and might make you very happy.

DUKE: Now it's very curious you should say that; my trustees and myself meet in committee on that subject at eleven tomorrow morning.

HELEN: They want you to marry?

DUKE: They insist.

HELEN: Are you going to?

DUKE: I have promised them an answer tomorrow at eleven.

HELEN: What is your answer going to be?

DUKE: I do not know.

HELEN: Come and dine with me tomorrow evening and tell me what you have decided to do.

DUKE: I'd adore to. That's charming of you; you're very sympathetic, Helen.

HELEN: I suppose it's because I like you.

DUKE: That's charming of you, really it is.

(*RICHARD returns.*)

RICHARD: George, I hope it amuses you to have made a woman cry.

DUKE: But I have said nothing that could possibly make her cry.

RICHARD: Didn't you in a sneering way accuse her of being forty-one?

DUKE: I did. But she is not crying because I said she was forty-one; she's crying because she is forty-one.

RICHARD: Bounder!

HELEN: Is she very upset, Richard?

RICHARD: I hope I will never see anyone as upset as she is again; I could do nothing with her; she even asked me to tell her that story to take her mind off her unhappiness.

DUKE: Did she laugh?

RICHARD: Laugh? It only increased her misery. I gathered the story was older than I was. (*To HELEN.*) Oh, by the way, Tom Leggatt and his wife came in through the garden, they are with her now.

HELEN: Why don't they come in?

RICHARD: They don't want to. (*Turning to the DUKE.*) Tom says he's content to see George in the 'Tatler' or the 'Sketch'.

DUKE: I wonder why people dislike me so much?

RICHARD: Because most times you're a damnable dislikeable feller, that's why.

DUKE: Do you know, I believe that's what it is. I'm almost sure it is.

HELEN: (*Smiling.*) I don't think so. Why don't you both come and sit outside, I must go and talk to the Leggatts.

DUKE: If you don't mind, I think it would be wiser if we stayed here.

HELEN: Very well. Help yourself, Richard, to a drink.

RICHARD: Many thanks.

(*HELEN goes into the garden.*)

DUKE: Water or soda?

RICHARD: I won't have a drink, thanks. Tom Leggatt has been telling me there's a rumour all over the city that you are broke.

DUKE: The city for once is correct. Tomorrow morning at eleven o'clock I have to decide which it's to be, marriage or bankruptcy. (*He pours whisky.*)

RICHARD: I'm sorry, very sorry.

DUKE: I'm touched, Richard.

RICHARD: But you couldn't have got through everything.

DUKE: (*Putting soda into his glass.*) I am given to understand that I have even eaten the grass my horses live on.

RICHARD: I am sorry.

DUKE: Thank you, Richard. And at eleven tomorrow, I, George, twelfth Duke of Bristol, a man whose very soul quivers with sentiment, whose heart beats only for romance, has to sell himself for money. It's a very serious thing, Richard.

RICHARD: I agree it is.

DUKE: But you don't know how serious it is. It means infidelity, Richard, that's what it means – infidelity!

RICHARD: It might not, I have known cases.

DUKE: For her sake, it's good for you to be an optimist, but you're wrong. I am a man who should essentially marry for love.

RICHARD: We all should,

DUKE: Lying in bed in the morning, how often have I pictured myself walking down a beautiful lane, and there at the bottom is a railway crossing, and with her heel caught in the line I see the divine woman of the world; in the distance I hear an express train. I dash,

I seize her in my arms – and as the train passes us,
I realise I have saved her – Wiping the blood from my
eyes – you will notice although I have saved her, I did
not come out of it unscathed myself –

RICHARD: I noticed it – it was a charming touch.

DUKE: I realize that I have met my divinity, from whom
I will never again be parted.

RICHARD: Most attractive! Most attractive!

DUKE: But – my financial position is such that
I dare not even go near a railway station.

RICHARD: I sympathise with you very deeply, believe me
I do.

DUKE: As much as you are able to, I am sure you do. But
to really understand is to be able to love as I could. (*He
looks in the direction of the window.*)

RICHARD: I, too, have loved.

DUKE: Quite so, but if you don't mind, I would like to
restrict this discussion to ladies.

RICHARD: And those are the only ones I have ever loved,
and not ladies – lady. I have loved for over twenty years
the most beautiful lady in all the world.

DUKE: Why haven't you told me about this?

RICHARD: One doesn't wear one's heart on one's sleeve.

DUKE: But one should. What's the fun if one doesn't?

RICHARD: A love like mine cannot be discussed.

DUKE: Do I know her?

RICHARD: Intimately.

DUKE: Who is it? – Who is it?

RICHARD: Maria Wislack.

DUKE: Richard, when I told you the tragedy of my life, the
depth of my feelings, I did not for a moment believe you
would treat it with levity – make jokes about it.

RICHARD: I'm not. I tell you I have loved her for more
than twenty years.

DUKE: Do you mean to tell me that you have loved that
old –

RICHARD: Silence! If I am not mistaken you were about to
call her by a name that would have prevented me ever
speaking to you again.

DUKE: Have a drink – or have you had too many?

RICHARD: I will have a drink. And I have not had too many.

DUKE: (*Pouring out a drink, which he brings to RICHARD.*) Richard, old boy, I love you as a brother, but I must say it, I'd rather see you dead.

RICHARD: George, I mean it. If you say one word again that reflects in the least way against Maria, Mrs Wislack, our friendship is at an end.

DUKE: Very well, but you can't stop me wishing you were dead. Did you know her late husband, Arthur Wislack?

RICHARD: Did I know him? Did I watch him with murder in my heart, treating that divine creature with cruelty, neglect – and eventually die of drink?

DUKE: He hated drink.

RICHARD: Then why did he?

DUKE: He chose it as being the most agreeable way of being unconscious whilst waiting for his release.

RICHARD: I warned you, George, I told you if you said another word that reflected –

DUKE: Sit down and don't be so damned dignified. Besides, you haven't finished your drink.

RICHARD: On that account only will I speak to you again.

DUKE: (*Picking up cigar-box.*) Have a cigar?

RICHARD: If you are apologising to me, George, I should prefer it in the form of one of your own cigars.

DUKE: Richard, if I have in any way hurt your feelings, I apologise. Now will you stop sulking and have a cigar?

RICHARD: Thank you. (*He takes one.*)

DUKE: Does she love you? (*Taking one himself.*)

RICHARD: How should I know?

DUKE: But haven't you asked her if she does?

RICHARD: Mrs. Wislack's income is at the least twenty-five thousand pounds a year, mine is three hundred.

DUKE: With or without income tax?

RICHARD: I'm not a fool, George.

DUKE: But I was always under the impression that you had at least fifteen hundred a year.

RICHARD: Yes, but unfortunately, all the horses I have been interested in have been entirely without ambition. They only run for running's sake.

DUKE: We have a great deal in common. But I take everything back; you have offered me a reason why you are right to love her. I applaud you.

RICHARD: What do you mean?

DUKE: She has twenty-five thousand a year.

RICHARD: Are you suggesting that the reason I love her is because she has money?

DUKE: I suggest it's the reason you should.

RICHARD: George, let us understand each other; my love for Maria has lasted through the years; I love her, not for what she has, but for what she is. If she were poor I'd ask her to marry me tonight.

DUKE: I had no idea you loved her as much as this, Richard.

RICHARD: Well, I hope you understand it now.

DUKE: I do, and I propose to help you.

RICHARD: How?

DUKE: I shall go to her at once, with a tremor in my voice. I will tell her of your love for her.

RICHARD: And then?

DUKE: I will wait for the answer and bring it back to you.

RICHARD: Thank you, but if there is to be any tremoring of the voice, I will be obliged if you will leave it to me.

DUKE: And tonight?

RICHARD: What do you mean?

DUKE: I am determined before the night is out that you will be under the impression that you are the happiest man in the world.

RICHARD: How do you propose to do that?

DUKE: You shall tell her here in this room of your love for her.

RICHARD: It's out of the question.

DUKE: I insist!

RICHARD: I haven't the courage.

DUKE: (*Looking at whisky.*) You shall have it.

RICHARD: My dear George, hundreds of times I have been on the verge of asking her, and my courage has failed me at the last moment.

DUKE: Ever tried brandy?

RICHARD: I have.

DUKE: No good?

RICHARD: One night I sat with a bottle of brandy in front of me, and I recited to it the language I would use when asking her to be my wife, with the result that when I entered the room I was unable to even wish her good evening.

DUKE: Bad luck!

RICHARD: No, no, I'm resigned to bachelorhood and solitude. Don't encourage me, there's a good fellow, it's hopeless.

DUKE: Richard, I give you my word of honour that a month from tonight you'll pop into her bed and say: 'Maria, here I am.'

RICHARD: George, that is an observation which I consider most unsuitable here or in the place that you suggest I should make it.

DUKE: I was speaking metaphorically.

RICHARD: I trust so.

DUKE: Loving her as you do, Richard, you must think what it would mean to you; someone to talk to, to be with, no money cares, no cares of any kind, just a happy, jolly fellow smiling his way through life.

RICHARD: Attractive – (*Shaking his head.*) but it's not for me.

DUKE: (*Appealingly.*) Think of the little ones prattling up and down the room – no, no, I take that back.

RICHARD: Why?

DUKE: Very well, if you insist.

RICHARD: Married life without children to me –
(*The DUKE makes a noise trying to stop himself laughing.*)
Are you laughing, George?

DUKE: Laughing? I have a cold coming on.

RICHARD: It's the sort of thing you would laugh at.

DUKE: Not as much as the children would, Richard.

RICHARD: What do you mean by that?

DUKE: Nothing! Listen, I'm going to help you. When she comes into this room I'm going to force myself to be nice to her. I am going to be at my best; I'm as it were, going to warm her up for you, to make your proposal, Richard; at the right moment I will persuade Helen to accompany me to the garden, thereby leaving her alone with you, and all that you will have to do will be to put the question.

RICHARD: No, no,

DUKE: I insist.

RICHARD: No, no.

DUKE: Richard, either you or I will ask her to marry you tonight.

RICHARD: How – how – would you advise me to begin?

DUKE: Well, I have always found it wiser to begin by putting both your arms round them, pausing for a second before speaking, and then saying 'God, how I love you.'

RICHARD: Yes, that might be a good plan with women that are married, but would it be with a woman that you want to?

DUKE: True! There you've got me. Let me think – yes – I think it would be; women love surprises.

RICHARD: She's had too many; and if it misfired, she's as strong as a horse.

DUKE: Then I should treat her softly; I should metaphorically coo at her.

RICHARD: No! I don't think so.

DUKE: Why not?

RICHARD: She's clever; she would metaphorically coo back.

DUKE: Then you must rely on instinct.

RICHARD: No, no, I can' t. She would think I wanted to marry her for her money.

DUKE: Nonsense! She is much too vain. I insist, Richard, – Understand?

(*HELEN laughs in the garden.*)

Ssh!

RICHARD: I'll try; but you will be nice to her, George?

DUKE: Even you won't know me. Richard, rely on me, I am
    going to pave the way for you marvellously.
    (*MARIA enters, followed by HELEN.*)

HELEN: You should have come out; it's a divine night.

DUKE: Had you and Maria been alone, we should have.

MARIA: (*Holding up the decanter.*) You seem to have drunk
    quite a nice lot of this.

DUKE: I'm afraid I did that; Richard let me down; he finds
    one whisky and soda in the evening is enough.

MARIA: I'm glad to hear it.

DUKE: Maria!

MARIA: Well?

DUKE: I apparently said something to-night, quite
    unintentionally, that offended and hurt you.

MARIA: Well?

DUKE: I'm sorry.

MARIA: Obviously you have been drinking.

DUKE: What makes you say that?

MARIA: You would never have apologised if you hadn't.

DUKE: You're wrong. I drank because I was depressed.
    Richard depressed me.

MARIA: Ho!

DUKE: Whilst you were in the garden, Richard has
    been pointing to me my limitations, so gently, so
    understandingly, that I was compelled to listen; he has
    made me feel that all is not well with George, the twelfth
    Duke of Bristol.

MARIA: Ho.

DUKE: The simplicity of his nature conquered me. I thought
    I had known Richard all my life. I was wrong – I did not
    know him until tonight. (*Patting him on the shoulder.*) Dear
    Richard!

MARIA: Ho!

DUKE: You haven't lost your voice, by any chance, have
    you?

MARIA No. Why?

DUKE: It's unlike you to be only able to say 'Ho!'

MARIA: I'm interested. I'm listening. Tell us what he told you.

DUKE: It wasn't so much what he told me about myself as what he told me about himself that affected me.

MARIA: As for instance?

DUKE: His gentleness and kindly feeling towards the world, his love of only that which is beautiful, his adoration for little children,

MARIA: How many has he?

DUKE: Richard is a bachelor.

MARIA: That hasn't answered my question,

DUKE: None.

MARIA: How do you know?

DUKE: (*Looking at RICHARD.*) He is not that kind of man.

MARIA: (*Also looking at RICHARD.*) I see. Go on!

DUKE: That – in effect – is all.

MARIA: Do you ask me to believe that in listening to that ridiculous nonsense you have become a better man?

DUKE: I have a feeling that tomorrow morning I shall find myself standing side by side with the most upright man that England has produced.

MARIA: I trust that tomorrow morning you will wake with a very bad headache and no recollection of the nonsense you have been talking to me tonight.

DUKE: Very well, I shall say no more.

HELEN: Oh, please do, I'm terribly interested.

DUKE: (*Crossing to HELEN and taking her hand.*) Helen, my dear, you and I are only very young –

MARIA: What?

DUKE: Perhaps we are right to believe all that is told us, but (*Turning to RICHARD.*) if Richard has lied to me tonight and has cheated me into believing he is all the things that the suggestion is that he is not, I will never speak to him again.

RICHARD: I said nothing I did not mean.

DUKE: And I believe you, Richard, and through you, I have a feeling tonight, and for the first time in my life, that I would like to get nearer to nature; I would like to walk on grass, inhale – (*He turns up towards the window during this.*) the scent of flowers, listen to the birds singing their simple songs of love. I feel it would help me to find myself more completely.

HELEN: Try the morning, birds don't sing at night.

DUKE: Not for you. Helen, would it amuse you to accompany me?

HELEN: I'd love to.

DUKE: I'm delighted. You will find me very silent.

HELEN: I don't mind.

(*They go into the garden.*)

MARIA: Well?

(*RICHARD smiles at her nervously.*)

Don't you wish to hear the birds singing their simple songs of love?

RICHARD: I rather felt he was exaggerating.

MARIA: Is that young man drunk, or has he acquired a habit of borrowing money from women?

RICHARD: Er – I don't quite understand.

MARIA: I don't know what's the matter with him because I know he hates me.

RICHARD: I think you are wrong. He said only charming things about you when you were outside.

MARIA: Tell me one.

RICHARD: (*Hesitating.*) He said you had a heart of gold.

MARIA: I knew he hated me,

RICHARD: Not at all. And many other equally nice things!

MARIA: Tell me some of those lofty thoughts which have made him wish to walk on grass.

RICHARD: It was nothing really; I was describing to him the loneliness of one's life, living alone, no one to talk to, no one to care for, the utter misery of it all; and the need men have for the affection of a good woman.

MARIA: Go on.

RICHARD: It would bore you.

MARIA: Not at all.

RICHARD: Thank you. I drew a little picture of returning to one's home in the evening –

MARIA: Where had you been in the afternoon?

RICHARD: Nowhere in particular.

MARIA: I see. Go on.

RICHARD: And there seated at one's dinner table, a divine lady who –

MARIA: To whom you would pass a few pleasant words on your way upstairs to dress to go out to dinner with someone else.

RICHARD: Not at all, I should stay and dine with her.

MARIA: Unusual but interesting. Go on.

RICHARD: I described to him the happiness one would feel in having someone one loved to dine with and talk to instead of sitting down miserably eating one's food as I do, alone.

MARIA: Horrid for you. Feeling as you do, Richard, I wonder you don't marry.

RICHARD: Ah! (*He sighs.*)

MARIA: Meaning – ?

RICHARD: The love of a good woman is not for me.

MARIA: Then try one of the others; there are any number of those to choose from.

RICHARD: No, no! There is and only has been one woman that I would care to share my life with.

MARIA: And have you asked her to?

RICHARD: No.

MARIA: Why?

RICHARD: She is too good, too beautiful, too noble, for such as me.

MARIA: If she is as you describe her, I agree. But she may not be quite all those things.

RICHARD: To me she is.

MARIA: Tell me more about her. Come and sit down.
(*He hesitates.*)
Come along, come along. (*Patting the seat beside her.*)

RICHARD: (*Sitting.*) No! I must for ever love her from a distance; I must for ever worship her in silence; I –

MARIA: Oh, shut up!

RICHARD: I'm sorry.

MARIA: How much longer are you going on beating about the bush instead of coming out in the open like a man and saying 'Maria, I love you. Will you or won't you be my wife?'

RICHARD: How did you know?

MARIA: How did I know? Haven't I had to listen to this meandering rubbish every time I ever met you?

RICHARD: And I had no idea you knew.

MARIA: You love me?

RICHARD: With all my heart, with all –

MARIA: Quite so, but let us proceed. Is your object matrimony or the other?

RICHARD: I would give ten years of my life to be your husband.

MARIA: I have no desire that our marriage ceremony should take the form of a burial service. Now, Richard, I should like you to know that I am very fond of you.

RICHARD: I cannot believe it. Why should you care for me?

MARIA: You would be wise in encouraging me not to dwell on that.

RICHARD: Quite.

MARIA: And in addition, you are the only man I know that I would for a moment consider marrying.

RICHARD: This is too wonderful to be true.

MARIA: Don't be too excited, you're getting the best part first. You agree, to be a successful business man you must be practical.

RICHARD: Most emphatically I do.

MARIA: Very well! So let us be practical. My income is twenty-five thousand pounds a year.

RICHARD: Many congratulations.

MARIA: Thank you. What is yours?

RICHARD: Mine?

MARIA: Yes.

RICHARD: Well, it varies; sometimes it's up, and then again it's down.

MARIA: How much is it when it's up?

RICHARD: Do you know, money means so little to me, I haven't really an idea.

MARIA: Where do you bank?

RICHARD: Anywhere – I simply don't care.

MARIA: Could you provide for me?

RICHARD: I could, but I'm not sure it would be in the way that you have been used to.

MARIA: Well, I could provide for both of us in the way that I have been used to.

RICHARD: That is true,

MARIA: So the money is of no consequence.

RICHARD: No.

MARIA: The only question is, would we be happy?

RICHARD: I should be very happy.

MARIA: As I am going to do the providing would you mind including me in your conversation? I said would we, meaning myself, be happy?

RICHARD: My life would be devoted to nothing else. You have known me long enough surely to know that?

MARIA: Having been married before, I know that it is possible that you are none of the things you appear to be.

RICHARD: I am described by my friends as a simple fellow.

MARIA: So was my late husband. He was so simple that I never understood one single thing he did for eighteen years. Richard, you said that you love me?

RICHARD: With all my heart, with all –

MARIA: 'I love you' embraces all that. Now I have a house in Scotland – what is today?

RICHARD: Tuesday.

MARIA: Tuesday – is it? Yes, Tuesday. Very well, I suggest that you and I on Thursday night by the midnight train travel there for one month.

RICHARD: It sounds delightful, but with what particular object?

MARIA: To all intents and purposes we will spend a month alone together as married people.

RICHARD: You and I spend a month alone together as married people!

MARIA: Yes.

RICHARD: You're not serious.

MARIA: I am.

RICHARD: But what an extraordinary idea. What an intensely good idea.

MARIA: I'm glad you like it. We will, so to speak, breakfast, lunch and dine together, just as if we were married.

RICHARD: But this is perfectly delightful! I really congratulate you most sincerely. Charming! And the courage of it.

MARIA: If at the end of the month I find that we think alike as it were, that you are a pleasant person to live with, I'll marry you.

RICHARD: And if I'm not, we will have had a grand time, and no harm done.

MARIA: None.

RICHARD: Really, I can't tell you how highly I think of it. It's daring without being unattractive, it's attractive, with no loss of beauty, it's wise without being cunning. Really, I do congratulate you! I never remember looking forward to anything so much. And the courage of it. (*There is a momentary pause, during which he looks at her.*) Ho! If there were only more women in the world like you what a happy world the world would be.

MARIA: Finished?

RICHARD: Not at all. I could go on for hours. I wish I could decide whether the wisdom or the courage of it appeals to be more.

MARIA: Finished?

RICHARD: Only for the moment. I'm so struck by the whole idea I have not been able to half express myself.

MARIA: Each night you will hear a clock in the hall strike eleven –

RICHARD: Now that's original. Really, I must congratulate you again.

MARIA: – which will be the signal for you to start putting your coat on,

RICHARD: With what idea?

MARIA: With the idea of going out.

RICHARD: But I shall have had all the exercise I need in the day. Oh, I know, the dog.

MARIA: On the hall table you will find a lantern, it will help you to find your way to the hotel a mile away.

RICHARD: Precisely for what reason do I go to the hotel?

MARIA: It's optional, but it's the place where you will be sleeping.

RICHARD: Ho! So I don't sleep in the house?

MARIA: You don't!

RICHARD: Ho! How about wet nights?

MARIA: I should advise your bringing a raincoat.

RICHARD: Yes – raincoat. I must say it seems to me you would learn a great deal more about me if I were actually in the house the whole time.

MARIA: I shall endeavour to learn all I want to know without that.

RICHARD: Very well, but –

MARIA: And I am not in the habit of staying in houses with a man alone.

RICHARD: I trust I am a gentleman.

MARIA: I shall be able to tell in a month's time. Well, what do you say?

RICHARD: I accept, of course. And I wish you to know I shall do everything in my power to prove to you that your happiness with me is assured.

MARIA: I don't want you to do anything – I just want you to be natural.

RICHARD: I could not be anything else.

MARIA: Then we leave midnight Thursday.

RICHARD: We do!

MARIA: You will call for me and take me to the station.

RICHARD: I will.

MARIA: Very well. My cloak, Richard.

RICHARD: You're going? (*He fetches MARIA's cloak from a chair.*)

MARIA: Yes! I had no idea it was so late.
(*He helps her with her cloak.*)
I make it a rule, Richard, never to be out of my bed after eleven thirty.

RICHARD: I shall be very happy to acquire a similar habit. I'll see you home.

MARIA: It's not necessary. I'll go through the garden. My house is only twenty yards away. Good night, Richard.
(*She offers her cheek for him to kiss.*
He hesitates, then kisses her.)
I hope I shall find that you are all that I think you are.

RICHARD: I hope you will find that I am a great deal more than you think I am.

MARIA: Good night.

RICHARD: Good night, darling.
(*MARIA leaves.*
RICHARD looks after her happily and then he helps himself to a whisky and soda.
The DUKE enters.)

DUKE: Do I, or do I not, see a happy man?

RICHARD: You do.

DUKE: She's accepted you?

RICHARD: She hasn't.

DUKE: She's refused you and you're delighted – and so am I.

RICHARD: She has not refused me.

DUKE: Well, what did she do?

RICHARD: That is entirely my business.
(*HELEN enters.*)

HELEN: Maria has gone away in a terribly good mood, Richard. Am I to congratulate you?

RICHARD: In a way, Helen dear, at all events you will be able to. A month from to-day you will look at me and say 'There's a happy man in the world.'

DUKE: Then you are engaged to her?

RICHARD: I tell you I'm not.

DUKE: Then what are you?

RICHARD: Well, I'm half engaged to her, and half married to her.

DUKE: Has the old lady been trying to find out what effect drink has on you?

RICHARD: Unless you are able to speak of my future wife in prettier language I shall ask you not to speak to me again.

HELEN: Why a month from today, Richard?

RICHARD: The position is this: owing to their being men in the world like George, we are in consequence all suspects. I leave on Thursday night for Scotland, with Maria, that we may spend a month together with the idea of discovering if we possess those things in common that would make for permanent happy married life.

DUKE: You and she go off to Scotland for a month alone to find out if you will be all right married.

RICHARD: I dislike your phraseology, but the answer is, we do.

DUKE: Very hot!

RICHARD: What do you mean?

DUKE: Well, isn't it?

RICHARD: I can see now why Maria mistrusts all men.

DUKE: But damn it, you can't say it's too good going away for a whole month with a woman?

RICHARD: We will, if you don't mind, in future refer to her as a lady. (*He hesitates.*) You are not suggesting that I would stay in the same house with her at night alone, are you?

DUKE: Aren't you?

RICHARD: How dare you! Only a man like you could have ever thought of such a thing. I sleep at the hotel.

DUKE: You mean to tell me that every night you leave her and go to an hotel?

RICHARD: What else do you suggest I should do?

DUKE: Stay in the house with her.

RICHARD: You cad!

DUKE: (*With a quick thought.*) Suppose it's raining?

RICHARD: I have thought of that. I am taking a raincoat.

DUKE: (*Looking at HELEN.*) What do you think about it?

HELEN To me it all seems very unnecessary. Nothing would induce me to go to Scotland at this time of year. If I cared for anyone enough, I should know him so well I'd marry him at once. (*She sits on the piano stool.*)

DUKE: I agree.

(*HELEN begins to play.*)

RICHARD: I'm sorry, but I see Maria's point perfectly. I think she is perfectly right.

DUKE: Do you think you will be able to convince her you are all right, Richard?

RICHARD: I am all right.

DUKE: Good! I wish I were there to help you. One minute!

RICHARD: Anything the matter?

DUKE: An idea is creeping into my brain. Richard, I am going to be of infinite service to you.

RICHARD: How?

DUKE: Every night you return to that hotel you will find me there prepared with what you have to say to her tomorrow.

RICHARD: What do you mean?

DUKE: My position in London is precarious. I wish to leave it; it is suggested I should make up my mind on a subject of considerable finality immediately. I do not wish to; it would suit me perfectly to spend a quiet month in Scotland.

(*HELEN stops playing.*)

RICHARD: And come and stay at my hotel?

DUKE: Precisely.

RICHARD: That would be marvellous. No! No!

DUKE: Why not?

RICHARD: If Maria knew she would strongly disapprove.

DUKE: She wouldn't know. I would enter my name in the hotel book as Smith. Only my manner and my appearance would suggest I am who I am.

RICHARD: I like the idea, but I must think about it.

DUKE: It's settled, Richard, I am coming. I leave by the midnight train on Friday.

RICHARD: No, no! It must be talked over very seriously.

DUKE: It shall be. Have you any whisky in your rooms?

RICHARD: I think so.

DUKE: We will adjourn there. Helen, I dine with you tomorrow – I look forward to it very much.

HELEN: Nine o' clock.

DUKE: To the minute. And thank you for an exceedingly pleasant evening. Good night.

(*He goes out by the door.*)

HELEN: Good night.

RICHARD: Good night, Helen dear. I can't tell you how happy I am.

HELEN: I hope you always will be, Richard.

RICHARD: I know I shall.

DUKE: (*Off.*) Come on, Richard. Good night, Helen.

RICHARD: (*Shaking hands with HELEN.*) Good night.
(*He goes off after the DUKE.*
HELEN remains for a moment thinking. Then suddenly she picks up the telephone.)

HELEN: Mayfair one – o – six – two. (*Pause.*)
Is that Mrs. Portious' house? Would you be good enough to tell Mrs Portious that Miss Hayle will be unable to dine with her on Friday night as she is going to Scotland – ? Thank you.

End of Act One.

ACT TWO

MARIA's house in Scotland. September. There are doors to the front porch, the kitchen and other parts of the house. The table is set for one person. HELEN is reading. MARIA enters from the kitchen.

MARIA: (*Looking at the clock.*) Twenty minutes to two. Hasn't that young man you like so much come in yet?

HELEN: No!

MARIA: Does he realise those beasts of servants left me at a moment's notice and we are doing all their work?

HELEN: Of course.

MARIA: Well, why isn't he here for his lunch at one o'clock, as you asked him to be?

HELEN: I'm nervous that something has happened to him.

MARIA: Nervous that something hasn't. The way you pander to this man, Helen, makes me ill with rage.

HELEN: (*Smiling.*) I'm sorry, darling.

MARIA: You follow him here. You persuade me to let him stay here – you wait on him hand and foot – ho! You make me so angry – I can't speak.

HELEN: (*Laughing.*) I'm sorry.

MARIA: There's nothing to be amused about. Having spent three weeks with him practically alone, haven't you discovered that he's one of the most odious creatures that ever lived?

HELEN: The only thing that I've discovered is that I'm the happiest woman in the world.

MARIA: You don't mean to tell me you still like him?

HELEN: I have never been so happy, darling.

MARIA: God give me strength! How can you tolerate his unutterable selfishness?

HELEN: Easily! It's only part of his education. But one of the only things the Duke of Bristol is unconscious of is his selfishness.

MARIA: And realizing that you still like him! Terrible! Terrible! (*HELEN gives MARIA a small box.*)
What's this?

216

HELEN: A present for you, darling. An appreciation of my gratitude to you. I telegraphed to London for it the second day I was here.

MARIA: But for what? (*Opening box.*)

HELEN: For being the cause of my spending three weeks practically alone with dear George.

MARIA: It's sweet of you, Helen dear, and I adore it; and all that I can say is, I hope you will always be as happy as you appear to be now. (*She kisses HELEN.*)

HELEN: Thanks to you, darling, I'm going to be.

MARIA: I take it he has asked you to marry him?

HELEN: Not yet, but he's soon going to.

MARIA: I hope you'll be happy. (*She looks at the clock again.*) Richard has been a long time gone to the village.

HELEN: The hill back from the village is steep and three miles long – and owing to your servants leaving you and the car not being available till this afternoon, he has had to climb it twice today.

MARIA: But he left here before twelve.

HELEN: It's a steep hill, darling, and three miles long.

MARIA: You'd find excuses for anyone. Helen, as a friend, what is your true opinion of Richard?

HELEN: I'm sure that Richard is the kindest, sweetest man I have ever known.

MARIA: That's what he appears to be. Do you think it's genuine?

HELEN: What do you mean?

MARIA: You don't think he's merely giving a good impression?

HELEN: No, I'm sure he's not. But if he is, darling, he's an unusually clever man.

MARIA: In what way?

HELEN: You haven't left much undone to find out if he has any particular weakness, have you, darling?

MARIA: How can you be so horrid? I've never been as nice to anyone as I've been to Richard. Are you suggesting that I haven't been nice to him?

HELEN: No; how could I suggest such a thing, when Richard described you as an angel?

MARIA: When did he?

HELEN: Last night, this morning, always when he speaks of you.

MARIA: Yes, but perhaps he said it hoping you'd repeat it.

HELEN: You must have discovered very little about Richard to even think that, darling.

MARIA: Anyway, I'm glad he said it, very glad.

(*The DUKE is heard whistling. HELEN smiles and goes to the porch door.*)

HELEN: Here's George. Isn't it divine to hear him so happy?

(*The DUKE enters.*)

DUKE: Tell me something more exquisite than Scotland on a beautiful day.

MARIA: You.

HELEN: Thank God! Nothing has happened to you, George.

DUKE: Why, did you think something had?

HELEN: I did rather. As you went out I asked you, as there were no servants, to be in to lunch at one, and when quarter to two came, I began to think something terrible had happened to you – (*She pauses.*) – as you knew we had no servants.

DUKE: Charming! Charming! I'm grateful.

(*He hands HELEN his hat and stick, which she hangs in the porch.*)

The fact of the matter is, I lost myself in a letter I was writing to the *Morning Post* on 'Why England always loses at games.' After lunch I will read it to you.

HELEN: That will be divine.

DUKE: I think it will cause a sensation.

MARIA: That you can write a letter at all will cause a great sensation.

DUKE: Writing it has quite exhausted me. Is lunch ready? I feel quite hungry.

MARIA: Lunch has been ready for three-quarters of an hour.

DUKE: No! I hope it isn't spoilt.

MARIA: (*To HELEN.*) He – he – hopes it isn't – (*Unable to speak any further.*)

HELEN: I'll bring it to you, George dear.
(*HELEN goes out to the kitchen.*)

DUKE: And what have you been doing, Maria dear?

MARIA: Don't be so damn patronising, I have been cleaning up your filthy untidy bedroom, and cooking your lunch.

DUKE: Ha! But if you hadn't quarrelled with your servants you wouldn't have had to do either.

MARIA: I did not quarrel with my servants.

DUKE: Then they quarrelled with you – which is a mere distinction without a difference.

MARIA: George!

DUKE: Yes, Maria dear?

MARIA: Look at me. Does my face at the moment express anything to you?

DUKE: No.

MARIA: Well, there is a hand at my side imploring me to let it smack your stupid face.

DUKE: I forgive you, because I realize either through their or your fault that you have lost your servants, and you are tired.

MARIA: Oh, Heaven, help me to remain something of a lady.
(*HELEN returns and places a plate one the table in front of the DUKE.*)

HELEN: There, George dear.

DUKE: (*Smiling at her.*) Thank you, Helen. Some bread?

HELEN: I'm so sorry.
(*She hurries out again.*)

DUKE: By the way, where is Richard?

MARIA: Richard at this moment is walking up that hill with things that you will eat for your dinner tonight.

DUKE: Good.

MARIA: Good!

DUKE: I hope he hasn't forgotten to bring me my *Times.*

MARIA: You hope he –
(*HELEN returns carrying a plate with bread.*)

HELEN: Bread, George darling.

DUKE: And some butter, dear.
(*HELEN goes out again.*)

MARIA: In the cellar there is champagne, Moselle, hock, claret – please let me fetch you something.

DUKE: Maria, you know I never drink at lunch.

MARIA: But I want you to. I want you to let me fetch it for you.

DUKE: If you will allow me to say so, your joke is singularly unfunny.
(*HELEN returns holding a plate in each hand.*)

HELEN: Butter, George! (*She puts the butter on the table and shows him some pudding.*) You would like some rice pudding?

DUKE: To say I would like rice pudding, Helen, would be as inaccurate as it would be insincere – but to say that I am hungry and will have some rice pudding is an entirely different matter. Where's the cream?

HELEN: There is no cream.

DUKE: What!

MARIA: Do you know what would give me more pleasure than anything else in the world?

DUKE: I cannot imagine.

MARIA: To rub your nose in rice pudding.

DUKE: Even if it is through one's own fault one is tired, one should endeavour to avoid crudity, Maria.

MARIA: Beast!

HELEN: I'm afraid I didn't put quite enough milk in it, George dear.

DUKE: I agree. But what it lacks in milk it makes up for in rice. (*He digs a fork into it.*)

MARIA: Throw it at him.

DUKE: I can quite see why you don't keep your servants, Maria.

HELEN: George, please!

DUKE: Have I said the wrong thing again?

MARIA: That is the second time you have suggested that it is through my fault my servants have left me.

DUKE: I'll put it another way. I suggest one has to like you very much to remain in the same house with you, Maria darling.

MARIA: Beast! (*She moves to him and pulls his nose.*) Beast!
(*She goes to the kitchen.*
The DUKE holds his handkerchief to his face.)

DUKE: It's too soon to tell, but I may have to ask you to
fetch me a doctor, Helen.

HELEN: Don't be ridiculous. Finish your lunch.

DUKE: To describe a kick in the face from a horse as
ridiculous is to me a little unsympathetic. Why isn't the
damned thing bleeding?

HELEN: I'm inclined to think it served you right. What
pleasure do you derive from always irritating Maria as
you do?

DUKE: I irritate her? I'm charming to her. Not once have
I, for Richard's sake, told her she's a disagreeable old
devil.

HELEN: She's not as bad as that.

DUKE: Why did her servants leave her?

HELEN: Because –

DUKE: Why do you hesitate? You told me yourself that if
you were a servant girl you would rather starve than
work for her.

HELEN: (*Looking at the door.*) I had no idea you would
repeat it so loudly when I said it.

DUKE: Let her hear it, it would do her good.

HELEN: Please, George. With all her faults, I am fond of
Maria.

DUKE: Do you think she's nice to Richard who adores her
and waits on her hand and foot?

HELEN: I think she means to be.

DUKE: You know that isn't true – you said so yourself.
(*HELEN looks at the door again.*)
I want her to hear me, I tell you. She nags him, orders
him about, won't let him do this or that – give me an
answer. Have you ever in your life met with such
selfishness?

HELEN: Yes. Once.

DUKE: You're lucky – I never have. It angers me so much
I have difficulty in controlling myself.

HELEN: George, dear, the more I see of you, the more
I realize you're cursed with too great a sense of humour.

DUKE: How true that is. I believe that if Maria were to
come into the room now – (*He holds his face.*) – and with
a pain still acute – and she were to say that she was sorry
I honestly believe I'd forgive her. (*He pauses.*) I'm sure
I should.

HELEN: I think that's wonderful!

(*RICHARD enters by the porch door, carrying parcels.*)

Richard, my poor sweet – twice up that dreadful hill!
You must be exhausted. (*She takes the parcels from him and
puts them on a sideboard.*)

RICHARD: Thank you, Helen. I am rather. Where's Maria?

HELEN: In the kitchen.

RICHARD: Is she all right?

HELEN: Perfectly.

DUKE: That is not true. Richard, I have some bad news for
you.

RICHARD: (*Anxiously.*) Maria's annoyed with me for being
so long.

DUKE: No! What do you think? She pulled my nose.

RICHARD: What for?

DUKE: I've no more idea than you have.

RICHARD: Ho! Well, it doesn't seem to have improved it.

DUKE: You – I can't believe it. As she pulled my nose
I said to myself: 'If anything will infuriate Richard with
her, this will.'

RICHARD: Well, it hasn't. And if she pulled your nose, she
had some excellent reason for doing so.

DUKE: And this is the return I get for coming up here to
stand by you, remaining under the most extreme
discomfort and insults to help you to win her –

RICHARD: Let me tell you something. I haven't a chance
in the world of winning her – but if I had, it would be in
spite of you. At least fifty times you've nearly damned
my chances.

DUKE: (*Indignantly.*) I wish to leave you. Richard – give me
my *Times*.

RICHARD: I hadn't time to get it.

DUKE: You mean to tell me you haven't brought me my *Times*?

RICHARD: I haven't.

DUKE: Well, of all the selfish devils that –

(*MARIA returns.*)

MARIA: So you're back. I suppose you forgot I told you I wanted these things at once? (*Looking at packages.*)

RICHARD: I know I've been a long time, but there were so many things to buy –

MARIA: It's all right. I expect you met a friend.

HELEN: Maria darling, you obviously have no idea what it means to climb that hill twice in one day.

MARIA: Nonsense: Just what he wants. Does him all the good in the world.

DUKE: Yes.

MARIA: (*To RICHARD.*) Yes. Were you able to buy everything?

RICHARD: Everything.

DUKE: (*Rising.*) That is not true – he did not bring me my *Times*.

MARIA: Sit down –

(*The DUKE sits.*)

and try and alter your monotonous voice.

RICHARD: I agree. It drives one mad.

DUKE: Don't pander to her, Richard, merely because you wish to make a good impression.

RICHARD: I am being perfectly natural. I agree with her.

DUKE: Then why did you tell me the night before we left London that my voice was my chief asset?

MARIA: Did you tell him that, Richard?

RICHARD: I may have done. I only know that unless you keep telling him he's something that he isn't he sulks. The gramophone records are in the brown paper parcel, darling.

(*HELEN looks over the parcels.*)

MARIA: Oh, that was nice of you to bring them. I'm so glad.

DUKE: I hate gramophones.

MARIA: You sent my telegram?

RICHARD: Ho!

MARIA: Richard, you don't mean to tell me you forgot to
send it?

RICHARD: I'm terribly sorry, but I'm afraid I did.

MARIA: This is too bad. Do you realise I won't have a
single thing to read for two whole days.

RICHARD: I know, and I can't tell you how sorry I am.

MARIA: What's the use of being sorry? If I'd known you
were not going to send it, I should have gone myself.
That's too annoying – But I notice you've brought all the
things you want.

(*HELEN whispers to RICHARD.*)

HELEN: Tell her to go to hell!

RICHARD: (*He starts.*) What did you say?

HELEN: (*As MARIA looks round at them.*) I said you looked
tired and not at all well.

RICHARD: I'm all right, really I am.

MARIA: Of course he's all right.

RICHARD: Maria, I would like you to believe me –

MARIA: Please don't worry – it was not important – it was
only my books, and I realise it's too much to expect
anyone to remember such a trivial thing. I should have
gone myself.

(*She goes to the kitchen.*)

DUKE: If I walked up that hill twice and a woman spoke to
me like that, I –

RICHARD: Well, as you haven't walked up once, mind
your own business. She asked me particularly to
telegraph for her books, and I realize it's most
disappointing, and I'm terribly sorry.

DUKE: You make me sick.

RICHARD: I will make you sick if you're not careful,
George.

DUKE: Helen, I would like you to walk with me. I am
anxious to read you my letter to the *Morning Post*.

RICHARD: If you have any decency you'll go and send
that telegram for Maria.

DUKE: I? Walk up that hill because Maria wants to read? Don't be funny. There's a book in the house she should read. Do you know what it is?

RICHARD: No.

DUKE: The Bible.

RICHARD: What do you know about the Bible?

DUKE: More than you think I do. It's full of examples to selfish women.

RICHARD: Any for selfish men?

DUKE: Yes. Read about Judas and you'll find he was the type of fellow who was too lazy to bring his friend *The Times*.

(*HELEN loads a tray at the table.*)

RICHARD: Do you know you're very nearly an idiot.

DUKE: Am I? Will you walk, Helen?

HELEN: If you mean it, George.

DUKE: I don't understand.

HELEN: So often after I've taken the trouble to change my clothes you've changed your mind.

DUKE: I mean to walk.

HELEN: Very well. (*To RICHARD.*) I was right when I told you to – (*Pausing.*) You didn't look at all well, Richard. (*She goes with the tray to the kitchen. RICHARD laughs gently.*)

DUKE: May I take part in the joke?

RICHARD: No, you can't. Ho! I nearly forgot – I met the telegraph boy coming up the hill and he gave me this telegram for you.

(*The DUKE takes the telegram from him, and puts it in his pocket unopened.*)

DUKE: Thank you.

RICHARD: Don't you open telegrams?

DUKE: Not the ones I send myself.

RICHARD: What did you send yourself one for?

DUKE: Tell me your joke and I'll tell you.

RICHARD: Very well. When Helen said 'I don't think you look at all well' I thought she said 'Tell her to go to hell.'

DUKE: I would have you know, Richard, my fiancée is not in the habit of using that type of language.

RICHARD: Fiancée? Are you and Helen going to be married?

DUKE: We are.

RICHARD: I feel hurt. I think she should have told me.

DUKE: She couldn't – she doesn't know herself yet.

RICHARD: What do you mean?

DUKE: You might have thought I'd been wasting my time here. I haven't, believe me. I have been studying Helen very carefully; and I have come to the profound conclusion, Richard, that she is in every way a fit person to be the Duchess of Bristol.

RICHARD: I agree.

DUKE: She has the disadvantage of having no family behind her as it were. Her father, unfortunately, was only a pickle-maker – but by nature she is a lady. And as I have to marry, Richard, I prefer to marry Helen than anyone I know, even though at first I realize my family will strongly disapprove. (*He takes out cigar-case.*)

RICHARD: Why should they? Helen is one of the nicest women in the world.

DUKE: I agree.

RICHARD: I didn't know you had any cigars.

DUKE: (*Putting cigar-case quickly away.*) I brought only fifty; consequently I only smoked them when you were not here.

RICHARD: You mean devil!

DUKE: Only where cigars are concerned. To continue; (*Lighting his cigar.*) I have resolved, Richard, to play my part. In addition to the position I give her, I am going to compel myself to make her a good and faithful husband.

RICHARD: Very kind of you.

DUKE: Let me tell you this: it's a most unusual thing in our family.

RICHARD: I suppose there is no doubt she will marry you?

DUKE: Leaving me out of it, are you suggesting that any woman would refuse to be the Duchess of Bristol?

RICHARD: No, that's true. (*Lighting a cigar of his own.*)

DUKE: Don't be childish. There isn't a mother in London with an eligible daughter who won't read the news with pain.

RICHARD: True! True!

DUKE: The relief at having made up one's mind is considerable. I can now return to London the same careless fellow you've always known me. Hence this telegram. I am urgently required in London, and I think I deserve a few days amusement.

RICHARD: Is Helen returning with you?

DUKE: Helen will return with you and Maria.

RICHARD: If you wait until tomorrow, I might be able to come with you.

DUKE: Why, are you going to leave the old – ?

RICHARD: George! Maria is expecting two more servants tomorrow and if they come there will be nothing more that I can do for her.

DUKE: You're through with her?

RICHARD: The reverse – she's through with me.

DUKE: Has she told you so?

RICHARD: Every time she speaks to me. I've got on her nerves, George – the poor dear simply can't bear me. It's a pity and I'm sorry, but there it is.

DUKE: Don't be a fool. She's always like this.

RICHARD: George, I've known Maria all my life. I've never known her like this.

DUKE: Leave her and come with me tonight.

RICHARD: Certainly not. Nothing would induce me to leave her as long as I can be of use to her.

DUKE: Noble I call it. An idea. The moment I'm married, you can make our house your home, Richard.

RICHARD: Thank you, George, that's charming of you.

DUKE: And I'll go further. My word, I'm a good friend. I'll insist on Helen making you a small allowance.

RICHARD: Certainly not!

DUKE: Very well. But don't you ever forget that I made you a damn good offer. (*He stretches himself out on the settee.*)

RICHARD: An offer you should be ashamed of. (*He sits on an armchair.*)

DUKE: Well, I'm not. I'm what an American friend of mine would describe as the far-seeing son of a gun. Nice cigar, Richard?

RICHARD: (*Settling himself apparently for sleep.*) Very.

DUKE: (*Sinking further into the settee.*) I shall live in the country a good deal when I'm married. It will keep one away from temptation.

RICHARD: I love the country.

DUKE: In my case I can see that marriage will have many advantages.

RICHARD: I can't begin to tell you how I envy you.

DUKE: And it's not as though one had not had a good time.

RICHARD: True.

DUKE: (*Closing his eyes.*) I have very expensive but very pleasant memories of women, Richard.

RICHARD: I have only loved one woman all my life.

DUKE: Pity. You've missed a good deal. It's fun while it lasts.

RICHARD: I've always believed that –

DUKE: You knew Molly?

RICHARD: Just.

DUKE: My word, she was expensive – but she was a sweet woman. Very sweet, I liked Molly. (*He pauses.*) Very much.

(*They are both asleep.*

MARIA comes into the room. She first notices the DUKE. Then she sees RICHARD, goes to his chair and is about to wake him – hesitates – deliberately crosses to the gramophone and starts it. RICHARD, waking with great suddenness, jumps up.)

RICHARD: Damn it, is there no peace in this house?

DUKE: (*Sitting up.*) I agree.

MARIA: That is very, very interesting.

(*The DUKE lies down again.*)

RICHARD: I am sorry, Maria. You frightened me, I was asleep.

MARIA: Really?

RICHARD: You know how one says things when one is half unconscious.

MARIA: Perfectly. The last person I was married to was frequently in that condition, and I found that was the only time he spoke the truth.

RICHARD: But you know I didn't mean it?

MARIA: Then why say it?

RICHARD: (*Irritably.*) Good heavens, woman, surely –

MARIA: And don't call me 'woman' and don't shout at me – I'm not deaf. And if you must smoke cigars, which I've told you I hate, you might at all events try not to drop your ash on the floor. Get something and clear it up.

RICHARD: Yes, darling. (*He turns to the fireplace and gets the hearth-broom and the coal-shovel and commences to sweep up the cigar-ash.*)

MARIA: There's another little bit there.

(*As MARIA directs him RICHARD obediently follows with the broom and shovel. At the last he is stooping with his back to the settee and the DUKE lifts his foot to kick him, but RICHARD just saves himself from looking indignant.*)

Richard – I am sorry your afternoon sleep was disturbed by me – very sorry. (*She goes out.*)

RICHARD: That, I think, has put the lid on it. What would you advise me to do?

DUKE: I've made it a rule in my life not to be concerned in any inquest. She's a most unreasonable woman.

RICHARD: I've never known her like this. And she always gave me the impression before I came here that she liked me. It's a great pity.

(*HELEN enters. She is dressed for walking.*)

HELEN: Anything the matter?

RICHARD: There is rather. Being a little tired, I unfortunately fell asleep, and Maria woke me with great suddenness by playing the gramophone; with the result I unhappily inquired if there was no damn peace in this house.

HELEN: Was she hurt or angry, Richard dear?

RICHARD: Hurt, I think.

HELEN: (*Nodding her head.*) I expect so.

RICHARD: I could kick myself. What do you think is the best thing to do?

HELEN: George dear, I wonder if you would see if I left a letter on the table by the front door?

DUKE: With pleasure.

(*He rises, goes out to the porch and looks behind the open outer door, closing it to do so.*)

HELEN: Tell her to go to Hell! (*Spelling.*) 'H – E – double L.' (*The DUKE returns.*)

DUKE: There is no letter here.

HELEN: Off you go, Richard – you'll be so much happier when you've made your peace with Maria.

RICHARD: You don't understand, Helen.

HELEN: Believe me, I do, Richard darling.

(*RICHARD leaves.*)

HELEN: There's one of the sweetest men I have ever known; and although I have known him all my life it was not until this three weeks which I've spent with him here that I realized how nice he is.

DUKE: I agree. I made him a devilish good offer just now, and he refused it. But I'm going to insist on him accepting it.

HELEN: I hope you will. Are you ready, George?

DUKE: (*Looking towards the window.*) Look! The sun's gone.

HELEN: (*Endeavouring not to show her annoyance.*) You mean you don't want to walk?

DUKE: Of course I want to walk, but I'm thinking entirely of you – the sun has gone. And incidentally, Helen, I've had some very bad news from London.

HELEN: I'm sorry! It means that you will have to leave for London at once, I'm sure.

DUKE: I've thought out every conceivable way in which I might avoid it – but alas! There is no way. I literally have to tear myself away tonight.

HELEN: I'm sorry. So we don't walk. (*Taking her gloves off slowly.*)

DUKE: If you don't mind very much.

HELEN: Not at all. I understand.

DUKE: That's where you're so delightful, Helen, you do understand.

HELEN: I hope you will always think so, George dear.

DUKE: I shall, believe me. You don't mind cigars?

HELEN: I like them.

DUKE: Helen, I am anxious to tell you something that has been in my mind for some considerable time.

HELEN: Please do.

DUKE: I beg of you not to consider it the impulse of youth, or the lack of much consideration.

HELEN: I won't, George dear.

DUKE: Very well. There is only one woman in the world that I would ask to be the Duchess of Bristol.

HELEN: That is very interesting, George.

DUKE: And if you will ask me who she is, I will tell you.

HELEN: Who is she, George?

DUKE: You, Helen!

HELEN: I am very touched, and very flattered.

DUKE: And I'm very happy. (*He kisses her on the forehead.*)

HELEN: Thank you, George dear. And I would like to tell you that I suppose in the whole world there is only one woman who'd refuse to be the Duchess of Bristol; and if you will ask me who she is, I'll tell you.

DUKE: Er – er – who is she?

HELEN: Me, George darling.

DUKE: Do I hear correctly that you refuse my offer of marriage?

HELEN: Your hearing is perfect.

DUKE: You refuse? You refuse – to be the Duchess of Bristol?

HELEN: I do.

DUKE: May I ask why?

HELEN: Only because you are the Duke, George.

DUKE: Only because – (*He looks at her in astonishment.*) Are you insulting me, Helen?

HELEN: Not nearly as much as you have insulted me.

DUKE: What do you mean?

HELEN: You should have only asked me for my money. You should not have included me with it.

DUKE: Do you suggest that I asked you to be my wife merely on account of your money?

HELEN: But didn't you?

DUKE: I indignantly and emphatically say I did not.

HELEN: Then (*She turns away a little and looks down.*) tell me the colour of my eyes.

(*The DUKE hesitates.*)

DUKE: Blue.

HELEN: (*Facing him.*) Look.

DUKE: (*Looking.*) Grey.

HELEN: So that was easily settled.

(*There is a pause.*)

I do hope it will not mean your having to send yourself another telegram, George.

DUKE: And I thought all this time that you liked me.

HELEN: Three weeks ago I adored you. If you'd asked me to marry you, run away with you without being married to you – if you'd asked me anything I would have done it. I adored you so much.

DUKE: Then why won't you now?

HELEN: I have been alone with you for three weeks.

DUKE: Well?

HELEN: And I realize you are charming until one gets used to you, to look at – (*Shaking her head.*) – but nothing else. It's been my greatest disappointment.

DUKE: You are telling me that I died on you, is that it?

HELEN: The second day.

DUKE: Indeed. Well, that is not the experience of other women who have known me, believe me.

HELEN: May I be frank?

DUKE: I insist!

HELEN: Other women who have known you put up with your boredom George, until they got the family jewels – and then they left you. But my case is rather different. I'm not only asked to return the family jewels, but I am asked to remain with the boredom!

DUKE: Refuse to marry me if you like, but don't be impertinent.

HELEN: You asked me to be frank.

DUKE: Boredom, indeed! It may interest you to know that I am always being asked to dinner parties because I am amusing.

HELEN: A dinner party lasts two hours – marriage has been known to last for two years. But you are not in that danger, George.

DUKE: I'm sure you won't believe it, but there are many women who would be delighted to marry me.

HELEN: I'm sure there are many women who would like to be the Duchess of Bristol. Frankly, I rather wanted to be myself, until I spent three weeks with you.

DUKE: Really, how kind!

HELEN: I know you hate being talked to like this, because you are unused to it. But your contribution to life, George, darling, is that you allowed your mother to bring you into this world, and having done that, you were quite satisfied that everyone else who has been brought into it is for the purpose of approving of you.

DUKE: I'm not aware of it.

HELEN: Of course you're not, I should be angry with you if you were. But take it from me who once believed she loved you – your conceit is beyond imagination, your selfishness has no comparison. May I give you a word of advice?

DUKE: It depends –

HELEN: Marry Maria.

DUKE: How dare you? Are you being funny?

HELEN: Not at all. But for selfishness, you would both win the cup outright. She has money – you'd have a grand time.

DUKE: If a man had said that to me, I would have knocked him down. Do you mean to tell me that I'm anything like that old –

HELEN: Only your clothing distinguishes you.

DUKE: It's a filthy lie – I haven't one single thing in common with her.

HELEN: Nonsense! If you don't get your own way about everything you sulk. So does Maria. If Richard, who has walked up that hill twice, forgets your *Times* you are injured. If he doesn't wait on her hand and foot, she is angry. So are you

DUKE: I've never allowed Richard to wait on me once,

HELEN: Only because you've been too busy allowing me to.

DUKE: But I thought you liked it?

HELEN: You thought I liked waiting on you as though I were a servant girl?

DUKE: You didn't say you didn't.

HELEN: George dear, there's one thing I like about you. You are the living illustration of the puerility of bringing a stupid man into the world with a title, and taking a useful man out of it without one.

DUKE: (*After looking at her.*) What an escape!

HELEN: Thank you, George.

DUKE: I was speaking for myself. Phew! I would have married you. Anyway, yours is a grand position – I envy you. It's something for a profiteer's daughter to have refused a duke,

HELEN: (*Controlling herself with difficulty.*) I can be a cad-girl too.

DUKE: I know it.

HELEN: Many years ago there was a butcher's shop. An august person passing it one day was not attracted by the meat in the shop, but by the butcher's wife. The butcher with an ambitious eye to a knighthood, encouraged him to pass it frequently – with the result he became a baronet. The butcher's wife was encouraged – she acquired an ambition – so she left the butcher, with the result a son was born a duke. So far as I can see, the only difference between our families is – my father only profiteered in pickles.

(*There is a pause – HELEN takes a cigarette from the box on the table and after lighting it gives it to the DUKE. He takes it quite naturally, puts it in his mouth and smokes it. She laughs.*)

DUKE: What are you laughing at?

HELEN: You're divine, George dear. I hope I shall always know you.

(*MARIA enters.*)

MARIA: Hasn't Richard brought tea yet?

HELEN: No. Poor darling, is he making tea?

MARIA: I told him to bring it ages ago, I thought you were going for a walk.

HELEN: George and I decided that as the sun was gone, and as it was very comfortable here, we wouldn't.

MARIA: (*Looking at the DUKE, who is gazing into space.*) Is anything the matter with him?

HELEN: George has had some rather bad news, Maria.

MARIA: Is it bad enough?

HELEN: I think so.

MARIA: That's splendid.

(*RICHARD comes in from the kitchen, carrying a tray of tea things.*)

RICHARD: Here we are, a little tea, a little cake, a little toast – and who cooked it, I ask?

MARIA: (*Starting to pour the tea.*) And who forgot to send my telegram, may I ask?

RICHARD: All right, I'll go down after tea and send it.

MARIA: And look sad all the evening. No, thank you, Richard.

RICHARD: If you had had the telephone put in you could send for a million books a day.

MARIA: I'm not in the happy position of being able to spend pounds for a telephone which one would only use for a few months in the year –

(*RICHARD takes tea to HELEN.*)

but perhaps you are.

HELEN: (*To RICHARD.*) You don't look at all – (*Spelling.*) H-E-double L.

RICHARD: Certainly not.

MARIA: Will you stop that whispering!

HELEN: (*Sitting beside the DUKE and touching him.*) Do you begin to see the likeness, George?

(*All through the preceding scene the DUKE has been sitting in deep thought. Every time MARIA speaks it appears to jar on him. He now jumps up and starts to walk out by the porch.*)

HELEN: Where are you going, George?

DUKE: I'm going to the village.

MARIA: What for?

DUKE: To send the telegram that Richard forgot to send for you.

MARIA: (*Dropping the teapot.*) Help!

RICHARD: (*Spilling some tea over his clothes.*) Look what you've done, you fool!

HELEN: Have your tea first, George.
(*MARIA pours it out.*)

DUKE: Very well.
(*MARIA passes him the cup.*)
Thank you very much, Maria, you are very kind.
(*MARIA starts, looks at him then at the others.*)

HELEN: Any sugar there, Richard?

RICHARD: Sugar? Sorry, I forgot it. (*He starts to go for it.*)

DUKE: (*Stopping him gently.*) You are tired, I will get it.
(*He goes out to the kitchen.*)

MARIA: All this before he sets fire to the house?

HELEN: (*Laughing.*) I don't think so.

RICHARD: But something is wrong with him. I believe he's dangerous. (*The DUKE returns and hands the sugar to HELEN.*)

DUKE: Sorry I've been so long.
(*They all look at one another.*)

RICHARD: Don't you feel well, dear old George?

DUKE: I feel terribly well, thank you.

MARIA: (*Whispering to RICHARD.*) He can't be. You know his grandmother was a little touched.
(*The DUKE walks to the gramophone and starts it.*)

DUKE: Pretty, don't you think?

MARIA: (*Clutching RICHARD's arm.*) Take it off, Richard, I'm suffocating.

DUKE: Sorry, Maria dear. I put it on for you. I thought you liked it. (*He stops the gramophone.*)

RICHARD: George, I've had enough of this.

DUKE: Enough of what?

RICHARD: This fooling. Can't you see that you're frightening Maria?

DUKE: I'm very sorry, Maria dear, I didn't mean to. I'm very sorry. (*He takes off his coat.*)

MARIA: Look! (*Shrinking back.*)

RICHARD: Careful, George old man, careful!

DUKE: (*Rolling up his sleeves.*) It's my turn to do the washing up. Don't hurry with your tea. I'm only going to put the kettle on. (*He goes to the kitchen.*)

(*MARIA walks on tiptoe to the door and looks out.*)

RICHARD: What's he doing?

(*Crash off.*)

MARIA: Ho! He's kicked the coal scuttle over. (*She starts.*) He's struck a match. No, no, it's all right, he's lit a cigarette. Richard, I'm going to my room. Fetch the doctor and ask him to take him away. And if George asks where I am, tell him I've gone for a long walk.

RICHARD: A long walk?

MARIA: A very long walk.

(*MARIA goes out.*)

RICHARD: What's the matter with him?

HELEN: Nothing at all. I put him on my knees and smacked him hard for the first time in his life. That's all. (*The DUKE returns.*)

Shall I see you before you go, George dear?

DUKE: (*Putting on his jacket.*) No.

HELEN: Very well. Good-bye and a pleasant journey. And if ever another girl falls in love with you, marry her the *next day*. It's your only chance, my sweet.

(*She goes out.*)

DUKE: Did you hear that?

RICHARD: Yes.

DUKE: She's been hurling those things at me in dozens.

RICHARD: I don't understand a damn thing you're talking about. Why are you behaving like an idiot, frightening Maria and all of us?

DUKE: I'm showing her, if I choose to be, I'm not a bit like Maria. Heavens! That hurt me badly.

RICHARD: What are you talking about?

DUKE: Now don't tell me I'm a liar, because I'm not. But what do you think she said to me when I asked her to marry me?

RICHARD: What?

DUKE: She told me that I'm an ass, I'm conceited, I'm selfish, I nag – I'm the descendent of a prostitute –

RICHARD: No, no!

DUKE: (*Angrily.*) I tell you I am! – or she says I am. I'm a bore. And I'm everything that's rotten.

RICHARD: Well, well, I'm amazed!

DUKE: What about me? What do you think I am? I've never been so disappointed in anybody in all my life. You know it's your old woman who's done this.

RICHARD: What old woman are you referring to?

DUKE: Yours.

RICHARD: Maria is exactly one year younger than I am.

DUKE: How old are you?

RICHARD: Forty.

DUKE: She's a liar. She's forty-one. Born on the same day as my stepmother.

RICHARD: I believe Maria. Anyhow, how is she the cause of it?

DUKE: This taking you away for three weeks and our coming with you.

RICHARD: Explain.

DUKE: Helen's found out thousands of things about me she didn't know – and she doesn't like a single one of them.

RICHARD: Did you love her, George?

DUKE: How can a man, harassed to death with financial troubles like I am! I'll go and get your old woman to turn you down and see how you like it!

RICHARD: Thank you, but I have more sense than you have, I'm not risking it. The moment the servants arrive tomorrow I leave a note telling her I am sorry but I've gone.

DUKE: Coward!

RICHARD: Not at all. I wish to spare her the embarrassment of telling me that I've failed her. What are you going to do, George?

DUKE: Something desperate.

RICHARD: George, we must make money.

DUKE: Try and forget I'm a duke and talk sense.

RICHARD: How did you lose your money?

DUKE: Women.

RICHARD: I mean how did you lose your big money?

DUKE: Women.

RICHARD: Well, I didn't. I lost mine –

DUKE: Look out!

(*MARIA enters.*)

MARIA: (*To the DUKE.*) Are you better?

DUKE: I was never ill.

MARIA: Well, I wish to tell you your behaviour was perfectly disgraceful.

DUKE: And shall I tell you why my behaviour was perfectly disgraceful?

MARIA: I should like to know

DUKE: Well. I wished it to be known that I had not one single thing in common, nor am I in the least like –

RICHARD: George!

DUKE: Very well, for your sake I won't. But I am writing to you, Maria.

(*He goes out to the kitchen.*)

MARIA: It would please me very much if you gave that young man up as a friend.

RICHARD: Oh, he's not a bad fellow – a little –

MARIA: I would like to think that you'd given him up.

RICHARD: I see your point.

MARIA: I've had a telegram. Those servants are unable to come.

RICHARD: Why?

MARIA: They've sent me an extremely rude telegram refusing.

RICHARD: Brutes: No matter, if you will allow me, I'll continue to do my best while you are here.

MARIA: Thank you, Richard. That's very kind of you. Although we've only been here three weeks I want to tell you something.

RICHARD: It's all right, Maria, I know.

MARIA: How do you know? Would you kindly be silent while I speak? What I have to say is a little embarrassing and you might realize it.

RICHARD: I know, and I'm sorry.

MARIA: I brought you here for the purpose of finding out, as you know, that if we married would there be a chance of us both being happy.

RICHARD: Quite. And I would like to say now –

MARIA: Would you please be quiet.

RICHARD: Sorry.

MARIA: When I left London, I liked you very much. I almost believed that you possessed qualities that would endear yourself to me.

RICHARD: I know. (*He shakes his head sorrowfully.*)

MARIA: But I had no idea, Richard, how nice you really are.

RICHARD: (*Amazed.*) What did you say?

MARIA: What I was going to say, when you interrupted me, was that you are a thousand times nicer than I thought you were. And I'm –

RICHARD: One minute – I –

MARIA: Would you mind waiting one minute whilst I finish what I was going to say?

RICHARD: Go on.

MARIA: I'm not only going to marry you, but –

RICHARD: (*Starting.*) What?

MARIA: Oh, don't keep interrupting. You're irritating me very much – But to prove to you how much I trust you, I'm going to settle five thousand pounds a year on you for life. Are you pleased?

RICHARD: Pleased? But I am delighted.

MARIA: Ah!

RICHARD: And all this time I thought I'd been irritating you to death. I almost believed you disliked me. You'll never have any idea how miserable I've been.

MARIA: But why?

RICHARD: You were so intolerant – so horrid to me.

MARIA: Horrid to you? What are you talking about? I've never been so nice to anyone in my life before.

RICHARD: One minute. Let us straighten this out. You know you've tried every way of provoking me to see whether I was bad tempered or not.

MARIA: I did nothing of the kind. I wouldn't descend to anything so mean.

RICHARD: Nonsense, you know you did. You know you used to nag the life out of me to see if I would answer back – and a thousand other things you did.

MARIA: What are you talking about?

RICHARD: (*Incredulously.*) Maria, you don't mean to tell me that has been really you all the time?

MARIA: Of course. Are you mad, Richard?

RICHARD: Is this how you would be if we married?

MARIA: Of course!

RICHARD: Heaven be praised.

MARIA: What for?

RICHARD: That you took me away for three weeks on approval.

MARIA: Tell me what you mean.

RICHARD: How much did you say you would settle on me?

MARIA: Five thousand a year.

RICHARD: My income is three hundred a year – and I know what it's like to feel a millionaire.

MARIA: Richard, are you insulting me?

RICHARD: How long did your late husband live with you, Maria?

MARIA: Eighteen years.

RICHARD: What a man! What a constitution!

MARIA: How dare you speak to me like that?

RICHARD: If you had the slightest idea how you've spoken to me during the last three weeks, you would be sympathetic. Maria dear, double that five thousand, treble that five thousand, give me every shilling you've got in the world, and then the answer would be 'No!'

MARIA: I – I – have never been so degraded in all my life.

RICHARD: When I left London with you I thought as I have thought of you all my life – the nicest woman in the world; the only woman I have ever liked. But obviously I never knew you at all. And these three weeks have made me realize that you are not and never have been one of the things I thought you. And as long as I live I will love you for having given me the opportunity of finding you out. I would have married you not knowing.

MARIA: You – you beast! Go away.

RICHARD: (*Drawing himself up to his full height.*) Before I go, Maria, I have only one other thing to say to you – may God bless you for your kindness and thoughtfulness to me.

(*He turns and goes out to the kitchen.*
MARIA weeps and screams. HELEN enters.)

HELEN: Darling, what is the matter?

MARIA: He – he – he –

HELEN: Calm yourself, darling. What is it?

MARIA: He has made me cry and –

HELEN: (*She pats her and comforts her.*) The brute! And for the first time in your life, darling. (*She smiles.*)

MARIA: I'm going to my room. I couldn't bear the beast to come in here and find he had been able to make me cry.
(*She goes out.*
Through the window snow can be seen falling.)

HELEN: (*Calling.*) Richard!

(*RICHARD appears at the kitchen door.*)

RICHARD: Has she gone?

HELEN: Yes.

RICHARD: (*Coming into the room a little.*) You're sure?

HELEN: Yes. Where is George?

RICHARD: Sitting in front of the kitchen fire, stunned by the shock you gave him.

HELEN: Maria's lying on her bed in the same condition. If anyone had told you and me three weeks ago that –

RICHARD: I wouldn't have believed them.

HELEN: Surely there must be deep down something rather nice about George for me to ever have been able to like him as much as I did.

RICHARD: I suppose there must be about Maria.

HELEN: Spoilt from the day of his birth – to make him a decent man he needs six months before the mast as a common sailor –

RICHARD: Alone with Maria.

HELEN: He needs to suffer the degradation and the humiliations of poverty –

(*The snow falls heavier.*)

RICHARD: Alone with Maria.

HELEN: Is there no way, Richard, we could do that for them?

RICHARD: There must be.

HELEN: Let's think.

End of Act Two.

ACT THREE

Three hours later. The room is empty.

HELEN comes in carrying a travelling bag; she hurries with it to the door of the porch. She puts the bag outside and closes the door again quickly. MARIA comes in, picks up a cushion and throws it across the room.

HELEN: Darling, you're losing control of yourself again.

MARIA: I – I could scream the house down.

HELEN: Why don't you? It might do you good.

MARIA: How dare he stay here tonight!

HELEN: You must be reasonable. There's no train until six in the morning. Surely you don't expect him to wait on a cold railway platform all night, do you?

MARIA: Yes, I do.

HELEN: Nonsense! Besides, it is not as though they were annoying you by being in the same room; they are sitting quietly together in the kitchen. (*At the door to the kitchen.*) Listen! Not a sound. You wouldn't know they were even in the house. And Richard will be gone by five.

MARIA: Ho! To think that I brought the brute here to find out if I like him, and he has the audacity the moment I tell him I do, to tell me he doesn't like me.

HELEN: Outrageous! But wasn't that the idea?

MARIA: What do you mean? I didn't bring him here to find out if he liked me.

HELEN: No. How silly of me.

MARIA: Anyway, I don't know which of us is the luckier: I to have lost the vulgar man, or you to have discovered in time that you were anxious to marry a congenital idiot.

HELEN: George isn't entirely an idiot!

MARIA: Yes, he is. Look at his face – 'idiot' is written in block letters all over it.

HELEN: All I will admit is his face betrays a lack of something, which is not unusual amongst members of very old families.

MARIA: Stop being a lady and say 'idiot'. Horrid man from the day of his birth.

HELEN: A month from today you won't recognise him, darling.

MARIA: That is my intention.

HELEN: I meant, he will be so different. Can you imagine George kindly, tolerant and unselfish – ?

MARIA: Oh, don't talk such rubbish!

HELEN: He's going to be.

(*The DUKE comes in from the kitchen. He is wearing an overcoat.*)

MARIA: Who asked you to come in here?

DUKE: No one. But I have the alternative of either sitting with two extremely unpleasant women in here, or one strong, silent man in there.

HELEN: Have you quarrelled with Richard?

DUKE: Ever since he ticked Maria off he is so conceited. There's no holding him.

MARIA: Is he boasting that he 'ticked me off' as you call it?

DUKE: Naturally.

MARIA: May I ask what sort of things he has been saying about me?

DUKE: He says he is going to make it his life's work from now on to make you a decent woman. And he says he has discovered the way to do it.

MARIA: How dare he say such a thing!

DUKE: I know! I told him not to be a conceited ass – but he says it can be done. He's very childish tonight.

HELEN: It sounds as though there were hope for you, George.

DUKE: If you have anything to say to me, would you kindly address me through a third person.

HELEN: Why are you wearing an overcoat, George dear?

DUKE: That is entirely my business. But if you must know, that kitchen is one mass of blasted draughts.

MARIA: I am sure you would find the station platform much less uncomfortable than my house.

DUKE: Richard and I talked it over, and we decided we would find it exactly the same.

MARIA: Let me tell you one thing. If ever I meet you again after you leave here at five o'clock tomorrow morning, and you even dare to speak to me, I'll cut you publicly.

DUKE: If I ever speak to you again, Maria, I hope everyone will cut me publicly.

(*HELEN laughs.*)

MARIA: Oh, Helen, how can you laugh at that horrid man.

HELEN: I'm not laughing, darling. I was shocked by his impertinence.

DUKE: Mrs. Wislack, may I have the key of the alcohol cupboard.?

MARIA: No, you may not.

DUKE: Very well, I won't, but may Heaven have mercy on you.

MARIA: Will you leave this room at once?

DUKE: I will not. I am suffering from rigour and I propose to continue with it in here.

(*RICHARD enters. He is wearing an overcoat, the collar is turned up. He is also wearing gloves. He is in a temper.*)

RICHARD: (*To the DUKE.*) You villain!

HELEN: What has he done?

RICHARD: He stood by the other side of the door –
I thinking he had found a place to avoid some of the draughts – when I discovered he was merely there to listen to your conversation in here.

MARIA: Ho! Is that true?

DUKE: Absolutely.

RICHARD: And I am not dull!

MARIA: Yes, you are

RICHARD: And I am not a vulgar little man.

MARIA: Yes, you are.

DUKE: You look vulgar, you are vulgar, and you're dull.
I wish to make a pronouncement. My rigour is on the increase.

RICHARD: Did you have that whisky and soda as I told you?

DUKE: No! She whom you once loved refuses to cough up the key.

RICHARD: She refused! (*To MARIA.*) Give me the key of that cupboard which should never be locked.

MARIA: I will do nothing of the sort.

RICHARD: Give it to me, I tell you.

MARIA: I will not.

RICHARD: Then you put me in the hideous position of having to reveal myself as a man who has always known where it was?

(*RICHARD crosses to a cabinet, puts his hand inside, finds the key and returns to MARIA.*)

MARIA: You – you – have had the audacity to go to that cupboard unknown to me?

RICHARD: Every night since I've been here I've covered my face – with the exception of that part which is used for the purpose of drinking – with shame.

MARIA: You – you –

DUKE: Do you mean to tell me that you had a whisky and soda every night without telling me about it?

RICHARD: You had your cigar. And only because you're cold will I give you one now. Helen, be good enough to fetch him a small whisky and soda.

MARIA: She will do nothing of the sort.

RICHARD: Silence! (*He moves to the door, opens it and speaks in a determined voice.*) Helen!

(*HELEN walks to the door; as she passes through he whispers.*) It's all right; I've put your bag in the car.

(*HELEN goes out, taking the key from RICHARD as she does so.*)

DUKE: How dare you whisper to my late fiancée?

RICHARD: (*Sentimentally.*) Ha! (*He blows a kiss to the door.*)

MARIA: Stop blowing kisses to a girl young enough to be your daughter.

RICHARD: Mrs Wislack! For me to be Helen's father, I should have had to be an enterprising boy of fifteen.

MARIA: Be quiet! You're having the same effect on me as a small boat in a very rough sea.

DUKE: (*Rising.*) Me too.

RICHARD: Where are you going?

DUKE: I wish to speak to Helen.

RICHARD: Are you going to speak to Helen – or are you
going to make that small whisky I ordered for you a
large one?

DUKE: How dare you, you cad!

(*The DUKE goes out.*)

MARIA: Oh! I could cry with shame!

RICHARD: Which is precisely what you are going to do,
lovey.

MARIA: Don't call me 'lovey', you hateful creature.

RICHARD: But you are Maria. During the last five hours
I have been thinking deeply, and I have come to two
conclusions about myself.

MARIA: I have come to one without thinking.

RICHARD: First, I realize you love me very much?

(*She looks at him.*)

Second, you are right to.

MARIA: The moment you came into the room I thought
I recognised the smell of cooking sherry.

RICHARD: And let me point this out to you: had it not
been for my constant fidelity to you during the last
fifteen years, I might be standing here tonight described
by the world as the Napoleon of lovers.

MARIA: On the other hand, it's possible you might not.

RICHARD: True! But I have no regrets; and further, I still
propose to remain faithful to the happy memories I have
of you before I found you out.

MARIA: Thank you very much.

RICHARD: My epitaph will be, 'He turned a woman who in
her youth was one of the most unpleasant of God's
creatures, into, in her middle age, a perfect pet.'

MARIA: Indeed! May I ask what I will be doing whilst you
are attempting to do that?

RICHARD: (*Smiling.*) Nothing! You won't know until it's
too late.

MARIA: Perhaps you will tell me what all this means.

RICHARD: (*Bending over her.*) It means that I have not
finally, as it were, given you up.

MARIA: Talk stupidities if you must, but don't breathe over
me – I hate it.

RICHARD: Try as I will, I still care for you, Maria.

MARIA: Don't waste any more of your time.

RICHARD: Nonsense! One word from me, and you know you'd fall violently into my arms.

MARIA: If you don't leave me I certainly shall – but not in the sense you mean it.

RICHARD: Do you realize, Maria, you are still a very beautiful woman?

MARIA: I do. And mind your own business.

RICHARD: It is my business. In a month from today you will not only be beautiful, but you will be one of the sweetest women in the world.

MARIA: Please don't think me impertinent, but assuming it is necessary, how do you propose to do that?

RICHARD: I expect so much from my idea that I even anticipate you will be so nice I shall find myself wanting to marry you all over again.

MARIA: Will you at once tell me what this is that you are threatening to do?

RICHARD: (*Taking a letter out of his pocket.*) The facts are in this letter, which it is my intention to place on that table before I leave for London.

MARIA: Give it to me at once.

RICHARD: Certainly not.

MARIA: Just as you like. Anyway, I don't suppose I shall ever read it.

RICHARD: You will read it again and again. And I have no hesitation in saying if the instructions are carried out it will make you the woman I thought you were three weeks ago. It may even mean that it will bring us such happiness that rather than ever be separated from each other again we – we –

MARIA: Will be the first married couple to swim the Channel.

RICHARD: Exactly.

(*She tries to snatch the letter from him.*)

Ha! (*He holds it away.*)

MARIA: Beast!

RICHARD: Your interest is awakened. That is all to the good.

MARIA: Go away – I'm going to cry.

RICHARD: You need not yet. That is part of the instructions in this letter. (*He puts the letter in his pocket.*)

MARIA: You bully.

RICHARD: The reverse. The most tender-hearted fellow in the world.

(*The DUKE returns. He is smiling; he is not in any sense drunk.*)

May I ask what's the matter with you?

DUKE: There wasn't any soda.

MARIA: Look at it, I ask you.

DUKE: Look well – you see it for the last time.

RICHARD: I'm ashamed of you.

DUKE: That's disappointing because I am delighted with myself. (*To MARIA.*) You naughty old lady, locking up such beautiful whisky.

MARIA: Go to bed, you disgusting creature. What can you do with it?

RICHARD: Nothing – it has never been able to do anything with itself.

DUKE: He who insults me takes from me nothing. He who takes from me my honour, taketh all. Shakespeare.

RICHARD: I bet you five pounds you don't even know who Shakespeare was.

DUKE: He was the fellow with a place at Stratford.

RICHARD: Give me that key,

(*The DUKE gives it him.*)

Why did you give it me without a protest?

DUKE: (*Smiling.*) I have my reasons.

RICHARD: You – you've drunk it all. If you have, George, you will pay for it, and pay very dearly.

DUKE: I fear nothing – that's the type of fellow I am.

RICHARD: Very well –

MARIA: You're not leaving me with this horrid little person, are you?

RICHARD: For the moment. I am going to see if my suspicions are correct.

(*He goes out.*)

DUKE: Boasting brute!

Mrs. Wislack, I don't wish to speak to you but I have to.

MARIA: I'm very sorry, but I don't wish to speak to you.

DUKE: Will you kindly be seated – I feel less frightened of you when you are sitting down.

MARIA: Say what you have to say and say it quickly. (*She sits.*)

DUKE: Very well. In the cause of both our futures, are you prepared to call a truce for the space of five minutes only of our dislike of each other?

MARIA: The reason?

DUKE: Love.

MARIA: Five minutes.

DUKE: In a few hours from now, Richard and myself will have left this house for ever.

MARIA: Thank Heaven!

DUKE: That isn't true. And moreover, if he goes tomorrow morning you may lose him entirely – he may never want to see you again.

MARIA: I hope he won't.

DUKE: Very well. (*He moves towards the kitchen door.*)

MARIA: Come here. What were you going to say?

DUKE: Are you going to stop pretending?

MARIA: Yes.

DUKE: Do you like him or not?

MARIA: Yes.

DUKE: Do you want him to catch that six o'clock train tomorrow morning?

MARIA: No.

DUKE: Do you love him?

MARIA: Don't shout.

DUKE: Do you love him?

MARIA: Yes – you beast.

DUKE: Then why don't you say so?

MARIA: I suppose a woman's entitled to some modesty.

DUKE: Not when you're on the verge of losing your loved one.

MARIA: You look ridiculous enough without looking sentimental. Having discovered all this, what does it mean?

DUKE: I don't want to leave here at five o'clock tomorrow morning.

MARIA: Why not?

DUKE: Because during the last few hours I too discovered that I am in love.

MARIA: With yourself.

DUKE: If it comes to that – (*He takes a white handkerchief out of his pocket and puts it on the table between them.*)

MARIA: What is that for?

DUKE: To remind us both there is a truce going on.

MARIA: Continue.

DUKE: I have discovered that I am on the verge of losing one of the world's most exquisite people. Forgive me – I close my eyes. I see her divine face, her little hands, her unusual figure – her –

MARIA: Shut up.

DUKE: (*Pointing to the handkerchief.*) Oh!

MARIA: I beg your pardon.

DUKE: Granted. And as you don't understand romance, I'll put it briefly. I love her.

MARIA: What are you going to do about it?

DUKE: I'm going to stay here. And – you don't deserve it – keep Richard here too.

MARIA: How do you propose to do that?

DUKE: In moments of seriousness such as this, damnable as it is, we must temporarily forget the word honour.

MARIA: That'll be easy for you.

(*The DUKE snatches up the handkerchief.*)

I beg your pardon!

(*He puts the handkerchief down again.*)

DUKE: Granted.

MARIA: What is your idea?

DUKE: We must in some way invent a means whereby we will all stay here a little longer, thereby gaining time to win them back again.

MARIA: How do you propose to begin?

DUKE: We must first cause a sensation.

MARIA: How?

DUKE: Well, I shall simply fling myself on the floor in an attitude worthy of a sick man and you will call violently for Richard.

MARIA: Then?

DUKE: You will describe to him my sudden collapse. How I clutched my heart and screamed with pain. That's funny – having mentioned the word heart I have a pain.

MARIA: Wind.

DUKE: I am a gentleman, Mrs Wislack.

MARIA: I beg your pardon.

DUKE: Granted.

MARIA: Do you think you will be able to convince him?

DUKE: As easily as one could a doctor – between you and me he's not very bright.

MARIA: How will you do it?

DUKE: I shall rely on simple groans.

MARIA: It might work, I suppose. Well, if we're going to do it, hadn't we better begin?

DUKE: You're right. Now where I wonder? The *mis-en-scène* is important. Here, do you think? (*Indicating chaise longue.*)

MARIA: Too comfortable. You said the floor.

DUKE: Oh, very well. (*He lowers himself to the floor at the foot of the chaise longue, first arranging a cushion which MARIA removes just before he lies down.*)

DUKE: Look here, whose side are you on?

MARIA: My own. I want this to work. Whoever heard of anyone collapsing on to a cushion?

DUKE: To me it seems a minimum requirement. However let it pass. (*He lies down.*)

MARIA: Are you ready for me to scream?

DUKE: Yes – no, wait. At the right moment I shall appear to recover a little and ask Richard to help me to bed. This will be your opportunity, Maria, to bring conviction to our plan by showing some practical solicitude for my welfare.

MARIA: What are you talking about?

DUKE: Well, for instance, I've forgotten my hot water bottle – you could offer to lend me yours.

MARIA: If I did they'd smell a rat immediately.

DUKE: Well, if you've got such a thing as a little Bengers Food in the house, some brought to me on a tray would not be unconvincing.

MARIA: I suppose you wouldn't like a band from London?

DUKE: And to ensure success you may find yourself having to wait on me a good deal.

MARIA: I knew from the beginning you'd get the better of this.

DUKE: Mrs Wislack, be good enough to call for Richard at once and remember I have undertaken the intelligent part.

MARIA: Ready now?

DUKE: Yes...no, one minute. (*He loosens his tie and disarranges his hair.*) It's the little touches that count, you know. Right.

MARIA: Richard, Richard.

(*HELEN comes in.*)

HELEN: Darling, what's the matter?

MARIA: George.

HELEN: He's been rude to you.

MARIA: (*Pointing to him.*) No. I'm wondering if he'll ever be rude to anyone again.

HELEN: George, darling. Whatever's happened? (*She kneels beside him. He groans and opens an eye.*)

DUKE: Kiss me, Hardy.

(*MARIA kicks him. He groans again.*)

MARIA: He must be delirious.

(*HELEN kisses him. RICHARD comes in.*)

RICHARD: Is something wrong?

MARIA: It's George. Poor darling, we were sitting here when suddenly he clutched his heart, screamed with pain and fell violently to the floor.

RICHARD: Good heavens!

HELEN: Richard, help him. I'm so worried.

RICHARD: Of course. I'll do whatever I can, Helen dear.

DUKE: Where am I?

MARIA: (*Irritably.*) I don't know.

DUKE: Mother. (*He groans; she slaps his face.*)

HELEN/RICHARD: Maria!!

MARIA: (*To others.*) Hysterical. (*To the DUKE.*) You're overdoing it.

DUKE: So are you. Where's my dear old friend Richard?

RICHARD: Here I am, old fellow.

DUKE: Take me to my bed. I feel I haven't long.

RICHARD: Oh, don't say that, old boy.

DUKE: Helen, Maria, forgive me.

(*RICHARD helps the DUKE out of the room.*)

HELEN: (*Anxiously.*) Is he terribly ill, do you think?

MARIA: Terribly. Nice little man, so courageous – I feel so upset.

HELEN: I shall go to him.

MARIA: (*Stopping her.*) Don't. Unless I'm very much mistaken he's persuading Richard at this moment to take his clothes off for him.

HELEN: I wish I hadn't been so horrid to him.

MARIA: He's forgiven you I'm sure. Nice little man, I misjudged him very much.

HELEN: Why doesn't Richard come back and tell me?

MARIA: I gather you still like him –

HELEN: Yes, I do. There's something about George you can't help liking, try as you will not to. Oh, why doesn't Richard come back?

MARIA: Patience, Helen dear.

HELEN: But I may be able to do something for him.

(*RICHARD returns.*)

Quickly – how is he?

RICHARD: Splendid!

MARIA: (*Angrily.*) Splendid. How can a man be suddenly splendid who collapsed in this room a minute ago as he did?

RICHARD: Too healthy I expect.

HELEN: What do you mean?

RICHARD: His pulse is normal, no temperature – he's –

HELEN: But shouldn't one of us go and fetch a doctor at once?

RICHARD: That's a good idea. I'll go and tell George at once.

MARIA: Oh, you unsympathetic, horrid man.

RICHARD: Not at all. I made a marvellous suggestion to him – I pointed out to him in the event of this being a long illness how much nicer your room would be than the one he was in.

MARIA: Did he agree?

RICHARD: He didn't say – but he is in your bed.

MARIA: I'm glad.

RICHARD: Oh, I nearly forgot – in the midst of some curious noises he was making, which I thought was singing and which he explained to me were groans – he asked me to send you to him at once.

MARIA: Why didn't you tell me that before?

RICHARD: I don't know – I was so upset to see old George looking so well I quite forgot it.

MARIA: I would never have believed that there could be anyone in the world so cruel and as unsympathetic as you are.

(*She quickly goes out.*)

RICHARD: Now's our chance.

HELEN: Will you explain to me what all this means?

RICHARD: George doesn't want to leave you tonight.

HELEN: He's only pretending to be ill?

RICHARD: And indifferently. Twice he had to put his head under the pillow to prevent me seeing him laughing. (*He walks to window, pulls curtains. It is snowing hard.*) In another hour nothing will be able to get away from here. (*He goes to the porch for a motor-coat.*)

HELEN: Maria told me the other day that she and her husband were once snowed up here for three weeks.

RICHARD: Let us pray this time it will be a month.

HELEN: Is it fair to take the car and leave them without a chance in the world of getting away from here?

RICHARD: Fair? It's the kindest thing that has ever been done for them. Such hell as a month alone here together will make them the nicest people in the world. (*He takes another coat down for HELEN.*)

HELEN: It's a cruel thing to do.

RICHARD: You mean you don't want to leave George?

HELEN: I don't, very much.

RICHARD: Do you love him?

HELEN: I think I do.

RICHARD: Then for heaven's sake do this for them; and then, I believe, I will be able to show you the two people we thought we liked. (*He puts the coat over her shoulder.*)

HELEN: But it may kill them both.

RICHARD: It will cure them both.

HELEN: I knew when it really came to it I should be weak.

RICHARD: I implore you to believe that I am right.

HELEN: In my heart I know you are.

RICHARD: Of course I am. (*He places a letter on the table.*) Thank Heaven I won't be here when she reads that. Ready? (*He crosses to the porch.*)

HELEN: Yes, I hate doing it but I know you're right. (*She follows him.*)

RICHARD: I know I am. (*He opens the porch door.*)

HELEN: (*Standing in the door.*) Poor darling George!

RICHARD: Poor sweet Maria,
    (*They leave, closing the door.*
    MARIA comes in expecting to find someone in the room.)

MARIA: (*Calling.*) Richard!
    (*There being no answer she goes to the kitchen door and calls again. Then she goes out for a moment and returns.*
    Motor horn off.
    She is moving to the window when she sees the letter on the table. She looks at the envelope, opens it, reads and screams. The DUKE comes in.)

DUKE: Has no one got the decency to come and see a dying man?
    (*MARIA waves him away, unable to speak.*)
    What's the matter?

MARIA: Read – read – read that.

DUKE: (*Taking the letter and reading.*) 'Maria and George – the snow is a foot deep – it will be deeper tomorrow – At heart you are both very nice people, but what you need is six months before the mast as common sailors – to suffer the degradations of the poor, and know the humiliations of their hardships – So that you may suffer

all these things, and more, Helen and I leave you alone –
we pray at least a month.'

(*He throws the letter down, runs to the outer door and opens
it. It is snowing harder. He stands in the door, looking at
something intently.*)

MARIA: Stop them. Stop them quickly. Oh, why don't you
stop them?

DUKE: Because I can't run forty miles an hour.

MARIA: Have they gone?

DUKE: (*Closing the door.*) Even the lights of their car have
disappeared.

(*MARIA screams.*)

Don't make that row. I'll never speak to either of them
again. (*He goes to the window.*)

MARIA: Nor shall I! If I have to stay alone in this house
with you I shall go mad.

DUKE: (*At the window.*) Look at it. Have you ever been
snowed up here before?

MARIA: Once, for three weeks.

DUKE: Oh, heavens! Will no one have mercy on us and
come and deliver us from each other?

MARIA: Nothing – nothing – will be able to get up that
hill.

DUKE: And you and I alone here – until – (*Pointing to
window.*) that stops.

MARIA: Yes.

(*The DUKE throws himself into an armchair. There is a pause.
They both gaze into space. Then MARIA moves to the door.*)
I – I shall go to bed until it does.

DUKE: Only the snow will want to come in. You need not
lock your door.

The End.

CANARIES SOMETIMES SING

Characters

GEOFFREY LYMES

ANNE LYMES

ERNEST MELTON

ELMA MELTON

Act I: The sitting-room in Geoffrey Lymes'
country house, near London.

Act II: The same. One month later.

Act III: The same. One second later.

AS TOM TITT SEES THEM:
Ronald Squire, Yvonne Arnaud, Mabel Sealby,
Athole Stewart.

Canaries Sometimes Sing was first performed at the Globe Theatre, London, on 21 October 1929, with the following cast:

GEOFFREY, Ronald Squire

ANNE, Mabel Selby

ERNEST, Athole Stewart

ELMA, Yvonne Arnaud

There are none of Lonsdale's customary nobility sitting around and waiting to be shot at in *Canaries Sometimes Sing,* but the author has found a new target – himself. Three or four years before the play was staged, Lonsdale declared:

> I write for money, and I should be telling damned lies if I said I didn't. The motive which makes an author sit down at his desk, dip his pen in the ink and write, is the desire for money, by which I mean a desire to winter in the South of France, or to buy a country house, or to hang pearl necklaces around somebody's neck. But when the motive has done its work – when, that is to say, it has locked his door and put the pen in his hand – it ceases to be of importance provided the man has any real stuff in him. He begins to write, and he no longer thinks of money. He is creating something, and the pleasures of creation are keener than any pleasures he can buy.

Geoffrey Lymes, the playwright in *Canaries*, says much the same, although the money he requires is not for the South of France, but to pay his wife's bills:

> ANNE: Yes, Augustus said at lunch what a pity it was you had sold yourself and only wrote for money!
> GEOFFREY: What does he write for, darling?
> ANNE: (*Smiling.*) Not for money, anyway.
> GEOFFREY: True! I read his last book, and I have never seen a man write so deliberately to stop the public reading that book than he did! And I don't believe it was intentional.

ANNE: Darling, are you right to be sarcastic about men like Augustus?

GEOFFREY: No, but they shouldn't say I write for money – I do, but they shouldn't say it!

ANNE: Darling, your plays are very amusing and all that, but they are for the moment only, aren't they? The end of your last play could have been more artistic, but you said, 'Not for you, there wouldn't be a bob in it!'

GEOFFREY: I'd just got your bills in for the lunches you had been giving for the fellows who are artistic.

ANNE: That's right. I knew money would come into it sooner or later!

GEOFFREY: Darling, only a joke!

Anne's pretentiousness is amusing, but there is usually in a Lonsdale play another woman who is witty yet down to earth, and who sorts out the silly chaps and their ladies. In *Canaries* it is Elma, a young actress, who sees through Geoffrey and exposes his insincerity and lack of genuine conviction:

ELMA: Do you know why you are a second-class playwright?

GEOFFREY: What do you mean?

ELMA: Because you are a second-class man. A plumber with a gift of dialogue. You neither have nor could furnish the world with an idea – you haven't the courage to have one.

Lonsdale's daughter, Frances Donaldson, said that the more her father's fame and reputation increased, the more restless, lonely and unhappy he became. I doubt, however, that he thought of himself as a second-class man, although he may have written Elma's lines about the second-class playwright with an ironic grin. Not long before, a reviewer had described Lonsdale as 'a second-class writer of tense situations and a first-rate writer of mirthful scenes.'

The plays in this volume were written by Lonsdale in the three acts and two intervals which were customary in the

1920s, and until well after the Second World War. Two intervals provided plenty of time for the scenery and the costumes to be changed, if required, and for the audiences to refresh themselves.

Acts II and III of *Canaries* are continuous in time, but the curtain still dropped in to provide a second interval. Today the fashion is more for a single interval, if possible, and it is not difficult to adjust Lonsdale to accommodate this. No damage will be done to his comedic intention.

For instance, Patrick Garland's revival of *Canaries* at the Albery Theatre in 1985 did not take a second interval, although the curtain was amusingly lowered for a token second. My production of *Aren't We All* went very well with just one interval. Everything is possible, so it comes down to a question of balancing all the factors involved.

Yvonne Arnaud in the original
Globe Theatre production

ACT ONE

A door in the sitting-room leads to the hall and the front of the house. Another door leads to the dining-room. There are French windows, but heavy curtains are drawn across them. There is a recessed window where the canary cage normally hangs, but the cage is now on a table, and GEOFFREY is feeding the canary. It is evening.

GEOFFREY: You're a naughty little feller that's what you are! And I have a very good mind not to give you your dinner! Why don't you ever laugh or sing? Eh? Why don't you? Perhaps you hate being in a cage? But we're all of us in a cage of some sort, little feller – and some of us are not alone in it! Good God, Percy, don't tell me the reason you never laugh or sing is because you are alone in it? You fool! Don't you realize how lucky you are – don't you know that I and millions of others would give nearly all we have in the world to change places with you! Ssh! In confidence! (*Whispering.*) Supposing you had someone in your cage like I have in mine – someone who bored you to death with her stupidities – every time she opened her mouth you nearly screamed – who does nothing that entitles you to divorce her – but who does a thousand things that entitle you to murder her! How would you like your cage furnished like this one is furnished – look at it – she'll tell you it's artistic! Look at the cloth on the piano – here – (*He rises, pulls the cloth off the piano and throws it into an oak chest.*) – that I won't stand any longer! (*He takes the two jazz cushions from the settee and also throws them into the chest.*) That's made you think a bit, hasn't it, Percy? You'd turn her out, you say! Getting them into your cage is as easy as getting them out is difficult; that's why only twenty thousand people get divorced a year! Supposing you had someone in there like that? Being a gentleman you would have to bear your mistake in silence – smile when you could strike – and to the world pretend a happiness that does not exist! If this were my case only, Percy, I would not speak, but I am telling you the story of countless thousands of men and women who smile in every other home but their own! Go on, don't be a fool, realize how lucky you are, and sing!

ANNE: (*Off.*) Is Mr Lymes at home, Morton?

MORTON: In the sitting-room, ma'am.

GEOFFREY: (*To the canary.*) Ssh! Here she is, back to my cage for the weekend. Listen to her when she comes in – then if you think I have exaggerated – been unnecessarily cynical – and you still want a mate – well, I'll hate doing it – but I'll buy you one!

ANNE: (*Off.*) Geoffrey!

GEOFFREY: In here, darling!

(*ANNE enters carrying some books and a packet of various letters.*)

Ah, my love, how are you?

ANNE: (*Putting up her cheek to be kissed.*) So tired, so terribly tired.

GEOFFREY: I was afraid you would be, darling!

ANNE: And so unhappy that little husband isn't pleased to see his wife!

GEOFFREY: What makes you say that?

ANNE: Because he didn't come to meet poor little wife in the car, and let her come all the way from the station alone in a nasty taxi!

GEOFFREY: You didn't let me know what train you were coming by!

ANNE: When we were first married you liked little wife so much you met all the trains!

GEOFFREY: True! True! Tell me, you've had a busy week, eh?

ANNE: (*Placing books on the piano, she sits and opens letters.*) Terrible! I've never stopped a minute! And I have such an awful week in front of me! Do you know, poor little woman has discovered she is on the committee of three charity matinées!

GEOFFREY: Why be on three?

ANNE: They insist! Even when I refuse they put poor Anne's name on the committee!

GEOFFREY: Ghastly for you!

ANNE: Three luncheon parties in my own house! Four dinner parties; and last night, tired out, they took me on to night club after night club – poor little wifey didn't get home until nearly four!

GEOFFREY: Little husband was in bed at ten!

ANNE: Little husband a very lazy man to live in the country as he does; he should come to London and help his little Anne!

GEOFFREY: You move in too high circles for me, Anne dear! I must say I feel a slight reflected glory when I read in the papers that Mrs Geoffrey Lymes, wife of the well-known playwright, was amongst the Duchess of Bristol's party at the – wherever it was!

ANNE: (*Her manner changes.*) What paper did you see that in?

GEOFFREY: I don't remember for the moment!

ANNE: It's too disgraceful – those beastly press-cutting people I belong to never send me anything; can't you remember what paper it was in?

GEOFFREY: I'm afraid I've forgotten!

ANNE: I'll write to them tonight! Brutes!

GEOFFREY: Tell me, have you discovered any new geniuses this week amongst your literary friends?

ANNE: No! (*Pausing; speaking indifferently.*) Letts lunched with me on Tuesday.

GEOFFREY: Letts? My word, that's a conquest, if you like – that's putting it across your friends with a vengeance!

ANNE: In what way? I don't understand?

GEOFFREY: The world's great writer – who never is seen in public, who hates photography almost as much as the photographer hates him. I call that a terrific triumph! How did you get him, Anne?

ANNE: How do you mean, how did I get him? I wrote and asked him if he would lunch with me.

GEOFFREY: How many times?

ANNE: Once, of course!

GEOFFREY: Well, that's marvellous! I was told he never even answers the first five invitations! He must have seen some of my plays and said to himself, 'A clever fellow like that must obviously have married an interesting woman! I'll go to lunch!'

ANNE: I don't think he even knew I was married to you. And when they were talking about you at lunch, he asked what plays you had written!

GEOFFREY: Crushed, b'God! Who did you ask to meet him?

ANNE: Lindsay Steele, John Hale, Augustus Gold.

GEOFFREY: My word, there's a gathering of literary celebrities for you. I wish I were a Highbrow. It's very sad!

ANNE: Yes, Augustus said at lunch what a pity it was you had sold yourself and only wrote for money!

GEOFFREY: What does he write for, darling?

ANNE: Not for money, anyway! (*He smiles.*)

GEOFFREY: True! I read his last book, and I have never seen a man write so deliberately to stop the public reading that book than he did! And I don't believe it was intentional.

ANNE: Darling, are you right to be sarcastic about men like Augustus?

GEOFFREY: No, but they shouldn't say I write for money – I do, but they shouldn't say it!

ANNE: Darling, your plays are very amusing and all that, but they are for the moment only, aren't they? The end of your last play could have been more artistic, but you said, 'Not for you, there wouldn't be a bob in it!'

GEOFFREY: I'd just got your bills in for the lunches you had been giving for the fellows who are artistic.

ANNE: (*Angrily.*) That's right – I knew money would come into it sooner or later!

GEOFFREY: Darling, only a joke!

ANNE: Joke? You meant it; every time I come down here, it's money – money – money – I'm sick of it!

GEOFFREY: Well, you are extravagant, aren't you?

ANNE: That's right, go on – tell me what the Income Tax is!

GEOFFREY: For Augustus – threepence!

ANNE: Doesn't posterity mean something?

GEOFFREY: Undertakers believe in it!

ANNE: I'm sick of it – I travel down on a beastly train every weekend to see you, only to be told how much money I spend, how –

GEOFFREY: And to tell me how badly I write!

ANNE: Well, everybody knows that!

GEOFFREY: Darling, I do wish you would remember to talk in your baby language; it means the same, I know, but it sounds so much less arrogant!

ANNE: I'm tired – tired to death of it all! (*Rising.*) I shall have my dinner in bed!

GEOFFREY: I'm sorry, I'm afraid you can't do that. My old friend Ernest Melton, whom I hadn't seen for years, and his wife are here for the weekend; they are dressing now.

ANNE: Why should I have to sit up and listen to those bores?

GEOFFREY: How do you know they are bores? – You've never met them, I haven't met his wife myself – I was out when they arrived!

ANNE: If they're friends of yours, they must be bores.

GEOFFREY: I daresay you are right! But he has one attribute that might appeal to you!

ANNE: I doubt it!

GEOFFREY: He'll be a duke one day.

ANNE: I don't care if he will be two dukes.
(*Moving up to door as ERNEST enters.*)

GEOFFREY: Ah, my dear Ernest! You've never met Anne, have you?

ERNEST: No, but I've been looking forward to it so much. (*Putting out his hand.*) It's charming of you to have us for the weekend.

ANNE: (*Her manner changes: she is charming and agreeable.*) I'm delighted – I tried so hard to get down early so as to be here when you arrived, but I –

ERNEST: Please! Please!

ANNE: They have given you a comfortable room?

ERNEST: Charming, thank you so much.

ANNE: Geoffrey dear, give Mr Melton a cocktail.

GEOFFREY: (*Taking one off the table.*) Waiting for you, old friend.

ERNEST: Thanks! Geoffrey has told you we are very old friends?

ANNE: Indeed he has! You were at Eton and Oxford together, weren't you?

ERNEST: By Jove, it seems remarkable that although we were inseparable both at Eton and Oxford, we have not seen each other for years!

GEOFFREY: A lot has happened in those years, Ernest, my boy!

ERNEST: We have both married.

GEOFFREY: We have!

ERNEST: And you have made a great success of life!

GEOFFREY: I wouldn't say a great success, I –

ERNEST: Nonsense. What is it like to be married to a literary swell like Geoffrey, Mrs Lymes?

GEOFFREY: What is it like, darling?

ANNE: One is very proud of him, Mr Melton.

ERNEST: I'm sure you are! When I was abroad and I read of Geoffrey in the papers, I used to boast that he was my greatest friend. The number of people who wanted to know him was quite flattering to me.

GEOFFREY: I hope you are staying with us for some time Ernest?

ERNEST: (*Laughing.*) Just the same feller. Not altered a bit, I congratulate you on having married the best fellow in the world, Mrs Lymes.

(*ANNE and GEOFFREY blow kisses to each other.*)

GEOFFREY: She knows it, old friend, don't you, darling?

ERNEST: I'm sure she does. What a jolly canary!

ANNE: Geoffrey, you naughty man, what is it doing on the table?

GEOFFREY: I've been trying to persuade the stupid ass that he has more to sing about than most people. Oh, I'm so sorry, Anne, but this telegram came for you just before you arrived.

(*He picks up a telegram.*)

ANNE: (*Taking the telegram and opening it.*) Oh, this is wonderful – but I'm afraid it means the poor darling can't get here until nearly nine. Do you mind very much dining as late as that?

ERNEST: Not in the least.

GEOFFREY: Who's coming, darling?

ANNE: Russiloff!
Ring the – no, I'll tell them as I go out! (*To ERNEST.*) Do ask your wife to be an angel and not mind.

ERNEST: Of course she won't.

ANNE: (*Smiling at him.*) Au revoir. Do ask for anything you want, won't you?
(*ERNEST opens the door for ANNE.*)

ERNEST: I will, indeed!
(*ANNE exits.*)
Charming, Geoffrey, charming!

GEOFFREY: She can be the most charming woman in the world, Ernest.

ERNEST: I'm delighted my old friend has been so wise and so lucky in his choice.

GEOFFREY: I don't believe I deserve it.

ERNEST: I differ. But it doesn't always follow that people get what they deserve.

GEOFFREY: If I have got what I deserve, I can think of nothing that I have ever done that deserves my getting it.

ERNEST: Frankly, I was a little nervous of meeting her; one reads in the papers of all the great people she entertains, and of course everyone has told me how clever she is.

GEOFFREY: Brilliant! But you needn't have been the least nervous: she hides it even more brilliantly.

ERNEST: Like all really clever people. She's charming! Forgive my ignorance Geoffrey, but who is Russiloff?

GEOFFREY: Not a notion! But you can take it from me he's a genius.

ERNEST: Really?

GEOFFREY: Anne is a perfect demon at discovering them; a genius has only to pop his head out of the window, and Anne has got him to lunch the next day.

ERNEST: Really? Really? You must find meeting them very helpful to you in your work?

GEOFFREY: Ernest, I don't! You see, I only write for money, and Anne's friends only write for art. I don't believe two per cent of them would know a pound note from a ten-shilling one. They are above such things.

ERNEST: Really?

GEOFFREY: In fact, in the circle in which Anne lives, to reach more than a hundred people signifies failure.

ERNEST: Really? How interesting.

GEOFFREY: Your wife is artistic, too, Ernest?

ERNEST: No, Geoffrey, she isn't!

GEOFFREY: (*To the canary.*) Listen; you might hear something. (*To ERNEST.*) She's a sports girl, eh?

ERNEST: No, Geoffrey, she isn't.

GEOFFREY: (*Nodding at cage.*) But you are very happy, old friend?

ERNEST: I am happy, Geoffrey.

GEOFFREY: (*Making a grimace at the canary.*) I'm glad.

ERNEST: It is very un-English, I know, and against all the teachings of Eton and Oxford to discuss one's wife in other than a favourable way –

GEOFFREY: I imagine the only exception both those institutions would make would be an old friend.

ERNEST: I feel that myself. And if your married life was, shall we say, not quite what you hoped it would be, you would confide in me?

GEOFFREY: I should consider it my duty to, Ernest (*He winks at the canary.*)

ERNEST: I agree. It's a long story!

GEOFFREY: Not in the way I hope you will tell it, old friend!

(*He moves the canary nearer.*)

ERNEST: Why do you keep moving that bird?

GEOFFREY: I'm always hoping that something might make him sing! Sorry. Go on, Ernest!

ERNEST: Very well. To begin. When we left Oxford, conditions, you remember, separated us. You to your work, and I to carry on the traditions of an English gentleman. Hating it, I shot! Fearing it, I hunted! Bored, I raced! But always conscious I was doing the right thing.

GEOFFREY: I'm sure.

ERNEST: Then to complete my education, I acquired the Bohemian spirit.

GEOFFREY: What does that mean?

ERNEST: You know! Taking a lady of the streets to dine at an hotel where your relations were dining. One was always expected to do something next!

GEOFFREY: Naturally!

ERNEST: Buying two front stalls for the entire run of a musical play.

GEOFFREY: You didn't use them?

ERNEST: I was always late. And then after the play, the fun of going around to the actresses' dressing-rooms and calling them by their Christian names.

GEOFFREY: What a fool I am. I never thought of doing that!

ERNEST: And it was in one of those rooms I met Elma.

GEOFFREY: Good!

ERNEST: I was fascinated by her; entirely unlike the women of my own class, she was gay – she was jolly! I took her to supper – I told her some of the things I had done in my life. How amused she was!

GEOFFREY: That I'm sure of!

ERNEST: And then – I drove her home in a taxi!

GEOFFREY: Now then!

ERNEST: On my honour, not meaning anything – with no ulterior motive – just carrying on the traditions of an English gentleman, as it were – I was fresh!

GEOFFREY: Good!

ERNEST: In a flash I knew I had made a mistake. Removing my arms, we drove in silence. I was conscious that whatever I said would be wrong! It was the longest drive I ever remember. She lived at a place called Streatham; I think it is somewhere near Eastbourne.

GEOFFREY: That's right.

ERNEST: Reaching her house, she got out, I jumped after her – it was obvious she had been crying – without saying good night or anything, she banged the door in my face! And then I started my long drive back!

GEOFFREY: Go on!

ERNEST: I realized what I had done – I had hurt a woman – good as our education is, Geoffrey, it is faulty. I remember my father telling me, 'Have fun with the girls, Ernest, my boy, but always play the game.' How the hell you can do both has always defeated me. I wish he had lived. I would have liked to have asked him what he meant!

GEOFFREY: He meant, never interfere in a woman's life, unless you are a great friend of her husband's.

ERNEST: Possibly! The next morning I wrote her a generous apology and some flowers! That night I was in my seat as the curtain rose – but never once did she look – I sent a message to ask her to speak to me – (*He shakes his head.*) – she was sorry, she was engaged. In despair, I rushed to the room of the leading man, who was famous for persuading young chorus-girls to go out to supper with old men of old families – he failed! He told me in confidence it was one of the first failures he had ever been connected with! He even went as far as to say it put his knighthood back two years. The next morning at eight o'clock I took my courage in both hands and went to Streatham.

GEOFFREY: Good!

ERNEST: I asked to see her – the maid returned and said she was sorry but she was out. I waited an hour – to be told she had been in all the time. Where do you think she was?

GEOFFREY: Where?

ERNEST: In the garden, gardening!

GEOFFREY: No!

ERNEST: Yes! With my own eyes I saw her. Geoffrey, who would have expected to find a chorus-girl gardening at nine in the morning?

GEOFFREY: Only another chorus-girl!

ERNEST: After a long time she forgave me. And nightly I drove her home to Streatham. Have you ever driven a beautiful but good woman home to Streatham with any frequency, Geoffrey?

GEOFFREY: No.

ERNEST: Then you don't know what suffering is. All the forces that Nature possesses are at work against you! A beautiful face, a divine figure, sweet-smelling scent.

A combination of things that even in the darkness show you clearly your slippers by the fireside; above the rattle of the taxi, the noise of the buses, you hear distinctly the patter of little feet; and although your mind and your imagination are working at their best, your arms remain paralysed, conscious that they are in the presence of a good woman.

GEOFFREY: My dear fellow!

ERNEST: Each night I determined to triumph over nature – to fight and conquer her – be just a friend – but each night I failed – so like millions and millions of men before me – I accepted the philosophy that although you cannot control the thoughts that come into your mind – you can at all events legalize them!

GEOFFREY: And she accepted you?

ERNEST: Yes. Conscious of the difference in our social position, she insisted that in the event of my family wishing the marriage to be postponed for six months or a year, I would agree.

GEOFFREY: Charming of her.

ERNEST: So to my father, who had regularly told me for twenty-five years that 'Whenever you are in trouble, my boy, come to your old father', I went. Before I was half-way through the story he called me a bloody fool and my fiancée a whore – with the result we were married in a fortnight.

GEOFFREY: (*Nodding his head.*) Quite! Quite!

ERNEST: But I defy you to show me any man who was happier than I during the first six months of our marriage!

GEOFFREY: (*To the canary.*) That's a long time!

ERNEST: It was perfect! Then for some inexplicable reason it all seemed to change. Our first serious quarrel was about the life of a bee!

GEOFFREY: Why?

ERNEST: I was listening to it on the wireless – determined to be master in my own house, I refused to take it off! Geoffrey, although there were some Americans in the last play she was in, nothing excuses the reflection she passed on my mother through me that night!

GEOFFREY: (*Smiling.*) She didn't mean it literally, old friend!

ERNEST: That's what she said – nevertheless, it was inexcusable! Soon I discovered she was without social ambition!

GEOFFREY: And she was on the stage? That's odd!

ERNEST: One night I introduced her to a cousin of mine, the Duchess of Bristol, and I admit her manner to Elma was a little haughty – but can anything excuse Elma saying to her, 'Do come nearer, I don't smell nearly so bad close?'

GEOFFREY: (*Delighted.*) She didn't!

ERNEST: I tell you she did!

GEOFFREY: Well, well, well!

ERNEST: Her simplicity of nature, her inability not to speak her thoughts aloud, ruined my career finally in the Army!

GEOFFREY: No! How?

ERNEST: I asked a distinguished General, whose influence might have been invaluable to me, to dine with us.
I consider it was her duty to listen to his long stories – think of my horror when she stopped him in the middle of one of his longest and said, 'General, as it is very evident there will not be another war in your lifetime, wouldn't it be more patriotic of you to leave the Army and join the chestnut trade!'

GEOFFREY: (*Delighted.*) She didn't – no – you're making it up!

ERNEST: I tell you I'm not!

GEOFFREY: What happened?

ERNEST: With soldierly fortitude, he controlled his angry blood from rising farther than his neck. (*Pause.*) Three weeks afterwards, without my regiment, I was ordered to China.

GEOFFREY: I see!

ERNEST: And there it was the same – men of importance who could discuss the old days of the Army and Navy bored her – she was intolerant of convention; ultimately our only friend was the manager of a provision store – her excuse was he made her laugh!

GEOFFREY: A provision store? In what odd places one finds rare things!

ERNEST: Dissatisfied – a man with no future – I sent in my papers and returned to England. But to what, Geoffrey?

GEOFFREY: What do you mean, old friend, I don't quite understand?

ERNEST: What is our life to be? Who are our friends to be?

GEOFFREY: Well, that's up to you, surely?

ERNEST: Up to me? I, who love edifying conversation, who would like to find at my table men of distinction, poets, writers, men with a breadth of vision – the dismissal of pettiness – narrowness – the –

GEOFFREY: Are you expecting to find these qualities amongst writers?

ERNEST: Certainly!

GEOFFREY: I see! I see! Well, if the food and the listening are good you'll have no difficulty in getting them!

ERNEST: But do you suppose if Elma didn't understand, or agree with what they were saying, she would keep quiet? No, Geoffrey, they would never come again!

GEOFFREY: I must say I am longing to meet your wife, Ernest!

ERNEST: Ah, she has a heart of gold, and all that is wrong with our marriage is, we have not the same tastes. Without the least reflection against Elma, I wish she were like your wife, Geoff!

GEOFFREY: (*To the canary.*) Cracked! (*To ERNEST.*) Feeling as you do, old friend, perhaps your lawyer could –

ERNEST: Geoff! I belong to the old school who believe that having made your bed, you must lie in it, with the woman for whom you made it.

GEOFFREY: Times have changed since you made that bed, old friend.

ERNEST: Not for me. Besides, if Elma had the least suspicion I was not completely happy, it would break her heart.

GEOFFREY: That makes it difficult!

ERNEST: No! I must train myself to like managers of provision stores and such like! I am hoping very much she will like you, Geoff!

GEOFFREY: I have a feeling I shall like her, Ernest.
(*ELMA enters.*
GEOFFREY rises to meet ELMA.)

ERNEST: Darling, this is my dear friend Geoff, whom I have talked to you about so often.

GEOFFREY: I can't tell you how delighted I am to meet you!

ELMA: (*Smiling.*) Thank you so much!

GEOFFREY: Where would you like to sit?

ELMA: Here, if I may.

ERNEST: We have just been talking about the old days, darling!

ELMA: I knew you had, Ernest! You were at Harrow and Cambridge with Ernest, weren't you?
(*GEOFFREY laughs.*)

ERNEST: Really, darling – if I have told you once, I have told you a thousand times – Eton and Oxford.

ELMA: I'm sorry, I'd forgotten, but I know it was some of those places!
(*GEOFFREY is very amused, and gathers she is having fun with ERNEST, who is quite unaware of it.*)

ERNEST: (*Almost indignantly.*) Some of those places! Really, Elma!

ELMA: Ernest dear, don't be such a snob about your schools; I went to a University at Streatham, but if people forget and call it Putney, I don't get excited!

ERNEST: Hardly the same, darling; is it, Geoff?

GEOFFREY: The results seem excellent in your wife's case. A cocktail, Mrs Melton?

ELMA: May I, Ernest?

ERNEST: If you would like one, dear!

ELMA: You know I would like one, but may I have one, darling?

GEOFFREY: Are they bad for your health? (*Giving her a cocktail.*)

ELMA: No, good for it! But they make me a little bright sometimes, and when I get bright, Ernest gets worried!

ERNEST: Really, darling, Geoff will think I beat you!

ELMA: Oh, no, he won't. (*To GEOFFREY.*) He's divine to me!

GEOFFREY: Of course!

ELMA: I love my little Ernest!

(*ERNEST laughs nervously.*)

Have I said the wrong thing, darling?

ERNEST: No, darling – but perhaps it's a little embarrassing for Geoffrey.

GEOFFREY: The reverse – I find it most attractive!

ERNEST: What a charming room, Geoff!

GEOFFREY: I'm glad you like it!

ERNEST: Charming taste, don't you think, darling ?

ELMA: I think it's wonderful!

ERNEST: Your wife is responsible for it, Geoffrey; it's no good – I know it.

GEOFFREY: My wife is entirely responsible for it, Ernest.

ERNEST: You will like her so much, dear!

ELMA: Yes, dear – I – I – only hope she will like me!

ERNEST: Of course she will! I'm hoping very much that you will be the greatest of friends – don't you, Geoff?

GEOFFREY: I can think of nothing I should like so much!

ANNE: (*Off.*) Geoffrey! Geoffrey!

(*ANNE enters. She almost rushes into the room. Her brightness and forced gaiety is nearly offensive.*)

Here you all are! I'm so sorry, so terribly sorry? (*Putting out her hand to ELMA.*) How do you do? So sweet of you both to come for the weekend. I've been looking forward to meeting you so much!

ERNEST: So have we – haven't we, darling?

ELMA: We've – we've talked of nothing else!

ANNE: Sweet! Has that wicked Geoffrey given you a cocktail?

GEOFFREY: Yes, darling!

ANNE: (*To ELMA.*) Do tell me you're not angry with me for having another guest who's making dinner a half an hour late?

ELMA: No!

ANNE: Horrid, careless man, hasn't a notion of the ordinary ways of society, probably go fast asleep in the train and never arrive at all!

ERNEST: I say, what fun to be like that. (*To ELMA.*) Don't you think so, darling?

ELMA: (*Obviously fails to see any humour.*) Yes, dear!

ERNEST: I was just saying, as you came in, in what perfect taste you have decorated this room!

ANNE: Laffinson did it. (*Turning to ELMA.*) You know his work?

(*ELMA looks blankly at her. ANNE turns to ERNEST.*)

ERNEST: Laffinson? I know his name, of course, but –

ANNE: Quite mad; if you didn't pander to the brute, quite capable of leaving you with the room half finished!
(*Crossing to the piano.*) Geoffrey, where's the rug for the piano?

GEOFFREY: Oh, I – I spilt some ink on it, and I sent it to the cleaners!

ANNE: And the cushions?

GEOFFREY: I sent them too.

(*ANNE pats him: he tries not to be irritable.*)

ANNE: How brutal! You're a naughty, naughty man! And to punish you, the moment it comes back, you'll find your little wife will take it to her house in London!

GEOFFREY: I'll ask the cleaners to send it to you direct!

ANNE: Nonsense! I – I wouldn't dream of taking it from my sweet little man! Of course, dear Mrs Melton, you were on the stage, weren't you?

ELMA: I was!

ANNE: How thrilling! Do tell me about it! I've always longed to hear what goes on in the theatre!

GEOFFREY: Anne dear, Mrs Melton left the stage some time ago, and I don't suppose –

ANNE: Be quiet, Geoffrey; I must know what goes on in the theatre! You don't mind telling me, do you, Mrs Melton?

ELMA: Not at all! What is it you actually want to know?

ERNEST: (*In a pacifying manner.*) You know, dear –

ELMA: I don't know, or I wouldn't have asked I –

ANNE: Everything! Did you play a part?

ELMA: I married my little Ernest!

ANNE: How thrilling! I must know all the terrible things that happen in a musical play. Do tell me!

ELMA: Well, you've got to be at the theatre half an hour before the play begins; you've got to stay there until it's over – and on Wednesdays and Saturdays you have to do it twice!

ANNE: Oh! Is that all? How disappointing! Is that really all?

ELMA: Occasionally a man comes round and offers a suggestion that would make it impossible for you to know his wife – but after all, that happens everywhere, doesn't it?

ANNE: (*Laughing.*) How sweet! I must tell Augustus that – he'll simply adore it! (*To ELMA.*) You like Augustus Gold's books?

(*ELMA has obviously never heard of him.*
ANNE looks inquiringly at ERNEST.)

You do?

ERNEST: Oh, indeed I do, indeed I do! (*To ELMA, excitedly.*) You know, darling, I gave you one of his books two days ago – 'Marigold'!

ANNE: (*To ELMA.*) Didn't you simply love it, Mrs Melton?

ELMA: (*Shaking her head.*) No!

ERNEST: (*Anxiously.*) But, darling, surely you –

ANNE: (*Laughing almost contemptuously.*) But how amusing – do tell us in your own way what you thought of it!

ELMA: I thought it the most awful muck that has ever been printed!

ANNE: Awful what?

GEOFFREY: Muck!

ANNE: (*Laughing in a forced manner.*) How terribly interesting! Poor Augustus! One of our greatest writers! Perhaps you didn't understand it, Mrs Melton?

ELMA: Perhaps that is what it was!

ANNE: I'm sure that is what it was! It is a passionate plea for the freedom of women, a demand that they should be free people in mind and body – it's the modern school, Mrs Melton!

ELMA: I wouldn't call it modern – nearly every nice old gentleman who drove me home in a taxi ten years ago tried to tell me about it!

GEOFFREY: I say, that's – (*He laughs – he appears to be unable to stop himself.*)

ANNE: You have amused Geoffrey, anyway, Mrs Melton. Oh, do stop, Geoffrey!

GEOFFREY: Sorry!

ERNEST: (*Who has been nervously trying to interrupt all the time.*) Anyway, I hope Geoff will make us laugh on Wednesday night; we've got seats for your play, old feller!

GEOFFREY: Good.

ELMA: And I am looking forward to it – everyone tells me it's splendid!

GEOFFREY: Yes, it is!

ERNEST: (*To ANNE.*) You like it very much, I'm sure, Mrs Lymes?

ANNE: Terribly! It's awfully good! (*She sighs.*) Oh, dear! I do wish Geoffrey would open the window sometimes.

ERNEST: (*Quickly.*) Oh, allow me – (*He starts to walk to the window.*)

GEOFFREY: Not that window, old friend!

ERNEST: Sorry! (*Turning back.*) Which one?

GEOFFREY: A spiritual window. Anne means opening the window that lets in great thoughts, helpful tit-bits, etc.

ERNEST: Oh, sorry! I thought for the moment –

(*ELMA laughs, though she makes every endeavour not to.*)

(*Angrily.*) Please stop laughing Elma – what is there funny about it?

ELMA. Sorry, darling!

(*GEOFFREY starts to laugh.*)

ANNE: (*Frigidly.*) Stop, Geoffrey! (*To ERNEST.*) You must bring your wife to stay with us often; she evidently makes Geoffrey laugh, and it is so good for him.

GEOFFREY: Sorry!

(*There is a pause.*)

Another cocktail, Ernest?

ERNEST: (*Angrily.*) Not for me, thank you!

GEOFFREY: (*To ELMA.*) You?

ELMA: No, thank you. –

GEOFFREY: Darling? (*To ANNE.*)

ANNE: (*Snapping.*) No!

GEOFFREY: Even if your friend is punctual, darling, he can't be here for another twenty minutes. Must we really wait for him?

ANNE: I have put dinner back half an hour! You don't mind, do you, Mrs Melton?

ELMA: Not in the least!

ERNEST: Frankly, I prefer dining late!

ANNE: What a charming guest! I'm so glad that you're fond of reading.

ERNEST: I almost prefer it to anything!

ANNE: That's delightful! I have quite a unique collection of books in my London house, and when you come to lunch with me one day I must show them to you.

ERNEST: I should like that more than I can tell you!

GEOFFREY: You haven't an altogether bad collection here, Anne darling!

ANNE: It's nothing like – but it is really a very attractive room. I think you would like it. Do come. I'll show it to you!

ERNEST: I'd like that very much.

ANNE: It would bore you to look at books, wouldn't it, Mrs Melton? No, you stay here and make Geoffrey laugh.

(*ANNE and ERNEST leave the room.*
Pause.)

ELMA: Would you do something for me?

GEOFFREY: Anything in the world!

ELMA: Go and send me a telegram saying my mother is dying and I must come home at once!

GEOFFREY: (*Laughing.*) Why?

ELMA: I'm miserable – I've made such a mess of it again!

GEOFFREY: Nonsense!

ELMA: I have – your wife can't bear me – Ernest is miserable –

GEOFFREY: Don't talk such rubbish!

ELMA: It's all Ernest's fault – he is always so certain that I'm going to do the wrong thing, that I get so nervous I do it! I'll catch it tonight when I go to bed!

GEOFFREY: What for, in Heaven's name?

ELMA: 'Why did you say you didn't like 'Marigold'? – why didn't you tell them some amusing things about the theatre? – why did you laugh and make me look a fool?' Why didn't I do this – why didn't I do that – oh, why haven't I the courage to just stay at home and grow fat?

GEOFFREY: (*Laughing.*) I hope you will do nothing of the sort – I hope you will come here often!

ELMA: (*Shaking her head.*) He's so stupid – he'd love to go away and visit his friends alone and be a pompous boy – but nothing will make him! It's the old story, I suppose, of married life!

GEOFFREY: In what way?

ELMA: If he went without me, he'd he miserable all the time because he would think he'd treated me badly – and people might say we are not getting on – so he makes me come with him – then I ruin the party! So either way he catches it, poor darling!

GEOFFREY: I know!

ELMA: I'm not sure married life isn't worse for men than it is for women – after all, an unhappy married woman can go to bed with a couple of boiled eggs and a detective story – and have a grand time – but a man can't, so he won't believe it!

GEOFFREY: There's a good deal in that!

ELMA: Oh, if they would stop bothering about making divorce easy – but marriage so difficult – what a happy place this world would be!

GEOFFREY: How do you suggest that could be done?

ELMA: I don't know. All I know is you go to a judge for a certificate when the damage is done, instead of having to go before him and convince him that there is a reasonable chance of happiness before it begins!

GEOFFREY: For example? What would have happened in your case?

ELMA: The judge would have said – 'Young woman, you are suffering like thousands of women before you from the glamour of an engagement – a not too attractive home – a modest fear that no other man will ask you! Certificate not granted – come back in a year's time!'

GEOFFREY: Then in the greatest indignation you would live together?

ELMA: Well, you do that if you marry, don't you?

GEOFFREY: Yes, but –

ELMA: And if it's a failure, you go on living like that!

GEOFFREY: Quite so! Then I take it if the first man is wrong you go on to another!

ELMA: Perhaps a third! Why not? Nobody says anything if a woman loses two of her husbands and marries a third! They call her a good old sport, and God bless her!

GEOFFREY: But there are the children to be considered!

ELMA: Isn't it wonderful how these little ones always come to our aid in our final hypocrisy?

GEOFFREY: True! True!

ELMA: Well, it's all very difficult. Anyway, in my case I know it's a failure – darling that he is, Ernest has never really left Eton and Oxford – at heart, though he says he doesn't, he loves his old pompous relatives – it irritates him to death that they don't like me – and irritates him more when they patronize me – so the poor darling hasn't one minute's peace of mind! It was very wrong of me! I oughtn't to have married the feller –

GEOFFREY: I think you're being very modest again!

ELMA: Not at all! He should have married some nice woman who, hating it, would have sat for hours on an uncomfortable shooting-stick watching him shoot – who would have loved giving little dinner-parties to dull people – who would have an engagement book full up to the brim a fortnight ahead – he would adore that – but as I can't do that for him, it's my duty to look for a nice suitable woman who can.

GEOFFREY: And when you have found her?

ELMA: I shall leave him, of course!

GEOFFREY: I applaud your unusual consideration! But I'm afraid you'll fail to accomplish it.

ELMA: Why?

GEOFFREY: Even if he wanted to, and I'm sure he doesn't, Ernest is the type that 'having once made your bed you must lie on it!'

ELMA: Nonsense! In six mouths I would be merely an incident of his youthful impulse!

GEOFFREY: In less than six months I hope he'd realize what a fool he was to let you go!

ELMA: Thank you!

GEOFFREY: I mean it.

ELMA: Anyway, even if you're right, and I don't think that you are – only experience would ever make Ernest realize it!

GEOFFREY: If he ever leaves you, I hope he'll marry some woman who makes his life such hell he'll come back to you on his knees asking to be taken back!

ELMA: (*Smiling.*) What fun that would be! I'd give anything to see Ernest on his knees asking to be taken back. Six months with a woman that he wishes so much I was like, might make a really nice man of Ernest!

GEOFFREY: Would you take him back?

ELMA: If he were very sad and miserable – I'm such a fat, easy-going lump – I don't know. Would you ever marry again?

GEOFFERY: I? Do you know, I have never thought about it – but now that I do, I don't believe I would. There may be another woman like Anne in the world, but I am not prepared to risk it!

ELMA: You must be great fun if one ever got to know you better!

GEOFFREY: I don't know about the fun – but I hope you'll know me better.

ELMA: I'm going to do my best!

(*ERNEST enters.*)

ERNEST: Geoff, old feller! (*He laughs.*) I wouldn't be you for a good deal!

GEOFFREY: (*Smiling.*) Be fair, Ernest, give Anne a chance, you've only been with her five minutes!

ERNEST: You know that I didn't mean that!

GEOFFREY: I'm glad.

ERNEST: (*Laughing.*) Stupid old ass! What I was going to tell you was, you have been lending a lot of your wife's books!

GEOFFREY: By Jove, so I have! What bad luck – she only goes into her library once a year!

ERNEST: And she's waiting to tell you what she thinks about it!

GEOFFREY: (*With meaning.*) I know!

ERNEST: Oh, by the way, darling, Anne – (*He laughs.*) – your wife has insisted on my calling her 'Anne', Geoff!

GEOFFREY: Good! Now I can call your wife Elma!

ELMA: Do, Geoffrey!

GEOFFREY: You were saying something!

ERNEST: Oh – she has asked us to lunch on Wednesday to meet – I have forgotten his name for the moment – some great Russian writer!

GEOFFREY: You're lucky! The only times I have been asked, they all spoke English! Anyway, I am not nearly so concerned about lunch on Wednesday as I am about dinner tonight. (*To ERNEST.*) You're a rotten guest; if you said honestly, 'Yes, I am hungry,' we wouldn't have to wait for this feller!

ERNEST: What does it matter, waiting a few minutes?

ANNE: (*Off.*) Geoffrey!

GEOFFREY: Charming voice, isn't it?

(GEOFFREY leaves the room.)

ERNEST *(Delighted.)* You like Geoff, dear?

ELMA: He's a pet. Terribly!

ERNEST: I knew you would. I'm so glad! I must say I'm liking being here most awfully!

ELMA: Has he always had a sweet nature like that?

ERNEST: Yes, of course – why? Are you surprised?

ELMA: I thought, through being married to her, he might have acquired it!

ERNEST: I don't understand.

ELMA: Well, you know – like grief – sometimes it makes the most horrid people kinder and pleasant!

ERNEST: I still don't understand!

ELMA: Her! Have you ever met a more awful poseur in your life than that woman?

ERNEST: Are you speaking of Geoffrey's wife?

ELMA: Oh, be friendly Ernest, don't always be such a blasted gentleman. I'm not going to shout it about! Anyway, you should know now what a nice wife you have got!

ERNEST: I don't agree with you at all. I think she is one of the most charming women I have met for years!

ELMA: You're not serious?

ERNEST: Certainly I am. She's so amusing, so well read – so clever –

ELMA: Only because you are not, darling.

ERNEST: You'll pardon me, Elma! You mustn't assume because you do not allow me to talk on serious subjects that I know nothing about them!

ELMA: Sorry, dear!

ERNEST: And I protest against your always suggesting that I'm a fool!

ELMA: I'm sorry.

ERNEST: And I must ask you – I insist – that you do nothing to jeopardize my friendship with Geoffrey and his wife!

ELMA: I promise not to even open my mouth!

ERNEST: *(Angrily.)* There you are – either you always –

ELMA: Darling! (*Crossing to cabinet for 'Sketch'.*) You must choose one of two things – either you must let me say what I like – then we won't be asked any more – or let me keep quiet and let them think you've married a fool!

ERNEST: I can't understand you – one of the most charming – clever –

ELMA: Ernest! One of these days you'll discover that she is quite the stupidest woman it has pleased God to put on earth. And when you tell me so, I promise not to say: 'but didn't I tell you so?'

ERNEST: I shall never say anything of the sort!

ELMA: Very well, dear.

ERNEST: And when she asks you to lunch on Wednesday, I would like you to accept.

ELMA: Of course I will, dear – and on Wednesday I'll have a headache and then you'll be able to go alone and talk on learned subjects without me being there to cramp your style!

ERNEST: Very well!

ELMA: She's done one thing at all events I have never been able to make you do!

ERNEST: What?

ELMA: She has persuaded you to go somewhere without me, which I've been praying you to do for years!

ERNEST: Well, the time must come if you won't –

ELMA: Of course, I will, dear – that's what I have been saying all these years!

(*GEOFFREY enters.*)

GEOFFREY: Ernest, my boy, my heartiest congratulations!

ERNEST: Why?

GEOFFREY: I can't tell you how grateful I am to you!

ERNEST: But what for?

GEOFFREY: I have at last introduced one of my men friends to the house that Anne likes!

ERNEST: I'm so glad!

GEOFFREY: My dear feller, you don't know what a success you've made with her! If you had heard what my wife says about your husband, Elma, you would be a very proud woman!

ELMA: But if you knew what a success your wife has made with Ernest, what a proud man you would be!

GEOFFREY: Good – I'm delighted!

ERNEST: She's charming, Geoff – so easy to get on with – and a brain – phew! You're a lucky feller!

GEOFFREY: So are you, old friend! (*Looking at ELMA.*)
(*ANNE enters.*)

ANNE: Dear, dear, sweet people – Geoffrey has been so cruel to me about keeping you waiting for dinner like this!

ERNEST: Oh, why?

ANNE: But if that horrid man isn't here in five minutes we'll start without him!

GEOFFREY: Good!

ANNE: And the moment the bell rings we'll go straight in – the brute will have to dine just as he is!

GEOFFREY: Good!

ANNE: Oh, my darling, and has no one played you for a whole week? I'm so sorry to have kept you waiting like this. (*Sits at the piano and plays.*)
(*ERNEST sits in an arm-chair facing the piano and strikes an attitude of knowledge of music.*
GEOFFREY sits by ELMA, looking at the 'Sketch'.)
(*Playing softly.*) But when dear Russiloff comes, I know that you will like him!

ELMA: (*Whispering to GEOFFREY.*) Who is Russiloff?

GEOFFREY: (*In a whisper.*) I think he's a poet!

ELMA: Oh! I hoped he was a conjurer!

GEOFFREY: Not in this house!

ERNEST: Charming! Charming!

ELMA: (*Whispering to GEOFFREY.*) Look! Ernest has chucked being a literary giant and become a composer!
(*GEOFFREY laughs.*)

ANNE: Making Geoffrey laugh again, you wicked little girl!

ELMA: I was showing him a funny picture in the 'Sketch'.

ANNE: (*Playing.*) Oh, what a fool I am – of course I'm dining with a relative of yours on Wednesday – Lady Joan – dear woman – insisted on putting me on her committee for canteens for the hop-pickers; we'll meet there, dear Mrs Melton?

ELMA: No – I'm afraid we won't.

ANNE: I am disappointed! Such a sweet woman – you like her, don't you?

ELMA: I – I –

ERNEST: (*Changing the conversation.*) What is it that you are playing?

ANNE: Guess!

ERNEST: Mozart?

ANNE: Wrong!

ERNEST: Beethoven?

ANNE: Wrong!

ERNEST: Let me think – Chopin?

ANNE: Wrong!

ELMA: (*To GEOFFREY in a whisper.*) He's trotting them all out, isn't he?

ANNE: Guess again!

ERNEST: Brahms?

ANNE: No!

ELMA: (*To GEOFFREY.*) Bollinger!

(*GEOFFREY laughs.*

ANNE has been watching ELMA and GEOFFREY the whole time.)

ANNE: It's by a little man I discovered myself – so clever – such a future! I don't believe you like Lady Joan, dear Mrs Melton?

(*GEOFFREY appears angry.*)

ELMA: I don't know her!

ANNE: Oh, why is that?

ELMA: I suppose because Ernest didn't marry a hop-picker!

GEOFFREY: (*Firmly.*) That answer should satisfy everybody.

ANNE: (*Pretending to be innocent.*) But, Geoffrey darling!

GEOFFREY: (*Angrily.*) Sufficient!

(*Door-bell is heard.*)

ALL: Russiloff!

GEOFFREY: (*In a whisper to ANNE.*) And just in time!

ANNE: (*To ERNEST, curtseys.*) Come along, sir – you shall take me in! (*Taking his arm.*)
(*ANNE and ERNEST go through the door to the dining-room.*)

GEOFFREY: Shall we emulate the old school, or just be modern?

ELMA: Oh, let's be both! (*Taking GEOFFREY's arm.*)

GEOFFREY: (*Laughing.*) Good!

ELMA: (*Stopping.*) Oh!

GEOFFREY: (*Almost anxiously.*) What is it?

ELMA: I've just discovered something!

GEOFFREY: What?

ELMA: What a wonderful wife your wife would make Ernest!
(*They go to the dining-room.*)

End of Act One.

ACT TWO

A month later. Afternoon.

The canary in its cage is in the window.

ANNE is seated at the piano playing – she keeps looking at ERNEST anxiously.

ERNEST listens, sadly looking into space, his face resting on his hand.

ERNEST: Beautiful! So beautiful!

ANNE: Ernest, you worry me – there's something the matter – I wish you would tell me!

ERNEST: (*Shaking his head.*) I doubt if you searched the world over if you would find anyone as unhappy as I am today!

ANNE: (*Stops playing.*) But why?

ERNEST: (*Looking at the door.*) Am I not your husband's best friend?

ANNE: Well? –

ERNEST: Have I not accepted his hospitality for a month – and three weeks of it deceived him in every way – have I not even descended to a trick to get him out of his own room that I might tell his wife I loved her!

ANNE: Well, if you won't tell her in front of him, how else can you tell her?

ERNEST: Is it becoming of an old friend to tell an old friend he loves his wife?

ANNE: Yes – if you do!

ERNEST: When you yourself are married to another woman!

ANNE: Yes, but you have told me a thousand times that –

ERNEST: I know I have. But what would happen to her if I left her?

ANNE: She'd marry again.

ERNEST: It is not so easy for women like Elma to marry again. No! I despair of ever knowing another happy moment!

ANNE: No one can help falling in love, Ernest.

ERNEST: That isn't true. We all of us can. I should have realized at once when I found myself drawn to you – that such happiness was not for me. I should have remembered my best friend – my wife, and left at once! I don't know why I didn't, it's so unlike me!

ANNE: You're not going to leave me, Ernest?

ERNEST: I have made a decision! Tomorrow morning I return to what Elma is pleased to call our home! (*He laughs.*) Home!

ANNE: Oh, why? But I shall see you again?

ERNEST: No!

ANNE: (*Quickly.*) You don't mean that, Ernest – please say you don't – you're just trying to frighten me!

ERNEST: I never frighten women.

ANNE: Then why did you tell me only two minutes ago that you loved me more –

(*ERNEST looks at the door.*)

Oh, it's all right, nobody listens in this house!

ERNEST: You cannot be too certain – I am married to a very unconventional woman!

ANNE: I wish she would hear – tell me you were joking – you don't mean that you will never see me again!

ERNEST: Yes!

ANNE: Ho! Then you don't love me!

ERNEST: Sapphire! Sapphire! (*Shaking his head sadly.*)

ANNE: Then why? I know – it's too much trouble – you are frightened of what people will say – oh, your wife has been talking to you!

ERNEST It is none of those things – in the most unexpected way, the most unexpected place – the shame of what I was doing was revealed to me.

ANNE: What do you mean?

ERNEST: Singing happily in my bath this morning – just an abandoned, cheery fellow – thinking of you – thinking how unevenly happiness has been distributed – a vision of what I was doing was thrust upon me – I saw myself as I am and not as I thought I was – my dishonour – my shame – was revealed to me – I was, as it were, held in a vice – that is bad enough – but that is not all – having indulged for some years in the luxury of turning on the hot tap with my big toe – held by my shame – I was unconscious of the heat until it was too late! It was two of the most unhappy experiences in one that I ever remember! The only satisfaction I have is – that I deserved it!

ANNE: But I don't love Geoffrey, Ernest!

ERNEST: But he loves you.

ANNE: He doesn't.

ERNEST: Again and again he has told me how little he knew of happiness until he married you!
(*ANNE starts.*)
Only last night he said to me – 'I wish I could tell you, old friend, what Monday morning means to me knowing I won't see Anne again until Friday night!'

ANNE: He said that, did he?

ERNEST: And many similar beautiful things! Why, only this morning he said –

ANNE: Thank you, I don't want to hear it.

ERNEST: Ah, exactly – (*He pauses.*) Because, like me, you realize how badly we have behaved.

ANNE: (*Wiping her eyes.*) You had no right to make me love you and then – (*Rising, going to ERNEST, putting her arms around him.*)
(*ERNEST nervously looking at the door, removes them.*)
Ernest! Ernest!

ERNEST: Think what his feelings would be if he discovered that I, his best friend, was cheating him like this – I don't believe he'd ever believe in anything again!

ANNE: I believe it's your wife – you don't want to leave her.

ERNEST: Do you think I find it amusing to be continually addressed as Rasputin and Sonny Jim, and in front of servants? No! It is only my strong sense of duty that makes me return to what is known as home!

ANNE: With your intelligence, what is your life going to be with her? Ernest – think!

ERNEST: (*Shaking his head.*) Ah! Ah!

ANNE: And what is my life going to be if you leave me?
Let us tell Geoffrey the truth, please!

ERNEST: And break his heart? As an honourable man, how
can I?

ANNE: But only a week ago you said you would like to
take me away this minute – rush into a booking-office
and say, 'Two tickets,' and when asked for where reply,
'Anywhere and everywhere – my happiness is such that
all places look alike!'

ERNEST: I did say it! Yes!

ANNE: You wanted to see the interesting places of the
world – the cathedrals – the museums – places of art –
all the things I had taught you to love!

ERNEST: Don't make it harder than it already is, Sapphire!

ANNE: Why, Ernest – why not chuck it all – you hate it –
you must – let us run to that booking-office! (*Putting her
arms around him.*)

ERNEST: (*Removing her arms.*) Please! Please don't do that,
Sapphire; you have no idea how silently Elma can come
into a room.

ANNE: But if you love me?

ERNEST: Please don't say it so loud, darling – Elma is
quite capable of being near that door!

ANNE: Well, what does it matter if she is? – Ernest, I must
tell you – I can't bear it!

ERNEST: One minute! You must let me look. (*He moves to
the door and opens it.*)
(*ELMA enters.*)

ELMA: Sweet man! (*To ANNE.*) He jumps up and opens the
door when you leave the room, and he's there ready to
open it when you come into it! What have you been doing?

ERNEST: What have you?

ELMA: I? (*Showing letters.*) I have just finished writing ten
letters! (*To ERNEST.*) Good girl?

ERNEST: Splendid!
(*ANNE nods her head to ERNEST, suggesting that ELMA
has heard nothing.*)

ELMA: I thought you were both going for a walk?

ERNEST: We were – but Annie began to play – and
     I forgot everything!

ELMA: I am so glad you have taught my little man to like
     music –
     (*ERNEST shudders.*)
     – and as soon as we get home, darling, I'll learn to play
     the pianola. We'll have some lovely evenings!

ERNEST: The pianola is hardly the same as the human
     touch, Elma!

ELMA: Oh, the advertisements say it's better. Anyway,
     I have written to some of the girls in the theatre and told
     them they must all come to us for the weekends – some
     of them sing just lovely – you'll like that, won't you,
     darling?

ERNEST: You are not serious when you say that you have
     written to them, Elma?

ELMA: Yes! Why not? Here are the letters! They are friends
     of mine, aren't they? And you like music! (*She pauses.*)
     What's wrong with them?

ERNEST: Nothing at all – but perhaps it won't be very
     amusing for our other guests to –

ELMA: Nonsense! (*To ANNE.*) You'd like to have a bit of fun
     when you come to stay with us, wouldn't you?

ANNE: (*Lucidly.*) I can't tell you how much I shall like to
     have a bit of fun!

ELMA: Of course! Won't Millie Gray make her laugh,
     Ernest?

ERNEST: Do you mean the lady who regularly throws her
     legs over her head without the slightest provocation?

ELMA: Yes!

ERNEST: I don't think she could make anyone laugh!

ELMA: Don't you? Well, she makes me – and she's a great
     friend of mine – and she's coming for the weekend!

ERNEST: Elma! I must ask you not to post any of those
     letters until I have discussed it with you!

ELMA: Why not?

ERNEST: Because I say so!

ELMA: (*Shrugging her shoulders.*) All right!

ERNEST: I'm sorry.

ELMA: I said all right.

ANNE: Why don't we continue this outside; it seems so wrong to waste such a lovely afternoon!

ERNEST: True! Yes! Let us do that! You'll come with us, Elma?

ELMA: No, thank you.

ERNEST: It would do you good.

ELMA: Thank you, I am very well.

ANNE: Anyway, I am going out! Don't bother about me, Ernest – I shall only go to the lake!

(*ANNE walks out through the windows.*)

ELMA: I wonder if she has any idea how few people there are in the world who would take her out of the lake compared to the number who would push her into it?

ERNEST: Elma! You are speaking of a very great friend of mine – whose guest we are – and I won't have it!

ELMA: All right, Sonny Jim; don't get excited because I don't like your girlfriend!

ERNEST: Ho! You promised me faithfully you would refrain from calling me by that most objectionable name!

ELMA: I know I did – but you annoyed me about my friends!

ERNEST: Good God! Haven't you a mind to rise above such people?

ELMA: No! And you are keeping your sweetie waiting – she'll give you such hell if you don't go after her!

ERNEST: What do you mean? It is a matter of the most profound indifference to Anne if I join her or not!

ELMA: Don't be silly – can't you take a joke?

ERNEST: No one enjoys a joke more than I do – but I don't call that a joke.

ELMA: Don't be a fool, Ernest – please go – she'll think I have kept you!

ERNEST: After the suggestion you made, I shall stay here!

ELMA: Do you want to be called Sonny Jim and Rasputin all through dinner? And worse?

ERNEST: If you dare, Elma!

ELMA: If you don't go and join that – oh, I nearly said it –
I'll call you names you don't even believe I know!

ERNEST: Elma, you are impossible!

(*He goes out through the windows.*
ELMA rises, walks to the windows, is looking out when
GEOFFREY enters.)

GEOFFREY: What are you doing at that window?

ELMA: I'm not sure that watching love doesn't give one the
next best thrill to being loved – anyway, both are very
beautiful!

GEOFFREY: Elma Melton! I insist on your coming away
from that window at once – to me there is something so
despicably unmoral about your watching your husband
making love to my wife that –

ELMA: Oh, isn't that beautiful – wicked little woman has
tapped him in her baby way with her fan! Did she put
that baby stuff over you when you were engaged?

GEOFFREY: Certainly not! It developed after we were
married!

ELMA: Oh, the little minx! She's tapped him again – and
the idiot likes it! Love is very beautiful!

GEOFFREY: Mrs Melton! This must stop – it isn't healthy
– it's indecent – and I insist on your taking your
husband away today and never entering this house again!

ELMA: (*Screaming.*) Geoffrey! He's lost his temper – he's
tumbled to her!

GEOFFREY: (*Moving quickly up to ELMA, in anxiety.*) What!

ELMA: Oh! No – no – it's all right, he's being a baby boy
too – he lifted his arm as though he was going to strike
her – but it was only to frighten wicked little girlie!
I wish he wouldn't give me such shocks! (*Looking at*
GEOFFREY.) It gave you a fright, duckie!

GEOFFREY: It did nothing of the sort.

ELMA: Then what did you rush to the window for?

GEOFFREY: It's a man's duty to show some interest if
another man threatens to strike his wife, isn't it?

ELMA: I don't know! It depends! Oh! Look at all the letters
I haven't written!

GEOFFREY: What do you mean?

ELMA: (*Opening an envelope – taking out a blank piece of notepaper.*) He thinks I have written to all my old friends and asked them for every weekend – oh, it was good work!

GEOFFREY: Elma, really, I –

ELMA: Don't be such a damned humbug!

GEOFFREY: Humbug! Sit down there! I wish to tell you that during my career as a playwright I have come in contact both on and off the stage with some desperate characters – but they all fade into insignificance when I think of you!

ELMA: He calls her Sapphire!

GEOFFREY: (*Eagerly.*) I don't believe it!

ELMA: He does, I tell you.

GEOFFREY: Did you laugh?

ELMA: Oh, it wasn't in front of me!

GEOFFREY: Then how do you know?

ELMA: I overheard by accident.

GEOFFREY: (*Angrily.*) Your lack of ordinary convention horrifies me.

ELMA: What have I done?

GEOFFREY: (*Angrily.*) What haven't you done! Amongst other things, you come into the home of two married people – and return their hospitality by what – not only taking your host's wife from him for your husband – but also have the audacity to ask him to be a party to it! It's un-English!

ELMA: I'm sorry!

GEOFFREY: Sorry? I don't believe such an appalling suggestion has ever been made in an English home before!

ELMA: I have only been to two weekend parties in English houses.

GEOFFREY: I don't know what you are suggesting, Elma – and I don't want to know – but I am certain, whatever the guests did, they had the decency not to let anyone else know what they were doing!

ELMA: None of the husbands seemed to know!

GEOFFREY: Exactly!

ELMA: (*Bending over and whispering.*) He wants to rush into a booking-office, take two tickets for anywhere, and run away with her this afternoon!

GEOFFREY: (*Eagerly.*) No! I don't believe it!

ELMA: It's true!

GEOFFREY: How do you know?

ELMA: I overheard by accident!

GEOFFREY: You listened?

ELMA: (*Looking away.*) I don't know what you mean.

GEOFFREY: (*Angrily.*) This must stop!

ELMA: After all, there is this to be said in his favour – he does love your wife!

GEOFFREY: The cad! The friend of my schoolboy days! (*Shaking his head.*) What a pretty advertisement for Eton and Oxford!

ELMA: And your wife loves him!

GEOFFREY: (*Angrily.*) That's a lie! My wife is much too clever to love anybody!

ELMA: Well, she understands him!

GEOFFREY: Yes! She understands him! But what exactly is my position in all this – am I to sit still and watch the deplorable behaviour of my friend and his wife – under my very eyes watch my home being broken up – and just say nothing?

ELMA: Never turn the hot tap on with your big toe!

GEOFFREY: I always do!

ELMA: Ernest burnt himself!

GEOFFREY: (*Eagerly.*) Where?

ELMA: I don't know – we are not on those terms!

GEOFFREY: Do you mean to tell me he had the audacity to discuss things of such a private nature with my wife?

ELMA: Artistic people are always abandoned!

GEOFFREY: Elma Melton – you are a very, very bad woman!

ELMA: I know! But if you hadn't told me the other night –

GEOFFREY: You are not going to refer to that most unfortunate alcoholic observation I made!

ELMA: But you did say it!

GEOFFREY: What did I say to you after the second glass of champagne that night?

ELMA: Your wife was the best little woman in the world!

GEOFFREY: Exactly! Be good enough to remember that!

ELMA: What did you say after the fourth glass?

GEOFFREY: (*Hesitating.*) It was bad champagne!

ELMA: You called me little woman – which annoyed me very much – and said 'that as I was different to any other woman you had ever met' you didn't mind telling me that your wife could be the most awful bore in the world!

GEOFFREY: Well, there's nothing very much in that – most men could say that about their wives!

ELMA: When you had finally said no to the brandy – you said that the only thing that prevented you hitting her sometimes was that everybody had told you all your life it was wrong to hit women!

GEOFFREY: Obviously only a remark!

ELMA: You never meant it?

GEOFFREY: Certainly not!

ELMA: Then why did you say to that canary this morning, 'Cheer up, Percy, there's a chance of freedom?'

GEOFFREY: Ho! ho! You listened – how could you, Elma?

ELMA: (*Indignantly.*) Wouldn't anyone listen to a man talking to a canary – mustn't it obviously be something he doesn't want anyone else to know?

GEOFFREY: True! Yes! That's fair!

ELMA: Of course!

GEOFFREY: Elma! It is very evident that there are some people in the world with whom there is nothing to be gained by being dishonest!

ELMA: Well?

GEOFFREY: So, I'll tell you the truth – I don't like it – but I will! All that I said in alcoholism – I think in sobriety! My wife is a bore – it is as much as I can do to sit in the same house with her without screaming – I crave for my freedom more than for anything else in the world – but I don't like the way I'm going about getting it!

ELMA: What's wrong with it?

GEOFFREY: I don't say it's wrong – but it's un-English!

ELMA: How would you like it done, then?

GEOFFREY: I would like them to be going on just as they are now – but you and I apparently unconscious of it – and when it had run its natural course – and they had left us both – for me to be able to say to you in horror, 'Had you any idea?' and you to reply indignantly, 'Do you suppose if I had known this was going on under my very nose, I would have stayed in your house for one moment?' In brief, I want to lose my wife but keep my self-respect! I want to be a gentleman!

ELMA: What do you want to be a gentleman for with all your gifts?

GEOFFREY: I hadn't thought of that – that's true!

ELMA: For goodness' sake leave something for men like Ernest!

GEOFFREY: That's true, too!

ELMA: Why don't you face it in a big way, like your wife has done?

GEOFFREY: My wife has behaved disgracefully!

ELMA: Magnificently!

GEOFFREY: What do you say?

ELMA: Listen – for years you have bored her!

GEOFFREY: (*Starting.*) I – I have bored her? (*Laughing ironically.*) You'll pardon me, Elma Melton! I bore nobody.

ELMA: Congratulations! For years she has craved for social position – what social position has a playwright?

GEOFFREY: (*Haughtily.*) I am under the impression everyone wishes to know him!

ELMA: Don't be ridiculous – he seldom has sex appeal and is rarely amusing – and only a third of the people who see his plays have got enough brains to know anyone wrote it!

GEOFFREY: How right you are!

ELMA: She would have had much more chance of social success if she had married an actor!

GEOFFREY: (*Indignantly.*) Elma! That I will never agree with!

ELMA: If you have only seen them act on the stage, I agree – but if you have seen them act on golf courses – entering a restaurant – or wherever two or three people are gathered together, then I do not agree!

GEOFFREY: It is seldom a man of letters has been so bitterly humiliated.

ELMA: And Ernest can provide for all her cravings – he has money – and one day a great social position – and he won't bore her any more than you do – and under our very noses she has without deceit – without scruple – without compromise – honestly set out to catch him – leave you and take him from me! Brushing aside my personal hope and prayer that she will succeed – she has behaved with such courage and fairness, I hope she gets him! Personally, I am going to give her all the help I can!

GEOFFREY: I hadn't looked at it in that way – do you think that I, too, should help her?

ELMA: If you have the slightest regard or affection for your wife you certainly will.

GEOFFREY: I am devoted to my wife – and I'll prove it! Ah! But what about my position with Ernest?

ELMA: What about it?

GEOFFREY: Knowing my wife as I do, is it fair to allow him to rush into this calamity without a word of warning? Am I, as it were, being a cricketer? That worries me! If he were a stranger to me, it would be a different matter – but to allow the friend of my schoolboy days to marry my wife without warning – doesn't it savour to you rather of cheating at cards?

ELMA: If he marries your wife, it is obvious that he must have done something to offend nature so deeply she is determined to be ruthless in her punishment!

GEOFFREY: (*Smiling.*) And I will comfort myself in the knowledge that nature has chosen me to be one of her chief instruments! Yes!

ELMA: The time has arrived when we must take some attitude –

GEOFFREY: Yes! I shall immediately ask your husband what his intentions are.

ELMA: You'll do nothing of the sort – Ernest at the moment thinks you're a fool and have no idea of what is going on – if you disillusion him he'll remember Eton – Oxford – the Oval – Sandwich – run like a hare, taking me with him!

GEOFFREY: He thinks I am a fool – and that I don't know, does he?

ELMA: Ernest is a gentleman! You don't suppose he would be such a cad as to make love to your wife if he thought you knew it?

GEOFFREY: Elma – I am unable to tell you how much I resent Ernest thinking me a fool – and it was in my mind to let him off and suffer myself – but now it is different – even nature has no idea how far I will go to help her!

ELMA: You'll have to be quick – we are leaving here tomorrow.

GEOFFREY: Did you overhear why he is leaving?

ELMA: He can't go on cheating his boyhood friend like this any longer! If you discovered him you would never believe in anything again!

GEOFFREY: That's bad! You don't think he wants to get out of it, do you?

ELMA: Why?

GEOFFREY: Well!, that's usually the stuff they put over when they are getting tired of the lady!

ELMA: How do you know?

(*GEOFFREY shrugs his shoulders.*)

GEOFFREY: To be a playwright one has to be informed of many things that are unhappy. But how do you suggest we should begin?

ELMA: When they come in, be nice to Ernest, but say something to your wife that will give her the chance to wipe away the tears that force their way into her eyes –

GEOFFREY: Nothing would make Anne cry!

ELMA: But Ernest doesn't know that yet!

GEOFFREY: That's true.

ELMA: And realizing the seriousness of the situation, as she does, the least thing will make her cry!

GEOFFREY: Why?

ELMA: Look at the strong position it puts her in with Ernest – poor little woman who has suffered so much in silence – and it strengthens his position with you so much!

GEOFFREY: How?

ELMA: Where is the dishonour of taking a woman from a man who makes her cry?

GEOFFREY: It seems to me he is coming out of this a hell of a feller! – but having discovered he owes me nothing – there's still you!

ELMA: I'll fix him all right! My business is at the psychological moment to burst in and say I know everything!

GEOFFREY: And then?

ELMA: I have faith in your wife!

GEOFFREY: Do I know?

ELMA: It comes as the most hideous shock you have ever known?

GEOFFREY: Yes, that's right! It would never do for me to have ever been even suspicious! No! It is imperative that I must be just a simple, trusting feller. Yes! But tell me this – ethically, are we not doing a most disgraceful thing?

ELMA: Logically, we are behaving splendidly!

GEOFFREY: How?

ELMA: If we don't make him marry your wife, what sort of life is mine going to be – the woman who stood between him and his happiness – jolly for me, wouldn't it be?

GEOFFREY: Terrible! In the event of this ending satisfactorily, what are you going to do, Elma?

ELMA: I suppose I had better go home to my mother!

GEOFFREY: Nonsense! Tell your mother to come here and stay here with us!

ELMA: I would like that – even if she can't come!

GEOFFREY: (*Laughing.*) I'm terribly fond of you, Elma. You're such a grand companion.

ELMA: I adore you!

GEOFFREY: You don't!

(*Voices heard off.*)

ELMA: Ssh! I shall be asleep!

GEOFFREY: And I shall be sitting innocently unaware that all is not well with my domestic life! But I'll give him hell when I do know!

(*ANNE enters followed by ERNEST.*)

ANNE: (*Laughing.*) You're the most ridiculous person in the world, Ernest!

GEOFFREY: No, no, not a word against my dear old friend!

ERNEST: Thank you, Geoff!

ELMA: (*Waking up, rubbing her eyes.*) I wish you wouldn't make so much noise!

ERNEST: Sorry, darling! You don't mean to tell me you two have been sitting in here on a lovely afternoon like this?

GEOFFREY: We have! She slept and I read a little – then I thought – how happy one is – a charming house – delightful friends – (*He pauses.*) – peace of mind! (*He sighs.*) Very, very charming!

ERNEST: I'm ashamed of you both. Anne and I went for a most attractive walk!

ANNE: I took Ernest to the wood and showed him where you work in the summer, Geoffrey.

ERNEST: It was charming. The sun was shining on the hills – the birds were singing – the trees were in blossom – it was all very beautiful.

ELMA: And what was most beautiful of all was that you weren't with your wife.

ERNEST: (*Indignantly.*) That was not my fault, Elma – I asked you to come.

ELMA: Oh, you asked me all right!

ANNE: We both begged you to come.

ERNEST: (*Looking at her, he is nervous of what she is going to say next.*) Geoff, old friend, I hope you will think it bad news – but you are losing Elma and myself tomorrow.

GEOFFREY: Not on your life I'm not! You don't go a day before Monday.

ANNE: That's what I said!

GEOFFREY: Oh, it doesn't matter what you said – it's what I say!

ANNE: (*Angrily.*) I suppose I may speak in my own house?

GEOFFREY: I can't stop you – if you mean to.

(*ANNE sinks into a chair – she endeavours to look as though she is trying not to cry.*)

What's the matter, Anne? (*To ERNEST.*) The old girl's tired! You're looking terribly tired, old girl – you haven't been looking your beautiful self for some time.

ANNE: (*Wiping her eyes.*) You beast!

GEOFFREY: Good heavens – I don't understand! Have I said anything?

ANNE: (*Crying.*) You meant to be horrid to me – you are always horrid to me.

GEOFFREY: Ernest, as my oldest friend, did I say anything that deserves my wife speaking to me like that?

ERNEST: Well, Geoffrey, frankly, I do think your manner was a little uncalled for.

ELMA: Rot! He said nothing at all.

ANNE: (*Sobbing.*) Oh! Oh!

ERNEST: Elma, be good enough to remember you are a guest in this house.

ELMA Isn't it about time you remembered it?

GEOFFREY: Oh, do stop it, Anne – making me out a brute in front of my oldest friend! Making an idiot of yourself like this!

ANNE: There! There! You're always the – the – the same – you're – you're always beastly to me.

GEOFFREY: Ernest, the truth. Did I say anything that entitles Anne to speak to me like that?

ERNEST: (*Nervously.*) Well –

GEOFFREY: (*Angrily.*) Did I?

ELMA: Did he?

ERNEST: (*To ELMA.*) Be quiet!

ELMA: How dare you speak to me like that?

ERNEST: I do dare – you have no right to interfere in things that are not your concern.

ELMA: It's as much my concern as it is yours – and if you think just because you are in love with another woman that I am going to stand here –

GEOFFREY: Elma! You are forgetting yourself! You're being silly.

ELMA: I'm nothing of the sort – I tell you he is in love with another woman –

GEOFFREY: I do not believe it – I know from what he has told me that he is in love with you.

ELMA: If you weren't a fat-headed –

ERNEST: Elma! Silence! If I am not mistaken, you are about to make a suggestion that you would regret all your life.

ELMA: Yes, I am. I can't stand it any longer – the position I have been put in for weeks, I –

ERNEST: Elma, please – please –

GEOFFREY: (*Patting ERNEST on the back.*) I am sympathetic, old friend – but let us remember that our little Elma is not herself – and –

ELMA: I am myself – and if you weren't a stupid, simple idiot you'd know it.

GEOFFREY Know what?

ELMA: That he is in love with your wife!

GEOFFREY: (*With great anger.*) It's a lie!

ELMA: It's the truth.

ERNEST: Oh, my God! – oh, my God!.

GEOFFREY: That is a lie, isn't it, Ernest?

ERNEST: Yes.

GEOFFREY: (*To ELMA.*) How dare you? How dare you? Having upset yourself excuses you – but only a little. (*Patting ERNEST on the back.*) Old friend!

ELMA: (*Beside herself with rage.*) Didn't you tell her in this room this afternoon that you loved her more than you could ever love anyone?

ERNEST: I did not.

ELMA: You – you – didn't tell her that you would like to rush into a booking-office and take a ticket for anywhere, as you loved her so much all places looked alike?

ERNEST: I did not.

ELMA: Do you mean to stand there and tell me that you didn't tell her you had scalded yourself in the bath this morning?

GEOFFREY: How dare you?

ERNEST: (*Starting.*) Oh, I did not!

ELMA: Didn't you kiss her and call her your little Sapphire?

ERNEST: No, I did not.

ANNE: May I speak?

ERNEST: No, no, please.

ANNE: Ernest, it is divine of you to protect me like this – and I shall always be grateful to you – but I cannot allow you to do so any longer.

ERNEST: Please, please, Sapphire – Anne!

ANNE: (*To GEOFFREY.*) All that – that – (*She pauses.*) – Ernest's wife says is true.

GEOFFREY: (*Horrified.*) No – no – my oldest friend – no, no!

ELMA: (*In a loud whisper to GEOFFREY.*) Too much.

ANNE: I'm sorry – but it's true!

GEOFFREY: I refuse to believe it – you're joking with me, Ernest!

ELMA: Can't you say anything, you Rasputin in the grass!

GEOFFREY: Silence!

ELMA: I won't.

GEOFFREY: Ernest – tell me it's a joke! I see it all – the three of you are in league to play this joke on me.

ANNE: Speak, Ernest.

ERNEST: (*Looking on the ground.*) No, Geoffrey, it's true.

GEOFFREY: It's – (*He pauses.*) – true – you – you – love my wife?

ERNEST: Yes.

GEOFFREY: And you have told her so?

ERNEST: Yes.

GEOFFREY: And she loves you?

ANNE: Yes.

GEOFFREY: I shall never believe in anything again.

ELMA: Thank heaven you have had the sense to get them both to admit it!

ANNE: (*To ELMA.*) One thing to me is evident – you were listening at the door.

ELMA: And another thing is evident – if either of you had any brains you wouldn't have said the things you said to each other with a door!

ERNEST: Elma, I can never forgive you as long as I live.

ELMA: And what makes you think that you will ever have the chance to – and let me tell you that anything you have to say to me, say now – because it's your last chance.

ERNEST: I have nothing to say to you.

ELMA: That has been my experience ever since I married you.

GEOFFREY: (*Holding his head.*) My home broken asunder – and by my best friend! For a playwright, how little I know of life!

ERNEST: What am I to say to you, Geoffrey?

ELMA: Don't ask such stupid questions!

ERNEST: Have you no regard for the seriousness of such a moment as this?

ELMA: None.

ERNEST: Well, kindly leave those of us who have. Geoffrey – I – I – must speak to you.

GEOFFREY: Ernest – I wish to hear nothing more! I couldn't stand anything more.

ERNEST: But I must – if I could have a few minutes with you alone.

ELMA: No! I'm in this – anything you have to say must be said before me.

ANNE: May I speak?

ERNEST: Please!

ANNE: It is perfectly true, Geoffrey – I love Ernest – I am sorry you have learnt that fact in the way that you have – I wish it could have been told you in a more ordinary way – but the fact remains that you do know it – I am not sorry – I'm glad – at the risk of hurting you more than you are already hurt – I'm happy that you know.

GEOFFREY: (*Putting his face in his hands.*) Go on.

ANNE: For years I have been unhappy and miserable –
perhaps it was not your fault – but for years I have
wanted my freedom.

GEOFFREY: (*Shaking his head.*) Go on.

ANNE: I never intended to like anyone else – but these
things happen when we least expect them – but now that
I do like someone else – and now that you know it –
I must tell you it is my intention to leave this house
tonight and for ever.

ERNEST: No, no.

GEOFFREY: Anne! Do you know what you are saying?

ANNE: Yes, Geoffrey.

GEOFFREY: And you mean it?

ANNE: Yes, Geoffrey.

GEOFFREY: I don't know what to say!

ERNEST: Could I – would you mind if I said something?

ELMA: Yes, we would.

ANNE: Please, Ernest. (*To GEOFFREY.*) I'm sure Geoffrey
agrees that there is nothing else I could do?

GEOFFREY: Anne! Feeling as you do – bitter as it is for
me – there is nothing else that you can do. (*Angrily.*) And
I only hope that villain will make you happy!

ELMA: Impossible.

ERNEST: Could I please say something?

GEOFFREY: No! Having ruined my life – I want to hear
nothing from you or ever see you again. Go.

ELMA: Yes, go and show her where you scalded yourself!

ANNE: Be quiet, you vulgar woman.

ELMA: How dare you speak to me like that!

GEOFFREY: Stop! Under no circumstances will I allow this
parting to end in a brawl. I insist that it is conducted
with breeding and convention.

ANNE: Thank you, Geoffrey. I'm going to take a few things
with me – my maid will remain the night and bring the
rest of my things tomorrow, if that is agreeable to you.

GEOFFREY: Perfectly.

ERNEST: Oh, please – don't let us do anything in a hurry –

GEOFFREY: Hurry? The moment Anne is ready I expect
you to be ready to leave with her!

ERNEST: But –

GEOFFREY: There are no buts, Melton – I have nothing more to say to you. You're not going to sit there and tell me you are not prepared to stand by your iniquity!

ANNE: Ernest, there is no – obligation for you to come with me unless you want to.

ERNEST: Of course I want to, but I must be allowed to explain to Geoffrey –

ANNE: Very well then – perhaps you would meet me in the hall in ten minutes! Geoffrey – I'm sorry if I have hurt you terribly – sorry. (*She turns and leaves the room.*)

ERNEST: (*Crossing to ELMA – anxiously.*) Geoffrey! – Elma, on my knees I implore you – I can't leave Geoffrey like this – I must speak to him!

ELMA: Well, why don't you?

ERNEST: But you would embarrass me! – Geoffrey, in memory of the old days – I know I don't deserve it – in memory of the day when you jumped in and took me out of the river –

GEOFFREY: Did you hear that, Elma – I saved his life that he might live to ruin mine!

ELMA: You ought to have known!

GEOFFREY: Yes.

ERNEST: Geoffrey, please, I implore you! I won't keep you a minute – and I must speak to you before Anne is ready. I may never see you again, Geoff.

GEOFFREY: And do you think I want to ever see you again? It's more than you deserve, but I will give you two minutes. (*To ELMA.*) For that time only, would you be good enough to leave us?

ELMA: Very well, if I'm not wanted!

GEOFFREY: (*Smiling at her.*) But you are wanted.

ELMA: Don't weaken.

GEOFFREY: Is it likely?

(*ELMA leaves the room. GEOFFREY turns angrily to ERNEST.*)

Well, what have you to say to me?

ERNEST: For God's sake don't speak to me like that, Geoffrey.

GEOFFREY: Well, how do you expect me to speak to you?

ERNEST: I know I've behaved like a cad – in fact, a much greater cad than you think I have.

GEOFFREY: I did not ask for details, Melton.

ERNEST: Call me Ernest.

GEOFFREY: I won't! Come – what is it you wish to say?

ERNEST: I'm shaking so much, could I have a little brandy?

GEOFFREY: (*Looking at him, he hesitates.*) Yes.

ERNEST: (*Goes to the tray.*) Thank you.

GEOFFREY: Bring the damn stuff here – I'll have one.

ERNEST: Yes, Geoff. (*Bringing the tray to a table and pouring out some for GEOFFREY.*) Enough?

GEOFFREY: No.

> (*ERNEST pours out more, gives it to GEOFFREY. Then he fills his own glass and sits.*
> *They look at each other.*)

I can't drink to your health – but for my wife's sake I hope you will make her a better husband than you have me a friend.

ERNEST: I realize I cannot make her a worse one, Geoff.

GEOFFREY: My God! Do you realize what you have done? You come into the house of your oldest friend – I can't go on – without a thought he trusts you with the best little woman in the world – and you end your visit by telling him that you love her!

ERNEST: (*Looking round at the door.*) But I don't.

GEOFFREY: What do you say?

ERNEST: That's what I've been wanting to tell you all the time – I don't love her.

GEOFFREY: (*Startled out of his life.*) You – you – don't!

ERNEST: For ten days I thought I did.

GEOFFREY: For ten days! What is your object in telling me this?

ERNEST: Because you love her – and want her with you.

GEOFFREY: You are not suggesting to me that you don't want her yourself?

ERNEST: Yes.

GEOFFREY: You blackguard Melton – you blackguard!

ERNEST: I'm not, Geoff.

GEOFFREY: You're the worst man I have ever known in my life.

ERNEST: But –

GEOFFREY: You make a woman love you – treat her as a play-thing – and the moment it comes to a climax, you're afraid of your conscience – of public opinion. No, you villain – that's not good enough for me – you're dealing with the wrong man. What you have done cannot be undone – leave this room at once and wait for her in the hall.

ERNEST: For God's sake, Geoff!

GEOFFREY: Go. I can forgive you loving my wife – but I will never forgive you for saying that you don't.

ERNEST: But I don't.

GEOFFREY: Ho, ho! Didn't you say to her in this room this afternoon that you would like to rush into a booking-office and take her round the world?

ERNEST: Of course! You didn't expect me to be such a cad as to say I didn't want to, do you? One is not without chivalry, I hope.

GEOFFREY: Chiv…you didn't want to take her for that trip?

ERNEST: My dear fellow, I'd have hated to.

GEOFFREY: Melton, if I were a gentleman, I'd knock you down.

ERNEST: But, Geoff, you don't seem to understand – I'm trying to give her back to you.

GEOFFREY: Oh, I see that very clearly, but you'll fail, Melton, you'll fail! And let me tell you this – you're provoking me to be a gentleman at any moment.

ERNEST: I don't understand – I thought you would be delighted.

GEOFFREY: At what?

ERNEST: When I told you I didn't love her.

GEOFFREY: (*Drinking.*) You callous – you – didn't you hear my wife say only a minute ago that she loved you?

ERNEST: Yes, but she'll get over it in no time.

GEOFFREY: It's a lie – I know my wife better than you do – she'll never get over it – it is obvious you are the only man she has ever loved or ever will love – if she knew you didn't love her, the shock would be so great I wouldn't answer for the consequences. Go to the hall at once. (*Pointing to the door.*)

ERNEST: No, Geoff – you exaggerate – you think that of her because you are fond of her – but I know better – in a week I would be merely a memory.

GEOFFREY: Let us get to the point, Melton; answer me this – are you going to marry my wife, or aren't you?

ERNEST: I'm not going to, Geoff.

GEOFFREY: For the last time, Melton – are you going to marry my wife, or are you not?

ERNEST: Geoffrey! You may strike me – you may maim me, you may stamp on my face – but I will not marry your wife.

GEOFFREY: Pass me that bottle before I lose control of myself.

ERNEST: May I help myself first?

GEOFFREY: No! What do you want it for?

ERNEST: I must, Geoffrey – my nerves are terribly upset. (*Helping himself.*)

GEOFFREY: What about mine?

ERNEST: I don't know why yours are. You love your wife – and you have got her back! (*Passing the bottle.*)

GEOFFREY: It must be only the fear that you might successfully retaliate that stops me hitting you. (*Pouring himself out brandy.*) Ernest, let me appeal to your better nature – are you – are you prepared to hurt a woman as much as you are threatening to hurt my wife?

ERNEST: Yes, Geoff –

GEOFFREY: You, a gentleman by birth, don't mind her thinking you are a cad until the last day of her life?

ERNEST: No, Geoff.

GEOFFREY: Ho! A woman that you kissed in this very room this afternoon!

ERNEST: I did not kiss her. At the most it could be described as a chivalrous brush of the forehead.

GEOFFREY: The same thing to a woman, Ernest.

ERNEST: I assure you not, Geoffrey.

GEOFFREY: So – so – loving you – you expect me to take her back?

ERNEST: But I see many advantages in that.

GEOFFREY: (*Angrily.*) Tell me one.

ERNEST: When she discovers how badly I have behaved – don't you see what a lesson it will be to her – she can appreciate you so much more than she has ever done before. No other man would ever appeal to her again – you'll have her with you for always.

GEOFFREY: Quick – pass the bottle – I'm going to faint!

ERNEST: Geoffrey, please, you've had three.

GEOFFREY: And I'm going to have thirty-three. (*Filling up his glass.*) You blackguard, Melton – you blackguard! (*After drinking.*) How did you tumble to her?

ERNEST: What do you mean?

GEOFFREY: You know what I mean – I don't care – poor little Elma will be disappointed, though; it's going to be an awful shock when she discovers she hasn't got rid of you.

ERNEST: What do you mean?

GEOFFREY: My word, she's a good sort – (*He laughs.*) We've had some grand laughs at you and Anne during the last three weeks.

ERNEST: You're not telling me you knew all the time?

GEOFFREY: Don't be silly!

ERNEST: Oh! And you did nothing to stop it!

GEOFFREY: If you had been married to my wife, and I was trying to take her from you, would you have tried to stop me?

ERNEST: No.

GEOFFREY: Of course not. How did you tumble to Anne, Ernest?

ERNEST: It will be painful, Geoff.

GEOFFREY: Go on! Go on!

ERNEST (*Pouring himself out another glass.*) When I first met her, Anne swept me off my feet – she discovered qualities in me that I knew I did not possess – she threatened to make me a great man – and generally she surrounded me with an atmosphere that was so unreal, so artificial, that for a little while I was unusually happy.

GEOFFREY: Go on.

ERNEST: Soon I discovered she was a bigger fake than she was making me – it was a great shock, Geoffrey.

GEOFFREY: Horrible.

ERNEST: And then she seemed to forget that my name was Ernest, and called me Tootsy Wootsy!

GEOFFREY: And playfully hit you with her fan.

ERNEST: (*Angrily.*) Sometimes I could have taken that fan from her and given her such a one that –

GEOFFREY: Same here.

ERNEST: When that feller you had to dinner the other night said England was effete, I nearly rose and said: 'How the hell can that be when Geoff has stuck this woman for six years?'

GEOFFREY: Six and a half!

ERNEST: Geoff, please don't think me impertinent, but how did you stand it?

GEOFFREY: God knows!

ERNEST: What are you going to do about it?

GEOFFREY: Now that you have failed me, what can I do? When you and Elma leave, couldn't I come with you?

ERNEST: Under the circumstances, wouldn't that be a little unmoral?

GEOFFREY: I don't know. There are a great many more men going round the world with a friend they don't know than with a friend they do. Let's have some champagne.

ERNEST: Yes.

GEOFFREY: No – it means waiting – let's go on with this! (*They help themselves.*)

ERNEST: You're not angry with me?

GEOFFREY: Angry with you – I'm proud of you!

ERNEST: And you don't think I ought to marry your wife!

GEOFFREY: I'd have you put in a home if you tried!

ERNEST: Geoff – you are a good feller!

GEOFFREY: So are you!

BOTH: Cheerio!

ERNEST: What do you think I should say to Anne!

GEOFFREY: I'll tell you all the things I think about her – and you repeat them to her as your own!

ERNEST: It's going to be a hateful scene, Geoffrey!

GEOFFREY: Write to her – why do you want to go and get yourself all upset because of my wife? – write to her – tear the address off the note-paper so that she doesn't know where to send you an answer!

ERNEST: Isn't that rather a caddish thing, not to face one's responsibilities in life?

GEOFFREY: No – don't be a fool! If you saw her, she'll get you!

ERNEST: I hadn't thought of that!

GEOFFREY: I had – you stand by me, dear old friend!

ERNEST: Geoff – you are a good feller!

GEOFFREY: So are you. Mind you, I have one thing against you – I can never forgive you for wanting to leave a charming woman like Elma!

ERNEST: Geoff, I could cry with shame when I think of the way I've treated her. This I would like to say in your wife's favour – if it hadn't been for her I should never have known what a treasure Elma was!

GEOFFREY: Quite right. Let's give credit where credit is seldom due!… I shall miss Elma – I love her very much!

ERNEST: (*Anxiously.*) You haven't been telling her so, have you, Geoffrey?

GEOFFREY: (*Starting.*) No – do you know, I never realized it until a few minutes ago – that's odd – because I realize now I love her very much – I suppose it's because I'm going to lose her!

ERNEST: Does she dislike me very much, Geoff?

GEOFFREY: She loathes you, old friend!

ERNEST: You'll help me, Geoff – you'll tell her –

GEOFFREY: I'm sorry I didn't make a fuss of Elma – I love her very much!

ERNEST: You're irritating me, Geoffrey!

GEOFFREY: Good!

ERNEST: If I thought for a moment you had taken
advantage of me during the time I thought I was in love
with your wife, I –

GEOFFREY: I didn't – but I am exceedingly sorry I didn't
– I love Elma very much! I'm going to miss her – I'm
going to be very unhappy – Indeed I am!

ERNEST: Look out!

(*ELMA enters.*)

GEOFFREY: Little Elma! My dear little friend!

ELMA: (*To ERNEST.*) Why are you still here?

GEOFFREY: The game's up, Elma!

ELMA: What do you mean?

GEOFFREY: Nothing doing – it's off. He's tumbled!

ELMA: He hasn't!

GEOFFREY: He has! And it's a terrible thing for me
because it means that I'm going to lose you – and I don't
want to lose you because I love you very much – indeed
I do!

ELMA: Are you positive of that, Geoffrey?

GEOFFREY: Absolutely! I love you very much!

ERNEST: Stop, Geoffrey. How dare you speak to my wife
in that way! Elma! Please listen to me – I'm terribly
sorry, I don't know what to say to you!

ELMA: You're not asking me to forgive you and take you
back again?

ERNEST: Yes! – I know I have treated you shamefully –

ELMA: Nothing will induce me to! (*Looking at ERNEST,
then at GEOFFREY, the speaking quietly.*) Besides, even if
I wanted to – it's too late!

ERNEST: What do you mean?

ELMA: I have been unfaithful with him!

(*GEOFFREY starts.*)

ERNEST: (*In anguish.*) It isn't true!

ELMA: It is!

ERNEST: Geoffrey! It's a lie, isn't it?

GEOFFREY: (*Hesitating – looking at the door.*) No, Ernest, old
friend, it's the truth!

ERNEST: My best friend – my best friend!

(*ANNE enters.*
GEOFFREY and ELMA exchange glances.)

ANNE: Ernest, Ernest! (*Looking at ERNEST.*) What does this mean – (*Shaking ERNEST.*) What is the matter?

GEOFFREY: Be gentle with him, Anne – he's had some bad news!

ANNE: (*Anxiously.*) What?

GEOFFREY: He has discovered that his wife has been unfaithful with me!

End of Act Two.

ACT THREE

One second later.

ANNE: Ernest!

  (*ERNEST shakes his head.*)

  Have you nothing to say to me?

ERNEST: Please, Sapphire – Anne!

ANNE: Oh, this is too dreadful! (*To GEOFFREY.*) Oh, stop smiling.

GEOFFREY: I won't – besides, I can't.

ANNE: (*Smelling glass.*) I thought so! (*To ELMA.*) You may have him, and I only hope that he won't bore you as he has me.

ELMA: I think you are very kind.

  (*ERNEST groans through all this.*)

GEOFFREY: Ernest, when nature gave you the gift of being able to make these curious noises, it was her intention that you should not use them publicly!

ANNE: Ernest, please, I –

ERNEST: No, no, I shall never lift my head again!

ELMA: No one can say that is bad news!

  (*GEOFFREY laughs.*)

ANNE: (*To GEOFFREY.*) When I leave this house directly, my prayer is that I will be spared ever seeing you again as long as I live!

GEOFFREY: Let us pray that your prayer will be favourably considered.

  (*ELMA laughs.*)

ANNE: I envy you your ability to laugh at nothing! But I am glad you can – (*Looking at GEOFFREY.*) because you will have every opportunity offered to you in the future! It is my intention to leave for London this instant, that I may see my lawyer tonight – do you understand what that means?

GEOFFREY: Perfectly! And you may tell him I will not defend – and the interview is to be charged to Ernest!

ANNE: I am grateful to you, Mrs Melton. I have wanted this opportunity for a long time!

(*She leaves, banging the door after her.*)

ELMA: Noisy!

(*Pause – the front door bangs.*)

She's gone to her lawyer.

(*ERNEST lifts his head, looks at them both.*)

Ernest, you haven't kept your promise!!

ERNEST: (*Shaking his head.*) My heart is broken!

GEOFFREY: That's a lie – the reason that you hid your face was because you were frightened that Anne would smack it – and after the cruel way you have treated her, you should have let her!

ERNEST: Be quiet!

GEOFFREY: I won't.

ERNEST: Tell me it isn't true, Elma – tell me you said those dreadful things to make me unhappy – to punish me – tell me it's a lie.

ELMA: I cannot tell a lie, Ernest!

GEOFFREY: Oh, I like that! That's funny!!

ERNEST: One more word from you, Lymes, and I'll throw you through that window.

GEOFFREY: Melton! I must ask you to remember that you are a guest in this house.

ERNEST: You can't love this man, Elma – you can't!

ELMA: How could I have done what I have done if I don't, Ernest?

ERNEST: No, no, you can't – I don't believe it!

GEOFFREY: Ernest, old friend – look at me very carefully.

ERNEST: Well?

GEOFFREY: Now can't you see why she loves me?!

ERNEST: I can see every reason why she shouldn't!

GEOFFREY: I hate men who can't drink like gentlemen!

ERNEST: If it were anyone else but this dreadful man! Look at him.

ELMA: I don't know – after all, you did leave me alone with him for weeks for a not too attractive woman!

ERNEST: I know – I know – (*Appealing to her.*) Elma,
I know I have behaved abominably, but if you will let
me, and this man will leave us, I can explain!

ELMA: Ernest, that you could have preferred Sapphire to
me, you never can explain!

GEOFFREY: Never!

ERNEST: I know, but –

ELMA: And it's too late! It may be propinquity! It may be
that having lived with a gentleman for six years one
imagines qualities in a playwright that do not exist, but
as far as it is humanly possible for a woman to know her
own mind, I believe I love him. I believe I love him
very much! But there is no obligation on your part,
Geoffrey – there is no reason why you should like me!

GEOFFREY: But I do! I realize I like you enormously –
I can't tell you how much – and if this man would leave
us a moment, I –

ELMA: Later!

ERNEST: Elma, for God's sake – is there nothing I can do?

ELMA: Nothing, Ernest, except do for me what Sapphire is
going to begin doing tonight for him – give me my
freedom.

ERNEST: If I tell you that I am prepared to overlook –

ELMA: I don't want you to overlook anything – I want you
to act on the information I have given you, and go to
London and see your lawyer tonight! That is your wish,
Geoffrey?

GEOFFREY: Absolutely! I insist!

ERNEST: Very well! Very well!

ELMA: Thank you! You're certain you want to go on,
Geoffrey?

GEOFFREY: I have never been more certain of anything!
It's difficult to tell you how much I like you in front of a
third person – but –

ELMA: There will be difficulties – unpleasantness!

GEOFFREY: What do I care!

ELMA: You're positive you like me enough to do this?

GEOFFREY: I have never been so positive of anything.

ELMA: I'm glad! I suppose for the moment I had better go home to my mother?

GEOFFREY: Certainly not! You will have your things packed and we will go together tonight!

ELMA: I would prefer that.
Ernest! Shall I see you before you go to your lawyer?
(*ERNEST shakes his head.*
ELMA leaves.)

ERNEST: I could kill you, Lymes!

GEOFFREY: I didn't quite catch what you said, old friend?

ERNEST: I say I could kill you!

GEOFFREY: Well, do speak up, there's a dear feller!

ERNEST: That you could have done such a thing to me!

GEOFFREY: Well, you did it to me for three weeks, and I didn't go about saying I wanted to kill you!

ERNEST: What did I do to you? I talked art, museums, Rome, literature, music, and all the other things your wife knows nothing about – is that immorality?

GEOFFREY: Of the worst kind.

ERNEST: You traitor!

GEOFFREY: I am not a traitor! I'm just an attractive feller who wins women without a word! I'm glad I didn't know my power over women before – it might have been very troublesome!

ERNEST: Stop smiling at nothing, you stupid ass! That you could have ever allowed my wife to be unfaithful with you is something I can't believe.

GEOFFREY: Oh! One moment! In self-defence – not a word against Elma, mind you – but there she grossly exaggerated.

ERNEST: What do you mean?

GEOFFREY: What I say! That she loves me there is no doubt whatever, but the infidelity she suggested was a gross exaggeration.

ERNEST: Are you telling me that Elma told me a lie?

GEOFFREY: It would be wrong of me to suggest that a woman I have just become engaged to could tell a lie – I only say she exaggerated!

ERNEST: I don't believe you!

GEOFFREY: Melton! Are you suggesting that if your wife had been unfaithful with me I would be such a cad as not to remember it?

ERNEST: Then why did she say it?

GEOFFREY: Ah, that's obvious! A determination to leave nothing unsaid that would make it possible for her to ever have to be alone with you again! You bore her terribly, old friend!

ERNEST: One moment! If she lied when she told me that, perhaps she lied when she said she loved you!

GEOFFREY: No, Melton, that is one of the few occasions when she will have ever told either of us the truth!

ERNEST: You conceited ass!

GEOFFREY: I'm sorry you say that; all my life I have tried in the hour of triumph to bear myself like all great men with artificial modesty!

ERNEST: Great men! Last night I picked up one of your plays; I read the first act – with the second I broke a window! You'll be known to posterity as a man who had the good fortune to live in an age when managers couldn't read!

GEOFFREY: Oh, what a mean way of attacking the Jews! (*ELMA appears at the French windows. She conceals herself behind the curtains listening, unknown to them.*)

ERNEST: Geoff, I'm sorry I said that – for God's sake – you don't love her, do you?

GEOFFREY: I certainly do – I didn't realize how much until I was going to lose her – all the time you left me alone with her I realize now, apart from the fact that it was helping me to lose Anne, I liked being with her! I liked it very much! Without knowing it, I was in love with her all the time!

ERNEST: Ho! Ho!

GEOFFREY: It's no good going on with those noises; nothing would induce her to go back to you!

ERNEST: If you sent her she would!

GEOFFREY: She wouldn't. And why should I? I adore the girl! She's attractive, amusing, a grand companion, and everything I like in a woman!

ERNEST: And another man's wife!

GEOFFREY: If you allowed yourself the privilege of forgetting it, surely I may?

ERNEST: If you really loved her you wouldn't drag her through this scandal!

GEOFFREY: What scandal! And supposing there is, what do she and I care about scandal? Melton, you're an impertinent feller! You leave your wife alone with me for weeks, you allow us to discover we have much in common – grow to like each other – and when you are bored with my wife you calmly say, 'Give me back my own!' You're an impertinent feller, Melton!

ERNEST: I love her!!!

GEOFFREY: So do I! And she loves me! And I am confident we could make each other very happy! I have no doubt our married life will be a great and permanent success! And let me tell you something else – I'm putting a woman in Percy's cage, because I realize now canaries cannot sing by seed alone. Anyway, I know I can't!

(*ELMA, unknown to him, blows him a kiss.*)

ERNEST: Won't you give her back to me?

GEOFFREY: No, I won't!

ERNEST: Very well, then! I shall divorce her at once!

GEOFFREY: Good!

ERNEST: And I know it isn't done – but I will do it – I will ask for the heaviest damages I can get! And settle them on her!

GEOFFREY: That's funny. The court will award you a lot when I tell them what you did.

ERNEST: And give your own wife away – (*He pauses.*) – that would be a charming thing to do, wouldn't it? But I'm sure you're capable of it.

GEOFFREY: Do what you like!

ERNEST: Pretty reading it will make. Large headlines: 'Playwright runs away with greatest friend's wife' – in larger headlines: 'Judge gives playwright severe dressing down – '

GEOFFREY: All his business is to pronounce the decree!

ERNEST: Very likely – but judges like their bit of fun like other people! Oh, a nice booing you will get on the next first night you have.

GEOFFREY: Who cares whether they boo or not?

ERNEST: You do, or you wouldn't have gone white!

GEOFFREY: I haven't! The brandy's worn off and I've become normal again!

ERNEST: Liar! And what a pretty reception you'll receive from club friends the first time you go in after having run away with your best friend's wife!

GEOFFREY: They'd have a damn nerve to criticize anybody else's moral life!

ERNEST: In self-protection they'd have to – they don't want to be found out! There are too many unhappily married men committed to marriage for life – too many men frightened they might lose their wives for them to let you get away with mine, scot-free! Those men will make your life hell, Lymes!

GEOFFREY: Pooh! What do I care?

ERNEST: Anyway, it would do one thing for you – it would save you ever having to bother again when the Honours list comes out – you'll know that you are still Mr Lymes.

GEOFFREY: Pooh! What playwright ever wanted to be a knight?

ERNEST: None – until they are offered it! And then they accept it, like the lawyers, for their wives' sake. Every time you enter a public room, you'll never know whether they are saying, 'That is Lymes, the playwright,' or 'Lymes, the home-wrecker' – you'll never know peace of mind again, Lymes – it may interfere with your work – it may even mean you will never write another play!

GEOFFREY: You're talking nonsense!

ERNEST: You know I am not! It takes the most enormous courage to do what you're doing, and only one man and a woman in thousands has the courage to do it! It's public opinion that keeps men and women together in this world! It's a much stronger bond than love!

GEOFFREY: What do I care for public opinion?

ERNEST: Then there's no point in my staying any longer –
I'll do what Elma asks of me!

GEOFFREY: One moment!

ERNEST: Well?

GEOFFREY: Come back here and sit down!

(*ERNEST sits down.*)
Understand this, Melton – if I were alone in this
I wouldn't hesitate – but I have to think of Elma. Do
you understand that?

ERNEST: I'm glad to hear it!

GEOFFREY: And if I appear to be weakening, it is solely
on her account – remember this, I like her too much to
do anything that would make her unhappy! And from
what you have described to me, I must ask myself,
'Would she be happy?'

ERNEST: If you did such a dishonourable thing, how could
she be happy?

GEOFFREY: Am I to understand that there is anything
dishonourable in taking an unhappy woman from a
dull man?

ERNEST: Nothing! But acknowledge it and you'll have to
find hotel accommodation for ninety per cent of the
married women of England.

GEOFFREY: That's true! That's terribly true! Melton!
I shall have to seriously reconsider my views of men
who look as stupid as you do!

ERNEST: Why?

GEOFFREY: Because from this conversation I have gathered
that underneath that incredible face and moustache there's
brains!

ERNEST: I am always being mistaken for a Conservative!

GEOFFREY: Belonging as you do to an old and aristocratic
family, I wonder you don't write articles for the papers!

ERNEST: I can't write.

GEOFFREY: Many other members of the aristocracy have not
been discouraged by that inability, Melton! But you have
made me realize the gravity of what I was threatening to
do – I must forget myself and think only of Elma!

ERNEST: I should think of myself, too – if I were you – it's you who will cop it worst.

GEOFFREY: What do I care what they say of me? Leave me out of it and think only of Elma!

ERNEST: Very well!

GEOFFREY: If I do the right thing and take her from you, I ruin her – if I don't, I make her terribly unhappy! I am in the unenviable position of either the public thinking me a cad – or your wife being sure that I am!

ERNEST: That's the position.

GEOFFREY: Do you dull men walking up the aisle of a church ever realize the responsibilities you are about to thrust upon some other unsuspecting man?

ERNEST: No!

GEOFFREY: Exactly! I am disturbed. I see no solution to the position you have put me in. One moment! The obvious end of this story is heroism and self-sacrifice on my part. Melton, painful as it is, I give you back your wife!

ERNEST: And rightly.

GEOFFREY: One moment! Will Elma agree to take you back? – I'd forgotten that!

ERNEST: Naturally, at first she will make a scene, but –

GEOFFREY: Scene? I cannot bear scenes with women, Melton!

ERNEST: I sympathize! But you'll have many if you marry her – and only one if you don't!

GEOFFREY: Odd you should look so stupid! Shall we run it as it were on the lines of honour?

ERNEST: Not much good with Elma! She's very likely listening at the door the whole time!

GEOFFFEY. What do you say?

Ssh! I won't be a moment, Ernest! (*Going to the door – opening it.*) You have no right to make suggestions of that kind against your wife. And I would be glad if you did not add to my already considerable nervous condition, Melton!

(*ELMA slips away into the garden.*)

ERNEST: You have nothing to be nervous about, Geoff –
after all, you are only doing a very honourable thing in
returning a woman to her husband!

GEOFFREY: Women hate having honourable things done
to them! There's going to be a scene, Melton! And I hate
scenes with women! I think it would be better if I wrote
to her.

ERNEST: Wouldn't that be cowardly, Geoff? You couldn't
do that – you must face her!

GEOFFREY: Melton! I will either write to your wife, or run
away with her! My sensitive nature forbids me to argue
with her!

ERNEST: Forget you are a writer and be a man, Geoff.
Listen! There are far greater things in the world than
love! To break asunder those who have been joined
together. It is not for you to have the unhappy married
people of the world pointing the finger of envy at the
one you love – and all the similar platitudes that men
have been telling women for years!

GEOFFREY: Melton! I will write all that to her.

ERNEST: She'll follow you – you'll have to have the scene!
And you could do it so convincingly!

GEOFFREY: I doubt it very much.

ERNEST: I'm certain you could.

GEOFFREY: You really think I could?

ERNEST: I shall be very surprised if I don't find myself
crying bitterly! If you can only get going, it ought to be
very beautiful. You have such an amazing personality,
Geoff!

GEOFFREY: Fetch her! One moment! In the event of my
being able to persuade Elma to take you back, what is
my position with Anne? Ah! That has to be considered.

ERNEST: After the things she has said to you, she couldn't
possibly expect you to take her back!

GEOFFREY: You're sure? Because if –

ERNEST: Of course! How could she! You're as free as
the air.

GEOFFREY: Fetch her.

(*ELMA enters.*)

ELMA: (*To ERNEST.*) Still here, Ernest? I thought you
    promised to go to your lawyer at once?

ERNEST: I know! But –

GEOFFREY: After you left us, Elma, he had what might be
    called a manly attack of hysteria – and I had no option
    but to let him stay!

ELMA: I've packed, Geoffrey – and I find there's a train we
    can catch at seven o'clock!

GEOFFREY: Yes – yes – we will catch it. Ernest, be a good
    feller and ask Morton to pack for me! –

ELMA: He has! Your things are with mine in the hall!

GEOFFREY: Good! Ernest, old chap, tell Morton to order
    us a taxi.

ELMA: I have already asked him to do that, too!

GEOFFREY: Good.

ELMA: Does this obvious endeavour to get rid of the good
    feller – and good chap – mean you wish to speak to me
    alone?

GEOFFREY: Good heavens, no! What makes you think
    that?

ELMA: I thought perhaps Rasputin had been busy during
    my absence!

GEOFFREY: Ras – Ernest has said only the most charming
    and attractive things about you, Elma!

ELMA: Really!

GEOFFREY: If your life with me would be happy, he is not
    only willing but anxious to give you your freedom at
    once!

ELMA: Why doesn't he do it?

GEOFFREY: His one thought is for you – he has none for
    himself.

ELMA: How nice.

GEOFFREY: His unselfish love for you has touched me
    very deeply – I never thought Ernest capable of such
    fine affection!

ELMA: I am a little bewildered – are you running away
    with me or Ernest? –

GEOFFREY: Elma! please! this is a very sacred moment.

ELMA: Sorry! But I thought if you were trying to get out yourself – it was a pity to waste all these words – as you only have to say so.

GEOFFREY: Elma! As long as I live – with you – or without – you – you will always be the most divine woman I have ever known!

ELMA: Then what are we waiting for?

GEOFFREY: Because before you take this plunge into the abyss of – of – I think it my duty to warn you of the grave step you are taking.

ELMA: Geoffrey, you've only got to say, 'Elma, I made a mistake – I haven't the courage – I am not big enough to face the criticism of the world,' and I shall be very understanding. I shall be very sympathetic.

GEOFFREY: I? I? What do I care for criticism? Good God! How curious women are! Here am I offering to make the greatest sacrifice I have ever made – and you suggest that I am thinking of myself! It's you I am thinking of. Supposing in the years to come you realize there are far greater things in the world than love –

ELMA: – Or had one the right to break the promise to the Vicar –

GEOFFREY: Yes.

ELMA: – Or is it a good example to those who follow us.

GEOFFREY: Yes, if you like!

ELMA: In brief – before I take this serious step, you feel I should consider all these things – do you suggest I should also consider returning to Ernest?

GEOFFREY: I realize to leave a man whom I now recognize as one who loves you very deeply – I am right, Ernest, in saying that?

ERNEST: Yes, Geoffrey.

GEOFFREY: For ever to have it on your conscience his lasting misery is due to you – I sincerely say we should both consider it very seriously.

ELMA: Your view being, it is wrong to accept any happiness at the cost of others – it is better to be miserable oneself than make another.

GEOFFREY: I say, conscious of the sorrow it will cause me, we should pause before doing anything so serious.

ELMA: Most touching. I had no idea you had such a beautiful nature, Geoffrey. Do you know why you are a second-class playwright?

GEOFFREY: What do you mean?

ELMA: Because you are a second-class man. A plumber with a gift of dialogue. You neither have nor ever could furnish the world with an idea – you haven't the courage to have one. You would sacrifice the greatest happiness in the world rather than be criticized by the man who lives next door – even though you don't know him. In your little life of egoism you never pass a church without hoping and wondering if there will be a lot of people at your memorial service. The only love you will ever understand, is taking a little flat and hiding the little lady in it. To possess the good opinion of all men you even cheat yourself – a man without an idea – a man without courage. (*To ERNEST.*) With all your faults you are a better man than your little friend.

ERNEST: I think so.

GEOFFREY: I protest. What I have suggested is purely out of consideration for you.

ELMA: If you believed your wife was still in this house and not on her way to her lawyer's, would you have made these suggestions?

GEOFFREY: Yes, I should.

ELMA: If it were proved to you – not loving her – that she cares for you as much as Ernest cares for me – would you sacrifice yourself and take her back? Why don't you answer?

GEOFFREY: If Anne cares for me as much as Ernest cares for you – I should.

ELMA: She does. Fetch her, Ernest – she is sitting in the hall, crying.

GEOFFREY: One moment!

ELMA: Fetch her, Ernest!

(*ERNEST goes out.*)

GEOFFREY: What does this mean?

ELMA: It means that I gathered from those tears that within a few minutes of your wife leaving this house for ever she who was contemptuous of everything normal, anything ordinary, realized that, after all, she was as conventionally-minded as you are. She discovered for the first time what being respectably married meant to her – she discovered it might be infinitely easier to live with a man you despise than face the smile of public opinion – in a flash she discovered what a silly thing she was doing – and having discovered how stupid it would be to live on only a little of your income instead of nearly all of it – she decided to return and tell you that she loved you.

GEOFFREY: But – but –

(*ERNEST and ANNE enter.*)

ERNEST: Be gentle with her, Geoffrey. She's very upset and unhappy.

ANNE: You want me, Geoffrey.

ELMA: Am I right in saying that you suddenly discovered within a few minutes of leaving your home for ever, your feelings as regards that home and your husband underwent a serious change – you suddenly discovered how deep your affection was for both of them!

ANNE: Yes.

ELMA: And I am happy to tell you Geoffrey feels the same – he feels that there are far greater things in the world than love – to break asunder those who have been joined together – and the many other platitudes all men discover when they don't wish to do a thing. In effect, Geoffrey has told me there is no other happiness in life for me other than with my husband – consequently there can be none for him other than with his wife – so, feeling as he does, I ask you to forgive him and take him back.

ANNE: Very well. (*She takes off her hat.*)

ELMA: I'm glad. So there's only one thing left for me to do – and that is to wish you all goodbye.

(*ERNEST rises.*)

Why do you move, Ernest?

ERNEST: I'm coming with you, aren't I?

ELMA: Don't be absurd. I'm not as good, perhaps, as
Geoffrey and Mrs Lymes – but I have courage, Ernest –
I could no more think of going back to that awful life
I have known with you than fly.

ERNEST: Where – where – are you going?

ELMA: I? I'm going to find another co-respondent.
(*ELMA goes out.*)

The End.